The Emergence of European Trade Unionism

The Emergence of European Trade Unionism

Edited by

JEAN-LOUIS ROBERT, ANTOINE PROST
and
CHRIS WRIGLEY

LONDON AND NEW YORK

First published 2004 by Ashgate Publishing

Reissued 2018 by Routledge
2 Park Square, Milton Park, Abingdon, Oxon, OX14 4RN
711 Third Avenue, New York, NY 10017, USA

Routledge is an imprint of the Taylor & Francis Group, an informa business

First issued in paperback 2018

© Jean-Louis Robert, Antoine Prost, Chris Wrigley and the contributors, 2004

The editors have asserted their moral right under the Copyright, Designs and Patents Act, 1988, to be identified as the editors of this work.

All rights reserved. No part of this book may be reprinted or reproduced or utilised in any form or by any electronic, mechanical, or other means, now known or hereafter invented, including photocopying and recording, or in any information storage or retrieval system, without permission in writing from the publishers.

A Library of Congress record exists under LC control number: 00053130

Notice
Product or corporate names may be trademarks or registered trademarks, and are used only for identification and explanation without intent to infringe.

Publisher's Note
The publisher has gone to great lengths to ensure the quality of this reprint but points out that some imperfections in the original copies may be apparent.

Disclaimer
The publisher has made every effort to trace copyright holders and welcomes correspondence from those they have been unable to contact.

ISBN 13: 978-0-815-39771-7 (hbk)
ISBN 13: 978-1-138-62095-7 (pbk)
ISBN 13: 978-1-351-14688-3 (ebk)

Contents

General Editor's Preface vii
Contributors ix
Introduction xi
Chris Wrigley

Part One   Territories, towns and industries

1 Trade unionism in the British, German, French and US iron
   and steel industries, 1850–1910 3
   Thomas Welskopp in cooperation with Odette Hardy-Hémery

2 Dockers' unions in the ports of London, Le Havre,
   Rotterdam and Hamburg, 1850–1914 33
   *Eric Nijhof in cooperation with John Barzman and
   John Lovell*

3 Trade unionism in textile towns and areas 54
   *Jean-Claude Daumas, Rémy Cazals, Marlene Ellerkamp
   and Alan Fowler*

4 Trade unions in medium-sized textile and machine-building
   cities: Ghent, Bielefeld and Monza, 1890–1914 91
   Karl Ditt, Giuseppe M. Longoni and Peter Scholliers

5 Large towns: Liverpool, Lyon and Munich 121
   *John Belchem, with the assistance of Karl Heinrich Pohl
   and Vincent Robert*

Part Two   Customs and representation

6 May Days 141
   *Gita Deneckere, Marie-Louise Goergen, Inge Marssolek,
   Danielle Tartakowsky and Chris Wrigley*

7 Workers, others and the state: a comparison of the
   discourse of the French, German and British labour
   movements at the end of the nineteenth century 166
   Antoine Prost and Manfred Bock

8	The constraints of the law *Norbert Olszak and Chris Wrigley*	184
9	Employers and trade unions in the late nineteenth century in Britain, France and Germany *Marie-Geneviève Dezès, Kenneth Lunn, Arthur McIvor and Klaus Tenfelde*	204
10	The multiple foundations of trade union organisation in nineteenth-century Germany, France and Britain *Michel Dreyfus, Sandrine Kott, Michel Pigenet and Noel Whiteside*	215
11	The structure and organisation of British, French and German trade unions before the First World War *Peter Berkowitz, Rebecca Gumbrell, Richard Hyman, Michel Pigenet and Michael Schneider*	233

Index   251

Studies in Labour History
General Editor's Preface

Labour history has often been a fertile area of history. Since the Second World War its best practitioners – such as E. P. Thompson and E. J. Hobsbawm, both Presidents of the Society for the Study of Labour History – have written works which have provoked fruitful and wide-ranging debates and further research, and which have influenced not only social history but history generally. These historians, and many others, have helped to widen labour history beyond the study of organised labour to labour generally, sometimes to industrial relations in particular, and most frequently to society and culture in national and comparative dimensions.

The assumptions and ideologies underpinning much of the older labour history have been challenged by feminist and later by post-modernist and anti-Marxist thinking. These challenges have often led to thoughtful reappraisals, perhaps intellectual equivalents of coming to terms with a new post-Cold War political landscape.

By the end of the twentieth century, labour history had emerged reinvigorated and positive from much introspection and external criticism. Very few would wish to confine its scope to the study of organised labour. Yet, equally, few would wish now to write the existence and influence of organised labour out of nations' histories, any more than they would wish to ignore working-class lives and focus only on the upper echelons.

This series of books provides reassessments of broad themes of labour history as well as some more detailed studies arising from recent research. Most books are single-authored but there are also volumes of essays centred on important themes or periods, some arising from major conferences organised by the Society for the Study of Labour History. The series also includes studies of labour organisations, including international ones, as many of these are much in need of a modern reassessment.

Chris Wrigley
Society for the Study of Labour History
University of Nottingham

Contributors

The European scholars contributing to this volume are John Barzman, John Belchem, Peter Berkowitz, Manfred Bock, Rémy Cazals, Jean-Claude Daumas, Gita Deneckere, Marie-Geneviève Dezès, Karl Ditt, Michel Dreyfus, Marlene Ellerkamp, Alan Fowler, Marie-Louise Goergen, Rebecca Gumbrell, Odette Hardy-Hémery, Richard Hyman, Sandrine Kott, Giuseppe M. Longoni, John Lovell, Kenneth Lunn, Inge Marssolek, Arthur McIvor, Eric Nijhof, Norbert Olszac, Michel Pigenet, Karl Heinrich Pohl, Antoine Prost, Jean-Louis Robert, Vincent Robert, Michael Schneider, Peter Scholliers, Danielle Tartakowsky, Klaus Tenfelde, Thomas Welskopp, Noel Whiteside and Chris Wrigley.

Introduction: the emergence of European trade unionism

Chris Wrigley

The renaissance of labour history in recent years has had several aspects, one of the most important being the fresh insights arising from comparative studies. There have been numerous excellent single-authored comparative studies[1] as well as important collections of essays focused on relatively short periods or themes.[2] This collection contains studies of the pre-1914 development of trade unions in Europe written by teams (or at least pairs) of historians of different nationalities.

This international study of European trade unionism was initiated by an international group of scholars, including Friedhelm Boll, Antoine Prost and Jean-Louis Robert, and the meetings of the authors were held at the Sorbonne under the aegis of Antoine Prost and Le Centre de Recherches sur l'Histoire des Mouvements Sociaux et du Syndicalisme. At preliminary meetings each team of authors set their agenda of issues to explore; each author then prepared appropriate material and, at a further meeting, comparisons were made collectively by each group, before the joint paper was written. Hence, this collection of essays represents sustained collaborative work. The essays are based on specialist knowledge of archival materials as well as a range of secondary sources often known to few beyond one country.

Part One of the book examines trade unionism in three economic sectors (iron and steel, docks and textiles) as well as considering its development in differing types of location (large and medium towns, textile and machine-making areas). After a discussion of the early May Days (1890–1906), Part Two provides assessments of major aspects of industrial relations. Several of the authors warn of the hazards and difficulties of attempting multinational comparisons. Nevertheless, the essays in both parts of the book provide fresh insights into the emergence of European trade unionism.

The team of writers on textiles (Chapter 3) emphasise that the differences which emerge from their analysis 'are not necessarily national ones' and urge more interregional comparative analysis. This is very good advice. For some parts of Europe one can go further, as labour markets were transnational and, for such instances, national studies could be too restrictive.

The economic sector studies in this book provide a range of

explanations for trade union success or relative failure in different industries. In iron and steel (Chapter 1) much explanatory weight is placed on industrial structure and the speed with which the transition from iron to steel occurred. In the Ruhr, after the tumultuous years of rapid expansion of the early 1870s, economic depression from 1873 apparently reduced many workers to a submissive state. In the UK, where production units were less large, trade unionism was strong relative to other European countries and there 'slower growth saved the conciliatory collective bargaining system'. In the case of dock labour (Chapter 2), the authors assess a range of structural factors affecting trade union growth, including whether parts were old or new, the types of cargo handled and the competitiveness of the labour market. The chapters (3 and 4) on textiles are among those which bring out the weakening effect on trade union growth of the presence of foreign labour (Alsatians in the case of Elbeuf) and of Catholic loyalties.

As for large provincial cities (Chapter 5), the team of writers argue that while they were not archetypal nineteenth-century strongholds of trade unionism, these urban areas 'did not necessarily impede trade union development'. Lyon, for instance, had a rich radical heritage which included the past struggles of 1831 and 1834. Such radical traditions – Paris and later St Petersburg are well-known examples – were very important in assisting radical mobilisations. Munich also had its heritage of being a relatively radical centre of more liberal (than Prussia) German states.

The early working-class May Days (Chapter 6) provided a focus for trade union issues, most notably the eight-hour working day, as well as for broader political issues concerning the extension of the franchise and avoidance of war. In Britain many of those turning out in London and around the country in the early 1890s were New Unionists, with New Unionism, Progressive wins in London county council elections and mass support for May Days all being aspects of an upsurge in the political and trade union consciousness of many unskilled workers. In Germany, it is argued, even modest May Day activities represented a rejection of a dominant culture of the Kaiserreich. The authors observe of the May Days that they offered unifying symbols and myths to the international labour movement.

In Chapter 7 the use of language by trade union activists is analysed by Antoine Prost and Manfred Bock. This provides a fresh understanding of the differing attitudes and beliefs of trade unionists in France, Germany and Britain, and is an innovatory approach to comparative labour history.

Two major influences on trade union growth are discussed in Chapters 8 and 9: the constraints of the law and attitudes of employers towards trade unionism. Although Britain and France were both viewed in the late nineteenth century as liberal democratic states, the dominant attitudes were notably different. In Britain the trade unions had secured a substantial degree of recognition and ability to engage in collective bargaining under 1871 and 1875 legislation. However, legal judgments between 1893 and 1901 undercut what they believed to be their rights. Hence the British trade union movement organised to press Parliament to redress the Taff Vale Judgment, 1901, and other adverse decisions. This included the TUC setting up the Labour Representation Committee (LRC) in 1900. The moves were successful in that the trade unions secured their legal objectives in the Trades Disputes Act, 1906. In contrast, the French trade unions operated in a hostile legal environment in which individualism was prioritised.

In Britain employers' attitudes were affected by the fact that they were faced with long-established trade unions which were clearly not socialist. In contrast, in Germany where socialist politics preceded mass trade unionism, employers had no difficulty in confusing trade unionism and socialism. Even more important in affecting employers' attitudes and actions in these countries and France were the natures of the state and the laws. Where the state backed, indeed encouraged, a line against trade unions then, not surprisingly, the employers were more intransigent than where the state was more liberal and the laws more accommodating.

The final two chapters (10 and 11) provide comparative studies of aspects of the organisation of British, French and German trade unionism. The first of these focuses on the friendly benefit side of trade unions. In Britain friendly benefits were a lever by which the unions could discipline members for disobeying union rules, and generally such schemes strengthened the trade unions and were very widespread. In Germany trade union benefits, notably sickness and unemployment pay, covered large numbers of workers after 1900. In France trade union benefit funds were less substantial. The second of these chapters adopts H. A. Turner's distinction between closed unionism, which restricted entry into its trade, and open unions, which could not and so had to depend on the strength of their members' united action to succeed in bargaining.[3] In Britain many skilled unions were sufficiently long-established and strong enough to be able to pursue closed unionism strategies. While there was diversity in trade union organisation in all three countries, there was less ability to control entry to trades in France and Germany. In Germany, with weaker local strength, trade unionism looked more to central power and organisation than the French or British unions.

Collectively the essays in this volume provide a fresh reassessment of Western European trade unionism in the four decades or so before the

First World War. In different ways, the different teams or pairs of authors offer comparative perspectives, and these are often unusual as the team perspective is often very different from that of even the ablest individual author who inevitably sees things from his or her specialist area of research. Hopefully, others will follow this approach for the trade union history of other periods and other places.

Notes

1. These include D. Geary, *European Labour Protest 1848–1939*, London, 1981; J. Haydu, *Between Craft and Class: Skilled Workers and Factory Politics in the United States and Britain, 1890–1922*, Los Angeles and Berkeley, 1988, and Gary Marks, *Unions In Politics*, Princeton, 1989; C. Eisenberg, 'Comparative View in Labour History', *International Review of Social History*, 34 (3), 1989; J. Breuilly, *Labour and Liberalism in Nineteenth Century Europe*, London, 1992; S. Berger, *The British Labour Party and the German Social Democrats*, Oxford, 1994; and N. Kirk, *Labour and Society in Britain and the USA*, 2 vols, Aldershot, 1994.
2. These include W. J. Mommsen and H.-G. Husung (eds), *The Development of Trade Unionism in Great Britain and Germany, 1880–1914*, London, 1985; L. Haimson and C. Tilly (eds), *Strikes, Wars and Revolution*, Cambridge, 1989; and C. J. Wrigley (ed.), *Challenges of Labour: Western and Central Europe 1917–1920*, 1993.
3. H. A. Turner, *Trade Union Growth, Structure and Policy*, 1962.

PART ONE
Territories, towns and industries

CHAPTER ONE

Trade unionism in the British, German, French, and US iron and steel industries, 1850–1910

Thomas Welskopp
in cooperation with Odette Hardy-Hémery

Introduction: The iron and steel industry and workplace-based trade unionism

Unionisation in the nineteenth and early twentieth centuries seems to have followed two distinct patterns.[1] The first pattern, I suggest, may be called 'artisanal unionism' which developed in the handicrafts and small workshop industries. Within this pattern, we encounter wide variations between countries, above all depending on the respective degree of business centralisation and, consequently, on the degree to which workplace and industrial relations became 'shopfloorised'. Only in workshops of a size sufficient to allow the formation of 'producer alliances' between skilled artisans and master craftsmen *vis-à-vis* a common employer, who usually did not work alongside his men, could a strong workplace-based bargaining position develop and serve as a basis for exclusive business unionism directed towards control of both the terms of employment and the local labour market. This was the case in most British and a considerable number of American trades. The German and French cases, by contrast, represent the other extreme of the spectrum: here, commercialisation transformed the handicrafts and export trades, organised in putting-out systems, long before both centralisation and the 'shopfloorisation' of industrial relations gained a firm foothold. Consequently, any drive towards unionisation had to confront the threefold problem of eroding, but still vital, guild structures, of the journeymen's mutual isolation in mostly very small workshops, and the proliferation of small master craftsmen in a precarious state of independence.

In this situation, all organisation was forced to take a detour via the formation of 'general', interprofessional associations, and producer cooperatives often appeared as a more plausible and realistic option than unions and strikes. In Germany, therefore, all organisation drives were pushed from the workplace into the public and politicised sphere of assemblies and *Vereine*. This explains why Social Democratic parties developed so early in Germany, why they won supremacy over labour unions, and how they came to serve as true obstetricians of a decidedly 'public' trade union movement which would otherwise have failed to materialise for a long time and which remained weak well into the 1890s.[2] In France, a dominant small town environment combined with the centre–periphery conflict between a hypercentralised Paris and the provinces to shape 'artisanal unionism' into a specific dual form. On the one hand, nationwide associations of journeymen (*compagnonnages*) continued to exist precariously between older guild traditions and informal trade union practices. On the other hand, artisans, masters and small shopowners, especially in small towns, formed neighborhood-centred syndicalistic networks that – in their anti-centralist radicalism – became the social basis of anarcho-syndicalism, which proliferated into small factory settings – for instance, in the metalworking trades.[3]

Although oscillating between elitist 'craft unionism' and socially inclusive 'all-round organisations' with a strong tendency towards socialism and anti-capitalism, 'artisanal unionism' displayed limits in its workplace power. This meant that it proved more susceptible to playing party political cards, whether in repeated 'single-issue movements' or in constant party affiliations of various kinds. The French version of this combination between unionism and politics: the 'revolutionary general strike', compensated union weakness and the inability to form centralised parties both by making the strike itself a political act and by capitalising on the country's political centralisation symbolized by the central importance of Paris for the system as a whole.[4] The *artisanal pillar* of the labour movement, so runs my argument, depended in its institutional appearance and ideological outlook mainly on the respective business structure of a given society. Since it tended to be politicised in various forms, even if only at times, it is here that we find the most decidedly *national* characteristics in the variations of trade union development.

The second pattern can be identified as 'strong craft unionism' in early workshop and process flow industries. These highly exclusive and elitist unions were deeply rooted in the workplace and drew their strength above all from their 'responsible autonomy'[5] in the work process, which was the consequence of the early firms' loose and fragmented management structure. Although unions of this kind sometimes participated in political 'single-issue movements', as organisations, they normally tended to maintain a decided distance from party politics and instead relied on their direct bargaining power. Coalmining, shipbuilding, some metal trades, and – as I will demonstrate in this chapter – the iron and steel industries were among the most important branches in which this type of union developed. In these trades, international similarities in the patterns of industrial relations were more pronounced than between the national variations of 'artisanal unionism'. Furthermore, as I am going to show for the iron and steel industry, existing differences between national trajectories have to be explained in terms of growth rates and industrial structure – that is, in terms of endogenous conditions – rather than in terms of interprofessional links and national party politics.

This conceptual differentiation may well provide a key variable for constructing a projected modern typology of trade union development in Europe and North America, even if it is certainly not fine-grained enough to exhaust the range of all possible types.[6] Yet the labour movements in Great Britain and the USA may be adequately portrayed as resting both on a massive pillar of strong craft unionism and a strong artisanal pillar modelled according to this prototype. In the American case, craft unionism dominated a largely party-independent labour movement well into the 1920s. The result was a predominance of pragmatic business unionism and the priority of unionism over party politics. Great Britain differed in detail, but not in principle. In France, and especially in Germany, the craft union pillar of the labour movement failed to materialise in its formative period, with longstanding consequences for its institutional development. The reasons for this divergence will subsequently be discussed for the case of the iron and steel industry. In Germany, the specifically 'public' and political artisanal labour movement singlehandedly dictated the structures within whose framework the expansion of autonomous trade unions, especially in the metal trades, later occurred. Here, the shifting of the balance towards industrial unionism did not gain ground until the 1890s. The result was a union structure dominated by centralised federations of weak craft unions, which grouped themselves around ideological camps – above all the Social Democratic Party and the Catholic Centre Party. This union movement failed to appeal to industries like iron and steel because it largely proved unable to cope with groups of workers whose group identity so strongly rested in the shopfloor context. Furthermore, between 1890 and 1910, by the time the German trade union movement gained its unprecedented strength, the employees in the iron and steel works lacked the resources to organise autonomously and to meet the central organisations half way from below. Despite all the institutional differences, its development in France was strikingly similar so far as its effects were concerned: here, both wings of the labour movement – the anarcho-syndicalist groups, which were strong in skilled metalworking occupations and small firms, and the socialist trade unions that flourished in the coalfields – proved incapable of penetrating the highly concentrated iron and steel industry of the French Nord.[7]

The specific significance of the iron and steel industry for studying trade union development in comparative perspective lies in the fact that this case reflects, in a most pronounced way, the mechanisms of workplace-based unionism under extremely dynamic industrial conditions – with political influence virtually absent. Until the 1890s, in the era of wrought iron production, this industry served as a prototype of strong craft unionism, except for the German case, where the social basis for such unions indeed existed, but economic conditions impeded formal organisation, and except for France, whose metal-producing industry only gained shape and strength once the new steelmaking processes were firmly established. The transition to steel production brought about the erosion of craft unionism and with this – for Germany, France, and the USA – the total demise of unionism from this industry until the 1920s and 1930s. It can be demonstrated that it was the slower and more protracted growth of the steel industry in Great Britain which facilitated the gradual transformation of the older ironworkers' craft unions into the strong steelworkers' unions of the 1890s and 1900s, which thereby secured their survival. Yet even the new industrial steelworkers' unions of the 1920s and 1930s in Germany, France and the USA remained syndicalist networks of plant-oriented informal work groups with their basis still overwhelmingly in the shopfloor context. Codetermination at the workplace and the 'micropolitics' of union plant leaders have since then been more important for unionism in the steel industry than centralised organisations with which those plant networks continued to maintain an ambivalent and sometimes strained relationship.[8]

The prime interest of this chapter lies in the British, French, and German cases; the complex nature of the interplay between workplace relations, organisation, and industrial relations, however, necessitates the inclusion of the American case as a mediating *tertium comparationis*.

The social milieu of iron production: socioeconomic conditions and the shaping of workplace relations

With the expansion of railway networks and increasing consumption in many commercial fields, the iron industry advanced to become a leading sector of early industrialisation. While Britain took an early lead, the US iron industry began to make substantial headway from the 1840s onwards and iron production in the German Ruhr district catapulted to a start in the 1850s.⁹ The mass production of iron took place in puddling furnaces where brittle pig iron was refined into a malleable material which then was rolled into rails or other products. Wrought iron was the principal product of heavy industry until the 1870s when the revolutionary Bessemer and open-hearth steelmaking processes started making successive inroads into product markets which had previously been dominated by wrought iron alone. Yet this replacement process proved protracted and uneven. The highest outputs of rolled iron products in the respective countries were not achieved until the mid-1880s, and the wrought iron sector of the industry cannot be described as marginalised before the early 1890s.[10]

Likewise, the distinct set of organisational structures and social relations on the shopfloor consolidated as a relatively stable social system of production which was not substantially transformed before the marginalisation of the iron industry as a whole. Iron manufacturing developed as a capital-intensive, highly competetive and extremely price-sensitive industry. Although differing considerably in size according to product profile, integrated puddling and rolling mills figured among the largest and most centralised industrial units of their time, often dominating regional labour markets. Notwithstanding these differences in scale, iron mills were characterised by a universal internal structure. This uniformity resulted from the inherent traits of iron production. The puddling process involved the manual treatment of the metal during its refinement. Reliance on manual handling limited the physical dimensions of furnaces and the weight of charges. This and the insufficiencies of reverbatory furnaces in general fragmented the production of wrought iron into a series of independent activities centred around the individual furnaces. Variations in the chemical composition of raw materials contributed to this fragmentation, since they had to be balanced by idiosyncratic manual interventions: puddling meant batch production. Consequently, puddling mills resembled rather simple aggregations of furnaces.[11]

The features of puddling impressed a similarly fragmented and serial structure upon rolling mills. The product of the puddling process consisted of iron bars which, after having left the furnace, were hammered or 'squeezed' in order to extract excess slag. They were then shaped and condensed in several passes on so-called 'roughing rolls', and finally weighed, sheared and stored in the mill yard according to quality. Since these units of metal were too small to be rolled directly, rolling mill workers had to build the small pieces into larger ones. This entailed a complex process of heating, 'piling', rolling, reheating and rerolling which made the manufacturing of rolled products a circular operation.

Rolling mills typically consisted of a number of specialised rolling facilities each comprising several trains of rolls driven by a central steam engine. Each rolling facility cooperated with a specific set of heating furnaces. Since heating furnaces shared most characteristics of their counterparts in puddling, including their cyclical performance, they imposed batch production on rolling. Thus, although the rolling process itself bore considerable potential for technical improvement and increase in productivity, the physical properties of the material, the circular arrangement of the stages of production and reliance on manual manipulation combined to reproduce the fragmented, decentralised structure typical of nineteenth-century iron mills. Like puddling, the rolling process split up into a series of loosely integrated discrete operations handled by small groups of workers.[12]

Throughout the three countries, iron mill society was divided into four constituent groups strictly separated by sharp social boundaries and distinguished by specific sets of workplace relations. The engineers tending the power machinery comprised a small body of usually young and low-paid semi-skilled workers whose tasks were only marginally integrated into the actual production process. A second, similarly small, group was formed by the foremen's staff. This group was in charge of the weighing of raw materials and products, of quality control, and of record-keeping. The actual production crew represented about 80 per cent of the total workforce. This body of workers fell into two categories sharply divided by the distinction between unskilled and skilled labour. The unskilled workforce in iron mills, comprising 40–50 per cent of the total, was organised in socially homogeneous 'gangs' closely supervised and directed by 'gang bosses'. They were chiefly engaged in the transportation of materials thus providing the links between the different stages of production. Other 'gangs' performed ancillary manual tasks around the furnaces and rolls. Still other unskilled 'gang workers' provided additional 'muscle' for the heavy lifting tasks of the skilled production hands at roll stands manufacturing large products. All unskilled labour, as it was seen by contemporaries, 'wait[ed] upon the skilled worker, the [actual] iron worker'.[13] As David Montgomery has pointed out, iron mills were characterised by a 'dichotomous structure' which had its roots in the system of production but was also consciously upheld by the 'social distancing' of skilled workers:

> The division of labor within an iron mill had created, on the one hand, common laborers, who fetched and pushed at the command of their gang bosses, and, on the other hand, large groups of craftsmen, who learned their trades by doing and who clearly directed their own work and that of their immediate helpers.[14]

Even when directly assisting production hands in particularly heavy tasks, 'gang' labourers were kept strictly outside the ranks of the skilled workers under whose direction they worked. As American union official Robert D. Layton testified in a Senate commission hearing in 1883:

> When we speak of a 'laborer' in the iron works, it is understood that we do not mean a man who performs any skilled labor. When you get above the laborer the men are designated by the character of the particular work in which they are engaged; they are called 'rollers', 'finishers' &c., and are skilled laborers.[15]

These skilled production hands formed autonomous 'teams', each attached to a particular puddling or heating furnace, train of rolls or set of shears. The decentralised, serial structure of iron mills split the skilled workforce into a corresponding series of discrete 'teams' each controlling one fibre of the fragmented process at the respective stage of production. This extreme horizontal division of labour accounted for the high proportion of top-skilled hands in the workforce.[16]

'Teams' worked autonomously and almost independently from one another, only receiving materials and passing them on after treatment. There was virtually no personal supervision and direction of the work process by the mill management during routine procedures. 'Teams' consequently exerted a remarkable degree of discretionary power over the organisation of their work. This functional autonomy became the hallmark of the skilled workers' 'team system' in iron production. This rested on three structural pillars.

First, puddling, heating, and rolling involved considerable metallurgical knowledge combined with an equally high degree of manipulative skill. With only imperfect equipment at their disposal, workers had to obtain acceptable production results by using simple tools to compensate for process insufficiencies and to balance variations in heat and input quality in a continuous sequence of on-the-spot judgements and proficient manual interventions: 'It was the kind of skill that was sight plus touch':[17]

> There is nothing but the crank that they turn to tighten the rolls, to determine the width of the bar that the iron is to be rolled into, and it requires a great deal of experience to do that properly, and for that reason the men get very high prices.[18]

This knowledge and skill was inseparable from the execution of manual labour. It was an empirical knowledge only gained in a protracted process of learning by doing, watching and imitating the work of more experienced men, and working up from the simplest to the most sophisticated tasks. It also was tacit knowledge since it was not transferable by theoretical training and since the consciously secretive iron workers jealously guarded their 'capital' in order to maintain control of access to their privileged segment of the labour market. In consequence, although the role of master puddlers, heaters, and rollers as heads of their 'teams' entailed 'significant managerial responsibility: the organisation and direction of a team of workmen of differing skills, all of whose coordinated effort was needed to manufacture a finished product',[19] their position remained bound to their manual performance. Furthermore, acting as group leaders and co-workers at the same time, they remained closely integrated into the 'team' structure and did not become 'part of management, as [their] twentieth-century counterpart[s] would be'.[20]

Second, in iron manufacturing, unlike in most other crafts and artisanal trades, top hands were not able to perform production work singlehandedly. The characteristics and physical requirements of iron production made teamwork a collective and coordinated effort to which both shared and complementary skills had to be applied. Although the team structure did serve as an informal apprenticeship system and internal skill levels varied correspondingly, at any given time a considerable number of helpers in puddling and heating were already fully trained hands capable of leading, and waiting to take over, a team of their own. Rolling, in particular, required the closely coordinated hand-in-hand cooperation of the entire group. To ensure effective work, the inner circle of underhands already had to be in command of the 'extraordinary skill required for this rhythmic performance'.[21] The functional autonomy of the skilled ironworkers' 'teams' both was exercised and reproduced in this internal coordination process which was directed by a team leader who himself was part of the work group he commanded.

Third, 'team autonomy' was a consequence of the iron mills' fragmented structure and of batch production. These combined to require a high frequency of production-related decisions in close proximity to the individual workplaces. This ruled out direct supervision by management. The fragmentation of the production process necessarily decentralised decision-making to the team level. This discretionary power, rooted in the work process itself, was the social basis of skilled iron workers' 'defensive elitism'. Elitism augmented their autonomy and at the same time served as an instrument both to usurp management's prerogatives in work-related issues and to shield their privileged social position in the mills.[22]

'Defensive elitism', as displayed by skilled ironworkers throughout the three countries, was anchored in the peculiar internal structure of iron mills. This structure differed fundamentally from any strictly linear or pyramidal notion of the organisation of business enterprises. Mill society was characterised by a dual structure, with the informal, autonomous hierarchies of the 'teams' on the one side, and the formal hierarchy on the other, ranging from the general superintendent at the top to the middle ranks of the mill superintendents and to the echelons of foremen and their staff on the departmental level. Between these two overlapping hierarchies, power relations resembled commercial and transactional links rather than a rigid system of domination and subordination. Power relations between the 'teams' and the firm's representatives were primarily governed by the 'cash nexus' of piece-rate wages.[23] Ironworkers' 'teams' thus 'made steel by using the employers' capital', autonomously working with 'the companies' equipment and raw materials', and they virtually resold the finished products to the company by the ton. '[All] the boss did', resumed David Montgomery, 'was to buy the equipment and raw materials and sell the finished product'.[24]

Both sides tried to capitalise on the fact that the organisation of the work process rested with the 'teams' and remained a largely impenetrable barrier to central control by management. Autonomy and collective indispensability allowed the 'teams' to 'extract ... more than an average wage' by linking tonnage rates to the selling price of the iron.[25] In boom periods, they thus secured a substantial share of soaring profits. The 'manufacture system', as this form of work organisation in wrought iron production came to be called, enabled the 'team leaders' to hire helpers 'without dictation from management', to organise work free from management's instructions and surveillance, and to pay their 'teams' at their discretion out of the tonnage price they received. Production was flexibly regulated by quantity and quality standards for materials and products which were contested subjects of an ongoing bargaining process between 'masters and men'. For the companies, the 'manufacture system' had the advantage of low overheads and organisational costs. Furthermore, their complex system of indirect performance evaluation did prove effective in maintaining work discipline since its findings directly affected wages. Moreover, the 'commercial relations' between companies and 'teams' placed a considerable share of entrepreneurial risks on the workers. In particular, piece-rates allowed for flexible cost reductions in slack times since the effects of falling prices could be immediately passed on to the 'teams'.[26]

As a consequence, relations between employers and skilled workers were in constant flux, closely tied to the ups and downs of the business cycle. While in boom periods the prospects of high profits and tightened labour market conditions made companies receptive to the 'teams'' 'attempts to denigrate, reject, or control the employers' property rights' in all wage-related issues,[27] slack times reduced the individual indispensability of skilled hands as unemployment among skilled ironworkers triggered job competition. Hard times, American ironworkers bitterly recalled, periodically eroded their bargaining position to a level close to 'the complete subjugation of labor to the will of the employer'.[28] Constantly balanced anew between companies and 'teams', industrial relations rhythmically oscillated between 'pleasant relations', which revealed workers' temporary dominance, and '[a] sort of warfare'.[29]

In this social context, skilled iron workers relied on their self-conscious 'defensive elitism' as a crucial social resource both to maintain or to recoup wage levels under varying business conditions and to safeguard their privileged segment of the labour market. In combination, the 'helper system', which placed the hiring, training, and promotion of underhands into the hands of the 'team leaders', the 'heat system' which openly restricted output and indirectly regulated working hours, and the 'one job system' which was designed to keep top hands integrated into the 'team structure' constituted the principal elements of skilled workers' control over labour market conditions. On the one hand, their functional autonomy in the work process enabled the 'teams' to influence working conditions by adopting an 'ethical code' governing the workers' conduct toward their fellow workmen and toward the company. The organisational capabilities inherent in the 'team' structure and in the command of top hands over their 'teams' rendered it possible to enforce work rules not by bargaining with the employer but by unilaterally imposing them on shopfloor relations by means of the collective conduct of 'honourable' craftsmen adhering to a shared 'mutualistic ethic'. Ethical conduct was largely habitualised through mill socialisation and embedded in group ritual although peer pressure and the threat of group sanctions added their weight to enforce compliance. On the other hand, mutual self-control had to be supplemented by the direct utilisation of group power in negotiating rules with the companies. The functional 'team' structures translated into an almost organic proto-organisational group cohesion which forged skilled ironworkers' collective indispensability in production into a direct veto power. Their skill- and group-based shopfloor power enabled the 'teams' to co-determine conditions of work to a remarkable degree in and through the production process even before unionisation.[30]

Yet 'team' solidarity, overwhelmingly fostered by the work groups' antagonistic power relations to 'a common employer upon whom demands must be made for any change in working rules or for an increase in wages', was always precarious and pressured.[31] Furthermore, at least in part, this solidarity must be interpreted less in terms of 'brotherly' affection for fellow workmen than in terms of hierarchial intragroup coercion by peers. As between masters, mutual ethical self-control, however decisive for maintaining group homogeneity and identity of interest, did not prevent frequent violations of output restrictions or apprenticeship rules for egoistic purposes. Likewise, in Britain and the USA, where the more rigid 'contracting' form of the 'manufacture system' prevailed, 'teams' and unions fought a running battle against the 'many jobs system' which placed 'contractors' as masters over fellow masters and loosened their ties to manual labour, thus threatening to undermine the social network on which the 'teams" group power rested.

The 'teams" internal structure, on the other hand, was far from egalitarian. 'Contracting', as described by Montgomery, was frequently handled by the 'teams' as a collective bargaining process that involved a complex hierarchical modus of consensus-building. In its more rigid forms, however, as commonly practised in Britain, it could come to mean outright exploitation of underhands by their 'team leaders'.[32] Generally, relations between top hands and helpers were often strained by latent conflicts over pay, apprenticeship rules and promotions. Their dominance as 'team leaders' allowed top hands to use their helpers as a kind of shock absorber in slack times. Their 'inner elitism', promoting the exclusive interests of masters as against all other social groups in the mill, tended to collide with the wider 'team elitism' which demarcated both masters and helpers from 'green hands' and unskilled labour and demanded that the masters also played by the rules of wider group discipline. On the whole, the mutual dependency of masters and underhands certainly remained the crucial factor in maintaining an 'organic' group discipline which served as the principal social resource of all skilled ironworkers in conflicts with management. Group consensus, however, remained fragile. Not surprisingly, this pressured solidarity proved easier to sustain in periods of industrial expansion than during recession or structural decline.[33]

The social origins of 'craft unionism' in the iron industry

These proto-organisational industrial relations in iron production provided the social seedbed for the formation of elitist and highly exclusive craft unions. This type of union simply extended informal group structures on the shopfloor into formal organisation. In an almost 'symbiotic relationship', such craft unions drew on the pronounced job pride, the firm primary networks and the formidable direct group power of the 'teams' as their specific social resources which determined both their elitist social outlook and their internal structure and institutional form. The unions, for their part, augmented the primary work groups' power through the organisational resources provided by inter-departmental and interplant network-building. In contrast to other forms of craft organisations which also built on job pride and 'craft solidarity' but whose organisational structure compensated for a lack of workplace power, the strong craft unions in the iron industry organisationally reinforced and supplemented the 'teams'' skill-based power of directly co-determining the conditions of their work. Characteristically, such unions maintained a decidedly syndicalist structure. The local 'lodges' constituted their chief components, and they were only loosely integrated by relatively weak central institutions.

Ironworkers' craft unions emerged as highly elitist associations of masters. They resembled a 'top heavy' type of organisation excluding most categories even of skilled helpers. Yet they represented a much larger organisational power basis than could be read from sheer membership figures, since the 'team leaders' channelled their proto-organisational group resources into the unions' collective force even before formally admitting their 'teams' into the organisation. Nevertheless, the unions principally served the masters' narrow 'inner elitism' and advocated the helpers' interests only insofar as all skilled hands' common exclusivity versus unskilled labour and their common position to management were concerned:

> As original leaders, [the masters] set up the rules and structure of the union in a manner that favored themselves. With the power to control access to jobs of the lesser skilled, they used their actual or potential power to surround themselves with relatives, friends, and sympathizers.[34]

Effective strike action was vitally dependent on securing the joint action of masters and helpers on the basis of informal conciliation, personal bonds, the authority of top hands as 'team leaders', and the factual indispensability of the masters for successful production which, in a majority of cases, forced helpers to comply with the former's decision to 'withdraw their skills' until management met demands. However, as occasional strikes of underhands against their masters and their recurrent readiness to act as scabs in cases of masters' walkouts demonstrated, the internal tensions in the 'team' structure did pose an existential challenge to the union. These strains translated into latent conflicts over the issue of proper representation of underhands at the organisational level. The second challenge the unions had to face were intercraft rivalries. More than a handful of walkouts were defeated when rollers and heaters denied puddlers on strike their support or vice versa. In those cases, companies could successfully bypass striking departments and thus avoid a total standstill of production. This increased their 'waiting power' and eventually helped them to 'dry out' such partial conflicts. The unions' approach to solving this problem was the amalgamation of sectoral organisations which proved, on the whole, an effective measure to force the trades to balance their interests in order to secure joint action.[35]

Industrial relations and collective bargaining in the 'age of iron', 1850s–1890s

Proto-organisational industrial relations in iron production and their close affinity to a specific, strong type of craft unionism provide a common enough starting point to trace and explain divergent developments among Germany, Britain and the USA. The most important difference between the cases is also the most conspicuous: whereas unions of the type portrayed above emerged in Britain and the USA in the 1860s, German ironworkers, although displaying a by now familiar propensity to engage in strike activities, failed to establish a formal union organisation throughout the period under investigation. Yet this divergence occurred on a remarkably broad basis of similarities in the patterns of proto-organisational social relations.[36] As I will argue below, a comprehensive interpretation of this German peculiarity primarily has to take into consideration the trade-specific industrial conditions whose variations between countries and regions proved favourable or unfavourable to ironworkers' craft union formation and survival. By contrast, an unqualified recourse to 'national' or 'political' factors, as was common in German labour history, fails to account for the emergence or absence of an organisational pattern that developed in close proximity to the shopfloor while keeping a conspicuous distance from the sphere of labour party politics. Such a view also ignores the far-reaching parallels in proto-organisational structures, and it tends to assign an undue weight to political factors which, in this case, may be seen as contributory rather than decisive. In addition, significant divergences in union structure and practice developed between Britain and the USA as well. I will demonstrate that these differences must likewise be traced back to differential economic and industrial conditions. Whereas the social networks of the 'team system' provided the 'necessary conditions' for the formation and entrenchment of craft unions, differential market and industrial processes, which directly affected industrial relations, represented intervening if endogenous variables that decided the divergent organisational outcomes of common proto-organisational social processes. As a result, the three cases will be shown to represent variations on a common pattern.

In Britain, puddlers and top hands of related crafts formed the Amalgamated Malleable Iron Workers of Great Britain (AMIW) in

1863.[37] A period of intense industrial conflict ensued from the adverse economic conditions of the late 1860s. Weakened by major strike defeats, the AMIW's membership dwindled away from 6500 in 1866 to a scanty 600 by 1869. On the brink of total collapse, the union leadership repeatedly petitioned in favour of arbitration. Reluctantly, regional employers' associations agreed to set up bilateral arbitration boards. Delicate prospects of economic recovery had spurred their decision, since only arbitration could advert the obvious threat of an inopportune revitalisation of the strike weapon by the ironworkers trying to retrieve wage losses suffered during recession. In the spring of 1869, the Northern Board was established, comprising one employer and one workers' representative from each affiliated plant. In 1876, the Midlands Board followed suit, consisting of 12 representatives from each side elected by delegates from each member firm.[38]

This pattern of regional multi-employer bargaining proved remarkably successful in reducing strike propensity. Eventually, the Boards adopted sliding-scale wage agreements designed to regulate fluctuations in piece-rates by formally linking them to movements of market prices within negotiated limits. General wage issues such as base rates and wage differentials between trades were determined by meetings of the full board. Local disputes were referred to joint standing committees of representatives not directly involved. If either panel of this two-tier system failed to reach a settlement, the cases in question were handed over to neutral third-party arbitration. Decisions on this level were binding on both sides.

The Boards proved effective as a stabilising force in industrial relations chiefly because British ironmasters had little incentive to break out of this system. Hampered both by cheap imports, channelled into the domestic market by independent iron merchants, and by a wide fringe of small domestic producers for whom these merchants continued to provide secure market outlets, even the largest producers fell short of accumulating a sufficient market share and, correspondingly, bargaining power to allow for the successful pursuit of alternative and potentially disruptive strategies.[39] Iron production in Britain remained 'amazingly scattered in small plants', and both fierce competition and the failure to establish oligopolistic market control forced employers to settle by means of arbitration instead of venturing into open conflict with organised labour.[40] Likewise, this combination and slow rates of overall increase in output helped preserve the industry's traditional structure during the transition from iron to steel. Whereas the Bessemer industry remained an isolated sub-industry with a quickly declining relevance for the trade as a whole, most iron firms expanded into steel production by gradually replacing puddling with small open-hearth furnaces. Unlike their German and US counterparts, British producers incorporated steel-producing technology into the industrial and social fabric of iron production. Their early concentration on high-quality steelmaking and the piecemeal nature of the transformation kept the social foundations of the 'team system' and the established collective bargaining scheme largely intact.

Although Board elections and procedures fell short of indicating formal union recognition, workers usually delegated AMIW's officials as their representatives. This increased the union's bargaining leverage while it lessened its dependency on the active maintenance of membership. In fact, craft unionism in the British iron and steel industry developed into a dual structure in which the workers' delegates came to represent the 'team leaders" *bona fide* bargaining agents. Subscribing to Board elections and working through its institutional system often served as a substitute for formal union affiliation.[41] The resulting stagnation of union membership had a twofold impact on the course of industrial relations in iron and steel. First, limited organisational strength virtually forced the AMIW both to utilise their strong institutional position to uphold authority and to comply with all Board policies. Second, their position provided little incentive to adapt union practices to changing structural conditions. In Britain, the divide between 'contractors' and helpers, who mostly received hourly pay, was considerably deeper than in Germany and the USA. Underhands had no representation whatsoever at the union level and, consequently, at the Boards. Since the AMIW did not seem vitally dependent on a strong, unified organisational basis, the union cultivated a highly exclusive version of the contractors' 'inner elitism'.

This recalcitrant policy eventually provoked the formation of separate helpers' unions. Growing at a fast pace into a powerful movement and broadening their social basis to include related crafts and lesser skilled iron- and steelworkers, helpers' unions managed to extend their grip into the expanding sector of open-hearth steelmaking which the AMIW had been too uninterested and elitist to organise. In particular, the British Steel Smelters Association (1886) gained considerable strength in a dynamic process of growth and won recognition in many open-hearth establishments. After usurping dominance in a number of regional Boards, thereby confining the AMIW to the traditional sectors of iron production, the helpers' unions succeeded in eliminating 'contracting' altogether. In exchange they jettisoned the most restrictive and elitist traits of the 'manufacture system'. For instance, they abandoned any claim to the regulation of output. Instead, they eventually achieved the implementation of fixed wage differentials between crew members, of direct payment and hiring by the firms, and of promotion lines governed by the principle of job seniority. The helpers' unions did maintain a filtered version of craft exclusivity, especially by discouraging unskilled labourers from joining the organisation. Yet, by undercutting the privileged skill status of top hands, the underhands managed to 'capture' the bargaining system from below. This limited step from craft to industrial unionism allowed them to adapt their organisations to the conditions prevailing in British steel production.[42]

In the USA, the Sons of Vulcan, a puddlers' organisation dating back as far as 1858, merged with the highly elitist Rollers' and Heaters' Union and their rival, a union of skilled rollhands and rolling mill helpers, to form the powerful Amalgamated Association of Iron, Steel and Tin Workers of North America (AA) in 1876.[43] Like its counterpart in Britain, the Amalgamated Association in its early years represented an association of masters and highly skilled rollhands. American 'team leaders' also reigned supreme by utilizing the union as an instrument both to reinforce their informal group power and to amass collective resources through horizontal organisation and amalgamation. Yet, unlike in Britain, neither labour nor employers in the US iron industry ever pressured for arbitration. In Britain, virtual stalemate in industrial relations had consolidated institutionalised collaboration between ironmasters and men. In the USA, by contrast, a much more erratically oscillating business cycle, higher growth rates in boom periods and a more rapid transition from iron to steel alternately propelled either labour or capital into periodically superior bargaining positions which they respectively tried to exploit and perpetuate at the expense of the other side. Subsequent reversal of economic conditions would then invariably provoke instant retaliation. This explosive configuration must be held responsible for the early and permanent displacement of multi-employer bargaining. Regional sliding-scale agreements had been negotiated in puddling and sheet rolling between 1865 and 1874. In the following year, a successful three months' strike by Pittsburgh puddlers and a temporary recovery of business led to the disintegration of the employers' united frontline.[44] Collective bargaining in the US iron industry subsequently split up into a series of single-employer negotiations. Usually, the AA would 'legislate' wage rates and 'by-laws' for the following scale year at its annual convention and then present a draft agreement to one of the prominent employers of the Pittsburgh area. If the offer was accepted, the majority of employers would likewise endorse the contract.[45]

Such firm-by-firm contracting had a pro-cyclical impact on industrial relations: it enhanced the union's position in times of overall union supremacy and during the period when the employers did not yet constitute too heterogeneous a group. In slack times, by contrast, and increasingly with the widening of differentials between medium-sized and large, integrated producers, strong opponents proved able to shut out the union altogether thus eventually setting in motion a downward spiral of union activity throughout the major iron and steel centres of the country. Individual contract negotiations, therefore, always directly or indirectly touched upon the very issue of union recognition and the survival of local 'lodges'.

On this basis, a pattern of intensely contested industrial relations evolved that became characterised by a high frequency of furious strikes and lockouts whose respective outcomes were largely determined by momentary economic conditions and the industrial structure of the firms involved. Conflicts over wages were most common. Yet local strikes against 'obnoxious rules', 'pretentious bosses' and employers' attempts to denounce union recognition erupted constantly, despite the union leadership's uphill battle to curb such spontaneous struggles.[46] At times, these 'frank trial[s] of strength' exhausted all participants alike and 'ended with disastrous effects to both sides'.[47] Single-employer bargaining and the enormous strike propensity evolving from this fragmented nature of industrial relations placed immense weight on AA policies concerning maintenance of membership. During the 1880s, therefore, the AA craftsmen, unlike the AMIW, increasingly turned towards broadening the union's social basis without renouncing craft exclusivity and control over union affairs. In order to enhance their striking force, they grudgingly gave in to the necessity 'to admit helpers into their organization ... [to] better enable [them] to control the helpers and thus eliminate the evils incident to their employment'.[48] In a piecemeal process, the AA developed from an association of masters into an organisation comprising 'all men working in and around Rolling Mills' 'except laborers'.[49] This structural shift, which accounted for the union's soaring membership figures in the late 1880s, augmented the 'team leaders'' organisational power as it brought 'team structures' and the social fabric of local 'lodges' into complete congruence. Thus 'team' cohesion and union discipline mutually reinforced each other:

> In our particular lodge the roller was also president of the union, and so it paid to be at the union meetings. You see if you missed a union meeting, the roller, if you worked on the rolling mill, saw to it that you got the most miserable job you could get, and he kept you on it for a day or two. You made the next meeting. The only thing is, he was the boss too.[50]

The integration of the entire 'team' fabric into the union structure did have a long-term impact on AA policies. In order to bypass the masters' overarching control over local 'lodges', underhands increasingly strove for the strengthening of the union's central institutions. To achieve this end, they adopted the organisation's annual conventions as a forum in which to assert their special interests. In particular, they persistently demanded that a more pronounced disciplinary authority over the 'team leaders' be exercised by the 'national' union leadership in order to enforce ever more detailed rules of conduct. However, this increasingly pervasive integration of helpers into the organisation kept them bound to an elitist craft union whose practices continued to be largely determined by top hands' interests while their own attempts to influence union policies stopped short of 'capturing' the AA from below. In contrast to Britain, this development severely reduced the organisation's flexibility and consequently its ability to expand into the rapidly growing steelmaking sectors of the industry. Its running battle to uphold group discipline and enforce compliance with union policies finally led to a significant shift in its practices from internally defining codes of behaviour to emphasising formal rules to be imposed on the employers in contract negotiations. Thus the union system in the mills, by the end of the 1880s, became increasingly pervasive and rigid.[51] In this situation, even disputes of marginal relevance frequently escalated into struggles for the very existence of the local union. Industrial relations in iron and steel reached a new climax of antagonism, when increasing union rigidity and militancy clashed with the stiffened resistance of employers bracing for the economic restructuring of the trade that was well under way in the late 1880s.[52]

The AA's internal development proved inappropriate in helping it adjust to the overall effects of structural change which at the same time spurred employers' growing determination to rid their mills of the constrictions of the union system altogether. Thrown back on the defensive in a fierce struggle for its very existence, which culminated in the bloody battle at Homestead in 1892, the union was almost completely driven out of the key sectors of the industry by the end of the fatal recession of the early 1890s that had decisively accelerated the replacement of iron production by steelmaking. The union had faced regional disparities in organisational strength almost from the outset. Whereas it claimed to control about two-thirds of all iron mills by 1890, it never gained a firm foothold in the large isolated rail mills such as Cambria or Bethlehem Iron. Likewise, it failed to organise the rapidly expanding Bessemer steel industry. Superior economic resources accounted for the former's power to withstand permanent unionisation. Working conditions in Bessemer works and steel rail rolling mills, on the other hand, generated patterns of group cooperation and work organisation fundamentally different from the 'team system'. Moreover, whereas by 1884 'no one could successfully fight the A.A. within the smoke of Pittsburgh' (Andrew Carnegie), and the Western iron centres generally had become the union's stronghold, 'for certain reasons, the East had never been successfully organised'.[53] Thus the union managed to defend its strong position in the industry only as long as the Western iron industry continued to expand spasmodically during the boom periods of the late 1880s and only as long as the dynamic steel industry remained relatively isolated in its sector of the trade. Increasing national market integration intensified cost competition and made the reverberations of the fierce competition in steel felt by the iron mills as well. Increasing centralisation of capital in multiplant enterprises and the subsequent structural contraction of the skilled ironworkers' labour market added their weight. The union's protracted agony finally gave way to wholesale defeat in the early 1890s.[54]

During the late 1880s, and particularly in the recession of the early 1890s, the union, albeit more successful than ever before in managing to secure joint action of masters and helpers, lost recognition in one mill after the other. The number of active lodges plummeted. Although major strikes failed in steel as well, the union received its death-blow on its own turf in the iron mills. It was not deskilling, as American labour historians suggest, but economic contraction and increasing corporate power that eroded its bargaining position structurally.[55] Job competition by drifting unemployed craftsmen, not by unskilled shipped-in strikebreakers, reduced skilled workers' individual indispensability and decisively impaired their direct and organised group power in the mills. This process finally paralysed the organisation until the new patterns of social relations in the steel mills had become a majority phenomenon throughout the industry.

Although iron production in the Ruhr district shared many, if not all, elements of the 'manufacture system' as established in Britain and the USA, German ironworkers stopped short of casting their 'defensive elitism' into formal union institutions. In the Ruhr, the iron industry expanded even more rapidly than in the USA, and this process took a far less cyclical course than in both Britain and the USA. Between 1860 and 1870, Ruhr ironworks increased their number of puddling furnaces by 124 per cent as compared to a growth rate of 40 per cent in the Pittsburgh area. Since skilled labour was in constant short supply in this period, at first migrant British and Belgian masters, and later their German successors, trained German puddlers and rollers in large numbers. Vast expansion and the virtual absence of cyclical downturns seemingly rendered the institutionalisation of craft exclusivity superfluous; intense competition between works for skilled labour put even individual workers and informal groups into an excellent bargaining position. Although German ironworkers did display the pronounced 'elitism' typical of their craft, the prevailing superb economic conditions reduced their need to adopt an openly 'defensive' posture at this early phase. The boom period of the early 1870s brought German ironworkers to the apex of their bargaining power. Strike activity reached an unprecedented climax. Employers saw themselves in a 'permanent state of partial strikes' during these years.[56]

Rapid and linear expansion must be said to have delayed craft unionism until a configuration arose which, thereafter, rendered organisation impossible. Prodigious growth rates had momentously inhibited the 'social closure' of the 'team system' in the Ruhr. Earlier than in the USA, for instance, a hybrid position between masters and management, the so-called *Obermeister*, emerged in the process that subsequently managed to wrest certain discretionary prerogatives from the hands of the 'teams'. Consequently, the 'team networks' in the Ruhr remained incomplete, lacking cohesion and full control over access to the trade, thereby rendering them much more vulnerable than the organisationally supported social fabric of British and American iron mills when depression struck after 1873. Furthermore, unlike in Britain and the USA, where iron-producing facilities continued to expand spasmodically well into the 1880s, this depression marked a watershed in the development of the German iron industry. Signifying a trend reversal rather than a cyclical downturn, the number of furnaces in operation dropped by as much as 50 per cent and subsequently continued to stagnate on a level far lower than during the boom years. Chronic underutilisation of capacities led to persistent unemployment among skilled ironworkers. Their lack of organisational support now backfired on them, and the structural crisis did everything but improve their organisational capabilities. '[T]oday', a Ruhr ironmaster stated pointedly, 'the worker is as submissive as one could possibly want him to be'.[57]

This trend reversal was caused by the peculiar structure of the iron industry in the Ruhr. It also signified a particularly early beginning of the transition from iron to steel which progressed more rapidly than both in Britain and the USA. Most iron mills in the Ruhr had been established as large integrated rail mills like those forming an isolated 'subindustry' and a major barrier to unionisation in the USA. Intense competition among rail producers in this district fostered a pronounced convergence of business structures which left little room for medium-sized firms that, as shown above, dominated the British iron industry and the Western iron districts in the USA. Fierce competition forced almost all the large iron producers in the Ruhr to invest in Bessemer facilities by 1870, and this nearly simultaneous move aggravated the subsequent crisis. Thus, unlike in Britain and the USA, steelmaking in the Ruhr was not confined to an isolated sector of the industry, but contributed to reshaping the structure of iron mills from the outset. In order to safeguard the enormous capital expenses already embodied in their steelmaking facilities in the severe deflationary crisis of the 1870s and 1880s, German ironmasters saw themselves forced to divert scarce resources from iron to steel production. Follow-up investments allocated to cutting costs by realising technological 'economies of scale and speed' in steel were given top priority in order to secure the economic survival of the firms as a whole, and this was accomplished at the expense of the iron establishments within the same enterprises. Thus competition between iron and steel was incorporated into the internal business structure of firms, and this, in turn, decisively hastened the displacement of iron by steel in Germany. Moreover, it further promoted the centralisation of capital and the accumulation of corporate power.[58]

In France, the transition from iron to steel progressed even more swiftly than in neighbouring Germany. Except for the older, slowly growing blast furnace industry, whose skilled employees displayed all exclusive traits of the 'team system' short of formal unionisation,[59] the actual steelmaking and rolling industry must be considered a true child of the Bessemer and Thomas Gilchrist process. From the outset onwards, therefore, the French steel industry emerged on the basis of the new steel-converting technologies and adopted the very structures that had destroyed all chances of unionisation in its German counterpart, proving to be hostile ground for any attempt at organisation.

France was a latecomer even according to German standards: the expansion of steel production did not make substantial headway before the late 1880s. Significantly, it relied heavily on Belgian and German experts for operating the new converter plants and rolling mills. Moreover, the French steelmaking enterprises appear even more concentrated than the oligopoly of large integrated producers that dominated heavy industry in the Ruhr. With its late take-off, the French iron and steel industry virtually bypassed the era of wrought iron and, with it, the social context within which ironworkers' craft unions had been rooted elsewhere.[60]

Industrial relations in the steel era, 1890s–1910

During the transition to steel production, the US and German steel industries set out to surpass their British competitor in terms of growth rates and plant sizes. Giant combined works centralised steel production in large-scale, hard-driven production facilities. In Britain, by contrast, this transition was rather a matter of degree. Firms remained predominantly medium-sized and ventured early into the high-quality niches of ship plate steel made in modestly dimensioned open-hearth furnaces. The centralised nature of the work process especially in the integrated converter steelworks of the 1890s and 1900s broke up the 'team' structure, and the high speed of operations and the lavish scale of both machinery and products combined to necessitate ever more hard, physical labour in order to allow the workforce to keep up with production. All work now, even the skilled tasks, had to be performed by large 'gangs' with a small skilled core and a wide periphery of unskilled 'muscle'. Because the skilled steelworkers were virtually swallowed by the inflated unskilled 'gangs', they had to succumb to the rules of 'gang' work and, alongside their ethnically diverse unskilled helpers, they were mercilessly driven by production foremen who themselves did not work physically but concentrated on their coordinating and supervisory roles as 'pushers'. In the social cosmos of the 'drive system', as this production arrangement came to be called on both sides of the Atlantic, mutual isolation, high turnover, low professional self-respect, and brutal repression combined to destroy informal group structures and to impede the genesis of new forms.

During the 1890s and the 1900s, the production milieu in German, French, and American steel mills left no room whatsoever for worker autonomy and group formation which could have served as a basis for organisation and collective action. Only with the harbingers of the full mechanisation of work processes from about 1910 on, which brought about the sharp reduction of unskilled labour and the expansion of the skilled workforce, did tightly-knit networks of skilled operatives – 'crews' – come to dominate plant life, and they eventually formed the shopfloor nucleus of the industrial unions which emerged in the 1920s and the 1930s. The great steel strike in 1919 marked the beginning of a new organisational era in the US steel industry, whereas the increase in wildcat strikes between 1917 and 1924 had a similar effect on German heavy industry.[61] The electrification and full mechanisation of production processes changed skill structures and work group composition in French steel mills correspondingly. The connection between this renewed workplace solidarity, based on new forms of skill- and plant-based group cohesion, and a new syndicalist militancy appears as a universal pattern among all the cases under consideration: in France, the years after 1919 were marked by unprecedented strike activity among steel and rolling mill 'crews' as they were on the other side of the Rhine.[62]

The 'drive system' consolidated the non-union status of the German steel industry structurally. Between 1890 and the outbreak of the First

World War in 1914, less than ten strikes were reported, all of them isolated, partial and unorganised affairs with less than 100 participants each. The workforce in the steel mills remained out of reach of the feeble attempts made by the unions in the neighbouring metal trades to organise them. In 1907 the Deutscher Metallarbeiter-Verband (DMV), by then the most powerful industrial union in the world, only counted 6904 steelworkers among its members in the Düsseldorf district, which encompassed the nation's principal steelmaking centre, the Ruhr. Steelworkers made up a scanty 15.9 per cent of the total regional membership, and only about 5.2 per cent of them were at all organised in the DMV. This situation would change dramatically after 1917, when the 'crew system' became firmly entrenched in the plants.[63]

The French iron and steel industry virtually came into existence in the era of the 'drive system', in the years between 1890 and the 1910s. Accordingly, it shared all its social characteristics, including the small and nevertheless hierarchically organised core of skilled workers, the overwhelming majority of unskilled labourers in the 'gangs', and the ensuing fragmentation and isolation of the workers in the anonymity of these 'gangs'. Correspondingly, strike activity was low and trade union influence weak and irregular. Unlike in Germany, it was the coalminers' union in northern France that tried to gain a foothold in the steel mills, especially in the heavy industrial region around Douai and Valenciennes, where coalmines and steel plants were located adjacent to each other and where the workforce of the mills was substantially recruited from coalminers' families. In these two decades, the level of organisation in the French iron and steel industry was as insignificant as it was in Germany and the USA: in 1911, only 345 steelworkers among the 8000 men employed in the two establishments of Denain-Anzin and Les Anciens were members of the union, and almost all of them were occupied in the maintenance and repair departments of the mills. In Trith-Saint Léger, near Valenciennes, only 200 steelworkers out of 2700 employees belonged to the union. These rates of union density of 4.3 and 7.4 per cent respectively roughly corresponded with the organisational level documented for the Ruhr in 1907.[64]

After the Homestead disaster in 1892 and a series of further defeats, the AA in the USA not only lost all its steel mill lodges but most of their bastions in iron production as well. Its membership of 24 000 in 1891, which had made the AA the strongest US labour union by that time, plummeted to a few thousand, restricted to the sheet mill sector of the industry where economic and technological change was particularly slow. In 1901 a disastrous strike against the newly formed US Steel Corporation led to the loss of about half of the sheet mill lodges. When US Steel finally staged a comprehensive lockout in 1909, the company succeeded in purging its sheet mills even of the last remaining lodges. Subsequently, the AA progressively became confined to the small niches of medium-sised independent specialist firms and stagnated in its elitist conservatism until it was forced by other unions and the mushrooming 'grassroots' movement to support the steel drive of 1919.

In Great Britain, by contrast, the peculiar structure of the steel industry and the gradual transition to steel combined to smooth out the disruptive effects of the 'drive system'. In fact, as far as workplace relations are concerned, the period between 1890 and 1910 must be viewed as a transitory phase between the 'team' and the 'crew system' rather than as a stable structural configuration in its own right. Unlike in Germany, France and the USA, therefore, the history of industrial relations in British steel is a history of continuity, and the history of steel unionism is a story of expansion and success. The organisations of underhands opposed to contracting, that had emerged in the 1880s, continued to grow, particularly in the open-hearth sectors of the industry, and they succeeded in expanding from Scotland, their original base, to England and Wales. The British Steel Smelters Association (BSSA), a union of skilled open-hearth workers, proved to be the most vital organisation, but blast furnace workers, sheet rollers, and ancillary workers followed suit. Between 1897 and 1913, the membership of all unions covering iron- and steelworkers rose from 30 000 to 80 000. In a lengthy process, these unions managed to amalgamate in the Iron and Steel Trade Confederation (ISTC) in 1917.[65]

The new unions in British steel combined direct recognition with a further development of the arbitration machinery. They therefore continued the iron industry's tradition of joint boards and two-tier bargaining on a regional basis. Yet whereas organisational fragmentation on the part both of most unions and most employers' associations confined bargaining and arbitration to product-specific and regional contexts, the BSSA succeeded in installing even a national bargaining machinery, which on the local level established a joint board and bipartite 'neutral commission' system for disputes not resolved by direct bargaining, and on the national level set up joint conferences which were composed of bipartite delegates of each establishment and trade union branch.[66] The emancipation from the elitist AMIW, the gradual and flexible transition from craft to industrial unionism, and the combination of direct recognition and arbitration combined to secure the survival of British steel unionism and to facilitate its firm entrenchment even under the conditions of economic and technological change. Yet it was decisive that this change was much less dynamic and disruptive than in Germany, France and the USA.

Conclusion

Craft unionism in the iron industry had its roots in specific workplace relations which have been shown to be universal in British, American and German iron mills between the 1860s and the 1890s. Yet the embeddedness of this social fabric in concrete market and business structures had to be taken into account in order to explain precisely why craft unions emerged or not, what institutional forms they assumed and which factors determined their varying ability to adapt to structural change. Thus I have here identified endogenous, rather than exogenous, factors to account for both similarities and differences between cases. Modest, but sustained expansion of the industry and the experience of repeated cyclical ups and downs seem to be the prime determinants which pushed ironworkers into institutionalising their 'defensive elitism'. The unions proved particularly viable and strong in industrial landscapes dominated by agglomerations of medium-sized firms that only gradually moved into steel and organised steel production on a limited scale. Large integrated iron rail producers persistently proved difficult to unionise on a permanent basis. This hints at the significance of corporate power in industrial relations which translated into superior 'waiting power' in case of conflict. Rapid expansion, structural crisis and a swift transition from iron to steel clearly inhibited union formation and provided existential challenges for established organisations as well.

The parallel expansion of steel production in large combined works accounts for the establishment of a non-union system in Germany, France and the USA after the 1890s, while slower growth saved the conciliatory collective bargaining system in Great Britain. Only after 1910 did the social conditions of steel production change in a way as to once more allow autonomous group formation and invite organisation drives as a new departure for the unionisation of the German, French and US steel industries.

On a deeper theoretical level, unionism in iron and steel bears an almost exclusively workplace-based, professional character. Its traits were universal, where – and as long as – similar economic and technological conditions prevailed, albeit with gradually diverging institutional outcomes. Despite this politics-distant and rather trade-exclusive character, iron and steel unions did contribute to the shaping of the national models of union formation: the strong craft unions of the 'age of iron' in Great Britain and the USA served as central proponents of the business unionism model which came to dominate the labour movement of these nations as a whole. In Germany, by contrast, the ironworkers' inability to establish formal organisations prevented them from pushing an exclusively artisanal labour movement further towards workplace-based craft unionism. This element was here only represented by the rather small printing and cigar-making trades. In the 1920s and 1930s, however, the plant-oriented new industrial unionism in German and US steel mills again helped shape the organisational landscapes of these nations to a considerable degree, with their characteristic and innovative combination of strong plant-related interest politics and a highly professional central bargaining machinery – a system which had emerged gradually during the transition from iron to steel in Great Britain.

Notes

1. Cf. V. C. Hattam, *Labor Visions and State Power: The Origins of Business Unionism in the United States*, Princeton, 1993.
2. Cf. F. Boll, *Arbeitskämpfe und Gewerkschaften in Deutschland, England und Frankreich. Ihre Entwicklung vom 19. zum 20. Jahrhundert*, Bonn, 1992, bes. S. 230 ff.
3. Cf. ibid.
4. Cf. ibid., 216 ff., 467 ff.
5. Cf. A. Reid, 'Employers' Strategies and Craft Production: The British Shipbuilding Industry 1870–1950', in S. Tolliday and J. Zeitlin (eds), *The Power to Manage? Employers and Industrial Relations in Comparative-Historical Perspective*, London and New York, 1991, pp. 35–51.
6. For a more detailed theoretical treatment see: T. Welskopp, 'Ein modernes Klassenkonzept für die vergleichende Geschichte industrialisierender und industrieller Gesellschaften', in K. Lauschke and T. Welskopp (eds), *Mikropolitik im Unternehmen. Arbeitsbeziehungen und Machtstrukturen in industriellen Großbetrieben des 20. Jahrhunderts*, Essen, 1994, pp. 48–106.
7. Cf. O. Hardy-Hémery, *De la croissance à la désindustrialisation. Un siècle dans le Valenciennois*, Paris, 1984; O. Hardy-Hémery, *Industries, patronat et ouvriers du Valenciennois pendant le premier XXe siecle: développements et restructurations capitalistes, à l'âge du charbon et de l'acier*, Éditions Sociales, Messidor, 1985.
8. This chapter is largely based on the research for my dissertation: T. Welskopp, *Arbeit und Macht im Hüttenwerk. Arbeits- und industrielle Beziehungen in der deutschen und amerikanischen Eisen- und Stahlindustrie von den 1860er bis zu den 1930er Jahren*, Bonn, 1994.
9. Cf. J. Haydu, *Between Craft and Class: Skilled Workers and Factory Politics in the United States and Britain, 1890–1922*, Los Angeles and Berkeley, 1988; D. Montgomery, *The Fall of the House of Labor. The Workplace, the State, and American Labor Activism, 1865–1925*, Cambridge, Mass., 1987; B. L. Elbaum and F. Wilkinson, 'Industrial Relations and Uneven Development: A Comparative Study of the American and British Steel Industries', in *Cambridge Journal of Economics*, 3, 1979, pp. 275–303; J. Holt, 'Trade Unionism in the British and U.S. Steel Industries, 1885–1912: A Comparative Study', *Labour History*, 18, 1977, pp. 5–35.

10. Cf. the detailed analysis in: Welskopp, *Arbeit und Macht im Hüttenwerk*, Chapter II.1; figures for wrought iron production in Germany, Britain, and the USA: L. Beck, *Geschichte des Eisens in technischer und kulturgeschichtlicher Beziehung*, 5 vols., Braunschweig 1899–1903, vol. 5, pp. 1053, 1056; *Directory to the Iron and Steel Works of the United States, 1873–1901*; P. Temin, *Iron and Steel in 19th Century America*, Cambridge, Mass., 1964; D. L. Burn, *The Economic History of Steelmaking: 1867–1930*, Cambridge, 1940.

11. Cf. M. Nuwer, 'From Batch to Flow: Production Technology and Work-Force Skills in the Steel Industry, 1880–1920', *Technology and Culture*, 29, 1988, pp. 808–38; for the puddling and rolling process in Britain and Germany see: A. Paulinyi, *Das Puddeln. Ein Kapitel aus der Geschichte des Eisens in der industriellen Revolution*, München, 1987; J. P. Roe, 'Manufacture of Wrought Iron', in A. O. Backert (ed.), *The ABC of Iron and Steel*, Cleveland, 1915, pp. 93–103.

12. See the description on the basis of primary sources in Welskopp, *Arbeit und Macht im Hüttenwerk*, Chapter II.2.

13. Testimony Layton, in: US Senate, Committee on Education and Labor, *Report of the Committee of the Senate upon the Relations between Labor and Capital*, 4 vols., Washington DC, 1885, vol. I, pp. 21, 27.

14. Montgomery, *The Fall of the House of Labor*, p. 28; M. E. Freifeld, 'The Emergence of the American Working Class: Roots of Division, 1865–1885', PhD thesis, New York University, 1980, p. 440–41; L. G. Schneider, 'American Nationality and Workers' Consciousness in Industrial Conflict: 1870–1920. Three Case Studies', PhD thesis, Columbia University, New York, 1975, pp. 86–90.

15. Testimony Layton, in US Senate, *Labor and Capital, Report*, vol. I, p. 21; for Germany: Hoesch-Archiv DHHU, Nr. 1946; J. W. Bennett, 'Iron Workers in Woods Run and Johnstown: The Union Era 1865–1895', PhD thesis, University of Pittsburgh, 1977, p. 10; B. Soffer, 'A Theory of Trade Union Development: The Role of the "Autonomous" Workman', *Labor History*, 1, 1960, pp. 141–63, at p. 142; R. Fremdling, 'Der Puddler – Zur Sozialgeschichte eines Industriehandwerkers', in U. Engelhardt (ed.), *Handwerkerschaft und Industrialisierung in Deutschland*, Stuttgart, 1984, pp. 637–65, at p. 641; K. von Borries, *Das Puddelverfahren in Rheinland und Westfalen volkswirtschaftlich betrachtet*, Diss. Bonn, Düsseldorf, 1929, p. 20; Elbaum and Wilkinson, 'Industrial Relations', p. 283.

16. Cf. detailed figures and tables in Welskopp, *Arbeit und Macht im Hüttenwerk*, Chapters II.2, II.3.

17. Historical Collection and Labor Archives, Pennsylvania State University (HCLA PSU), United Steelworkers of America Oral History Project: Interview no. 28 with Les Thornton (1970), p. 3.

18. Testimony Layton, in US Senate, *Labor and Capital, Report*, vol. I, p. 21.

19. F. G. Couvares, *The Remaking of Pittsburgh. Class and Culture in an Industrializing City 1877–1919*, Albany, NY, 1984, p. 18; Montgomery, *The Fall of the House of Labor*, p. 11; Freifeld, p. 440; Fremdling, p. 659.

20. Montgomery, *The Fall of the House of Labor*, p. 12.

21. J. McHugh, *Alexander Holley and the Makers of Steel*, Baltimore and London, 1980, p. 235.

22. Ibid.; cf. also Nuwer, 'From Batch to Flow'; Soffer, 'A Theory of

Trade Union Development'; Montgomery, *The Fall of the House of Labor*, Chapter 1; for Britain: Elbaum and Wilkinson, 'Industrial Relations'.
23. Cf. the analysis and primary material for Germany and the USA in Welskopp, *Arbeit und Macht im Hüttenwerk*, Chapter II.3; cf. also: T. Welskopp, 'Arbeit und Zusammenarbeit im Hüttenwerk. Deutsche und amerikanische Beispiele, 1860–1930', in O. Dascher and C. Kleinschmidt (eds), *Die Eisen- und Stahlindustrie im Dortmunder Raum*, Dortmund, 1992, pp. 149–79, 153–62.
24. D. Montgomery, *Workers' Control in America: Studies in the History of Work, Technology, and Labor Struggles*, Cambridge, Mass., 1981, p. 12; see also K. Stone, 'The Origin of Job Structures in the Steel Industry', in R. C. Edwards et al. (eds), *Labor Market Segmentation. Conference on Labor Market Segmentations*, Harvard University, 1973, Lexington, Mass., 1975, pp. 27–84, 27, 30.
25. A. Dawson, 'The Paradoxy of Dynamic Technological Change and the Labor Aristocracy in the United States, 1880–1914', *Labor History*, 20, 1979, pp. 325–51, at p. 329.
26. Elbaum and Wilkinson, 'Industrial Relations', pp. 283–7.
27. A. Dawson, 'The Parameters of Craft Consciousness: The Social Outlook of the Skilled Worker, 1890–1920', in D. Hoerder (ed.), *American Labor and Immigration History, 1877–1920s: Recent European Research*, Urbana, Chicago and London, 1983, pp. 135–55; 139–40.
28. Testimony Weihe in US Senate, *Labor and Capital*, Report, vol. II, p. 12; Soffer, 'A Theory of Trade Union Development', p. 155; D. Brody, *Steelworkers in America. The Nonunion Era*, New York, 1969 (first published in 1960), p. 58; W. T. Hogan, *Economic History of the Iron and Steel Industry in the United States*, 5 vols., Lexington, Mass., Toronto, and London, 1971, vol. 1, p. 85.
29. Address by President John O. Edwards, 'Sons of Vulcan', *Vulcan Record*, I (7), December 1870, pp. 3–4.
30. Cf. the analysis in Welskopp, *Arbeit und Macht im Hüttenwerk*, Chapters II.3, II.4; Welskopp, 'Arbeit und Zusammenarbeit', pp. 156–63.
31. J. H. Ashworth, *The Helper and American Trade Unions*, Baltimore, 1915, p. 90.
32. Montgomery, *The Fall of the House of Labor*, pp. 9–13; Freifeld, 'The Emergence of the American Working Class', pp. 440–60; Elbaum and Wilkinson, 'Industrial Relations', p. 283.
33. Welskopp, *Arbeit und Macht im Hüttenwerk*, Chapter II.4.
34. Soffer, 'A Theory of Trade Union Development', p. 154.
35. See the detailed accounts in Freifeld, 'The Emergence of the American Working Class', pp. 440–60; J. S. Robinson, *The Amalgamated Association of Iron, Steel and Tin Workers*, Baltimore, 1920; C. D. Wright, 'The Amalgamated Association of Iron and Steel Workers', in *Quarterly Journal of Economics*, 7, 1892–1893, pp. 400–32; for Britain and the USA: Holt, 'Trade Unionism in the British and U.S. Steel Industries', pp. 5–17; Elbaum and Wilkinson, 'Industrial Relations'; Welskopp, *Arbeit und Macht im Hüttenwerk*, Chapter II.4.
36. The extent of similarities as between Germany and the U.S. is demonstrated on the basis of primary sources in: Welskopp, *Arbeit und Macht im Hüttenwerk*, Chapters II.3, II.6, II.7.

37. Elbaum and Wilkinson, 'Industrial Relations', p. 285; Holt, 'Trade Unionism in the British and U.S. Steel Industry', p. 6.
38. Elbaum and Wilkinson, 'Industrial Relations', p. 286; A. J. Odber, *The Origins of Industrial Peace: The Manufactured Iron Trade in England*, Oxford, 1951.
39. Cf. Burn, *The Economic History of Steelmaking*.
40. T. H. Burnham and G. O. Hoskins, *Iron and Steel in Britain 1870–1930*, London, 1943, p. 236.
41. Cf. Elbaum and Wilkinson, 'Industrial Relations', p. 287; A. Pugh, *Men of Steel*, London, 1951.
42. Elbaum and Wilkinson, 'Industrial Relations'; Holt, 'Trade Unionism in the British and U.S. Steel Industry', pp. 6–33.
43. For a detailed account of craft union formation in the US iron and steel industry see Welskopp, *Arbeit und Macht im Hüttenwerk*, pp. 120–4; Robinson, *The Amalgamated Association*; Wright, 'The Amalgamated Association'; J. Jarrett, 'The Story of the Iron Workers', in G. E. McNeill (ed.), *The Labor Movement: The Problem of To-Day*, Boston and New York, 1887, pp. 268–311.
44. Jarrett, 'The Story of the Iron Workers', p. 304.
45. *National Labor Tribune*, 9 May, 1885; 30 May, 1885; 6 June, 1885; 13 June, 1885; 20 June, 1885; 27 June, 1885; Robinson, *The Amalgamated Association*, p. 141; Jarrett, 'The Story of the Iron Workers', p. 305; Amalgamated Association (AA), *Proceedings of the 16th Convention*, 1891, p. 3357.
46. AA, *Proceedings of the 14th Convention*, 1889, p. 2786.
47. Jarrett, 'The Story of the Iron Workers', p. 290.
48. AA, *Proceedings of the 12th Convention*, 1887, p. 1953.
49. *Vulcan Record*, I (6), August 1870, p. 20; AA, *Proceedings of the 6th Convention*, 1881, p. 682; J. A. Fitch, *The Steel Workers*, New York, 1910, Appendix II, pp. 257–8; US Senate, *Labor and Capital*, vol. I, p. 1140; Elbaum and Wilkinson, 'Industrial Relations', p. 289; Robinson, *The Amalgamated Association*, pp. 42–5.
50. HCLA PSU, United Steelworkers of America Oral History Project: Interview no. 32 with Harry Viren, 1967, pp. 25–6.
51. J. H. Bridge, *Inside History of the Carnegie Steel Corporation*, New York, 1903, p. 202; S. R. Cohen, 'Steelworkers Rethink the Homestead Strike of 1892', *Pennsylvania History*, 48, 1981, pp. 155–77, 161–3.
52. Welskopp, *Arbeit und Macht im Hüttenwerk*, Chapter II.7.
53. Cited in Bridge, *Inside History*, p. 185; Jarrett, *The Story of the Iron Workers*, p. 287; E. Murasken, 'The Amalgamated Association of Iron, Steel and Tin Workers. A Study in Unionism', MA thesis, New York University, 1937, p. 70.
54. Cf. the analysis based on a statistical breakdown of all strikes in the industry until 1895 in Welskopp, *Arbeit und Macht im Hüttenwerk*, Chapter II.7. A valuable account of the Homestead strike is the recently published study: P. Krause, *The Battle for Homestead 1880–1892. Politics, Culture, and Steel*, Pittsburgh and London, 1992.
55. The older view is represented by Stone, 'The Origin of Job Structures'; Montgomery, *Workers' Control*; Brody, 'The Breakdown of Craft Unionism', in *Steelworkers in America*.
56. Testimonies Wintzer, Schlinck, and Massenez, in Eisen-Enquête-

Kommission, *Protokolle über die Vernehmung der Sachverständigen durch die Eisen-Enquête-Kommission*, Berlin, 1878, pp. 259, 372, 398.
57. Testimony Massenez, in ibid., p. 393; Welskopp, *Arbeit und Macht im Hüttenwerk*, Chapter II.6, provides full documentation of the German development on the basis of primary sources.
58. See ibid., Chapters II.6, II.7. For the development of business structures in the US iron and steel industry and the survival of market niches for small-scale firms where the AA managed to keep up collective bargaining cf.: J. N. Ingham, *Making Iron and Steel: Independent Mills in Pittsburgh, 1820–1920*, Columbus, Ohio, 1991.
59. Cf. G. Hardach, *Der soziale Status des Arbeiters in der Frühindustrialisierung. Eine Untersuchung über die Arbeitnehmer in der französischen eisenschaffenden Industrie zwischen 1800 und 1870*, Berlin, 1969; R. Fremdling, 'Die Ausbreitung des Puddelverfahrens und des Kokshochofens in Belgien, Frankreich und Deutschland', *Technikgeschichte*, 50, 1983, pp. 197–212; R. Fremdling, *Technologischer Wandel und internationaler Handel im 18. und 19. Jahrhundert. Die Eisenindustrien in Großbritannien, Belgien, Frankreich und Deutschland*, Berlin, 1986.
60. The sections on France are based on Hardy-Hémery, *De la croissance*, and Hardy-Hémery, *Industries, patronat et ouvriers*.
61. For a detailed discussion of the succession of production systems and the traits of the 'drive' and 'crew system' see Welskopp, *Arbeit und Macht im Hüttenwerk*, passim.
62. For France cf. O. Hardy-Hémery, 'Strikes in the Coal and Metal Basin of the Nord: New Work Force, New Ideas. Three Years of Indecision: 1919–1921', *Annali*, 1990/91, pp. 45–64.
63. *25 Jahre Arbeitnordwest, 1904–1929*, Berlin, 1929, p. 25; Welskopp, *Arbeit und Macht im Hüttenwerk*, pp. 35 ff., 414 ff.
64. O. Hardy-Hémery, 'On the Trade Union Movement in the French Iron and Steel Industry, 1880–1914', MS, Lille, 1996, p. 3.
65. Elbaum and Wilkinson, 'Industrial Relations', p. 294.
66. Ibid., p. 295; Board of Trade, *Report on Collective Agreements between Employers and Workpeople*, London, 1910.

CHAPTER TWO

Dockers' unions in the ports of London, Le Havre, Rotterdam and Hamburg, 1850–1914

Erik Nijhof
in cooperation with John Barzman and John Lovell

The problem: structural or national differences?

Unions of dockers, like those of other workers, have often been studied in a rather narrow context: as local organisations, as a part of the national labour movement, or as partners in industrial relations. The latter approach offers better perspectives for explaining specific developments and features, but national or even international models may also play a role. A comparative study of the development of dockers' unions that pays tribute to these different perspectives is therefore helpful. We have selected the dockers' unions of four North Sea and Channel ports, belonging to nations with very different economic and labour movement structures (United Kingdom, France, Holland, Germany).

We treat each port in the same way: after a history of the growth and struggle of the unions, the latter's organisational characteristics are linked to an analysis of the social structure of dockwork, such as the type of port and traditional demarcation lines among workers and employers. A detailed list of these factors is given in the Appendix. After this brief sketch we return to our question: to what extent were the differences due to specific circumstances in each port, or to the wider framework of national characteristics?

Struggles and structures

London

The establishment of the lightermen's union in 1866 opens the record of formal organisation in the port of London. After them, only the stevedores, engaged in loading general cargo in the enclosed docks on the north bank of the Thames, and the corn porters, engaged in the manual unloading of grain in the docks on the south bank, founded additional stable organisations. Other groups only produced ephemeral initiatives.

A major revival of unionism occurred during and after the 1889 strike. Both the lightermen's and stevedores' unions expanded rapidly: membership of the latter rose steeply from 2500 to over 4000 in 1889–90, giving a union density of 80 per cent. On the south bank the corn porters (re-)established the South Side Labour Protection League with some 5000 adherents. A new organisation grew out of the small Tea Operatives' Union as a result of the strike, to constitute itself as the Dock, Wharf, Riverside and General Labourers' Union (the Dockers' Union) that enrolled 25000 members in July 1890, most of them port workers. It was to be the largest union and the main instrument of mass mobilisation in the port, although its position was weakened by the survival, and indeed proliferation, of independent unions. Apart from the stevedores, lightermen and south side union, there were newly established occupational unions of crane drivers, tugboatmen, shipworkers in the short sea trades, coal porters, ballast heavers and so on. Since these groups included many of the more skilled elements among the dock labour force, the Dockers' Union was placed in a position of strategic weakness.

Union membership in the port peaked in the summer of 1890, when 100 per cent organisation was briefly attained in many sectors. The closed shop was achieved for a time, but could not be preserved by the unions. Thereafter, a decline set in that affected all unions. Some of the smaller occupational unions disappeared, and this fate would also have befallen the Dockers' Union had it not extended its organisation beyond the London waterfront. In London the union suffered heavy membership losses in 1891 but retained a major foothold at the Victoria and Albert Docks – the busiest in the port. When this too was lost after the 1900 strike, it retained only a nominal presence in London for the ensuing ten years. Given the purely local character of the south side union, the only organisations capable of exerting any real influence in the port during the first decade of the new century were the unions of stevedores and lightermen. When a National Transport Workers' Federation was established in 1910, these unions provided the principal officials of the new body.

In August 1911 there was a major revival of unionism, comparable to 1889, with a general strike of port transport workers. On the eve of the strike, union activity and membership lagged behind that of other ports, but now the Dockers' Union membership multiplied from 2000 to over 22000, whereas the Stevedores' Union doubled from 4000 to 8000.

Once again the Dockers' Union was the largest organisation in the port, but it had to share the floor with the stevedores and lightermen. In the absence of a controlling interest exerted by any one union, the Transport Workers' Federation – to which all port unions were affiliated – came to play a crucial role in London during 1911–12. With a union rate approaching 100 per cent in many sectors, the closed shop became a major issue, as it had been in 1889–90. This issue led to renewed confrontation with port employers in 1912. The protracted strike that year, conducted by the Federation, led to a severe defeat for the London unions. In contrast to the national union membership trend, unionism in the London port declined between 1912 and 1914. The Stevedores' Union's membership fell back to 5000 and the Dockers' Union lost two-thirds of its membership, its decline being arrested only by the outbreak of the First World War.

London, an old tidal port with closed docks, was the greatest port in Europe, with a tonnage of 38 million in 1909 and about 25 000 workers. These were divided by many traditional demarcation lines, derived from cargo-handling practices on sail-ships, which may be summarized as follows.

First and foremost, there was the distinction between work on ship and on shore. On ship, loading operations required more skill than discharging or handling the winch; the transition from sail to steam reduced the need for expert stowing but replaced it with the need for rapid and safe cooperation between the gang members and the deckman. Other shipworkers stood on shore or in a barge, transporting the cargo from or to the ship.

Shore work was divided into quay labour (receiving or dispatching goods to or from cargo vessels) and warehouse labour (handling and preparing goods for sale in the warehouse, often situated outside the docks). Hand trucks were used for dispatching goods on the quay, an unskilled and rather light job done by 'boys' and 'second-rate' workers. Once the goods were on the quay, the work of sorting and further transporting them to their final destination could be done at a more moderate speed and was, therefore, spread more evenly throughout the year. Quay labour was carried out in the docks and at the riverside wharves where the goods were delivered by lighters.

Quay work for export purposes was different: long-distance vessels normally called at a number of ports, and consignments therefore had to be taken on board in a specific order, according to their various destinations. The correct stowing of such vessels depended on the shore worker, who marked the various articles and brought them in the proper order to the ship's side; they constituted an elite and were better paid.

The stowing of export goods inside these ships was monopolised by a specific group of shipworkers (not the unloaders) who constituted a kind of craftsmen's group from time immemorial – the *stevedores*. Their identification with loading activities was mainly based on the general dock companies' (London and East and West India Companies') monopoly of discharging operations on the north bank; on the south bank (Surrey) and in Millwall stevedores also unloaded. Even after the break-up of this monopoly in 1891, the stevedores succeeded in maintaining their privileges, thanks to their strong professional group cohesion and the continued existence of small master stevedores specialising in specific types of cargo; after 1891, they faced little competition from the general dock companies which had become less interested in shipwork. But this new situation revived old disputes between stevedores and the remaining *dockers* on the validity of these traditional demarcation lines, which was not favourable to unionism.

To complicate matters, shipwork on the short-distance vessels, outside the docks, was performed by a body of workers, distinct from either stevedores or dockers, that was itself divided into different groups, of which the *steamshipworkers* were the most coherent, as they were employed by contractors.

Cutting across all these demarcation lines were divisions based on the different goods handled. In the warehouses, distinct groups of workers were engaged in storing tea, and other colonial goods (such as sugar, coffee, cocoa), wool, frozen meat and so on. The work was rather unskilled and each group was haunted by its own slack season, but all enjoyed a certain reputation and stuck to their job. Moreover, the handling of bulk goods gave rise to many additional divisions, both on shore and on ship, sometimes sharpened by spatial isolation (the south bank). Before the introduction of the elevator in the 1880s the *corn porters* of Millwall and Surrey, two distinct groups, enjoyed high wages, thanks to the heavy, unhealthy (dust) and responsible (weighing) character of the job, which gave them higher status than the ordinary quay workers. The handling of soft wood – different from hard wood – required distinct skill, especially on the quay: thus these *deal porters* were paid better wages and had higher status than the *lumpers* on the ships. The professional identity of all these workers was reinforced by their spatial isolation on the south bank.

Quite apart from these occupational groups related to ship, shore or specific goods, we have to distinguish the *lightermen* who transported general cargo by barges or lighters from the vessels to the docks or warehouses or vice versa. Their work was considered skilled as they had to navigate well and possess a sound knowledge of the tides, and because they trained their own apprentices. The qualified lightermen were freemen of the Watermen's Company established in 1556 (which surely had much older predecessors). The appearance of tugboats affected their skill but not their strategic position.

The structural oversupply of workers (many of Irish origin) was aggravated by these impermeable partitions of the waterfront labour market, each compartment preserving its own broad fringe of casual and irregular workers around a more privileged nucleus of regulars, varying from tiny and almost insignificant in the unskilled, low-status and low-wage trades to considerable in the more skilled trades such as the stevedores, export workers, tea workers and lightermen. Moreover, these sectional divisions were sharpened by an intense feeling of sectionalism cultivated by all categories and most notoriously, of course, by the more priviliged trades. This sectionalism was reinforced by a parallel partition of the living conditions: further, each trade had its own residential quarters in the immediate proximity, thus creating a vast archipelago of small and coherent working-class communities. Another boundary arose from Irish descent which, though no longer considered a separate 'race', was associated with a distinct religion and reputed clannishness.

This sectionalism strongly reduced the effectiveness of the high union density achieved in some trades, and the outbreaks of great strikes, in which a combination of sectional and general demands could mobilise the great majority of all port workers, are, in this light, to be considered as exceptional events, always followed by a steep fall in union membership and the re-emergence of divergent interests. That the unions nevertheless succeeded in gaining some results, including one successful general strike, was due to a degree of disunity among the various groups of employers almost equal to that among the workers.

Le Havre

Until 1879 no public association with the features of a trade union appeared for more than a few weeks. After that, the development of labour organisation may be divided into three main periods. From 1879 to 1888, many professional trades established short-lived organisations that either disappeared during the 1882–89 depression, or did not belong to the port proper (or both); only the sailmakers and the port day-labourers created more durable unions.

At the beginning of the 1889–99 period trade revived, giving more opportunities for workers' actions. Major strikes of over 1000 workers erupted first at the Compagnie des Docks and Entrepôts (D&E) and then among the port day-labourers, with smaller strikes and petitions among the sailmakers, sail riggers and coal porters. All were considered successful. In their wake five trades revitalised or created unions: the sailmakers' union prospered again; that of the port day-labourers was refounded (after its dissolution in 1882); and the coal porters, hauliers and tally clerks became organised for the first time. On the other hand, the D&E workers (at the time, the only group who properly could be called dockers in French) accepted a paternalistic system whereby 168 delegates represented their shopmates to the managers, rather than form a real union. The development of a broader class-consciousness made some strides, as shown by the fact that the notion of solidarity between permanent and casual workers was central to the D&E strike which mobilised 400 monthly-paid employees (*embrigadés*) together with 600 casual workers (*auxiliaires A et B*), and that port unions joined with workers of other branches to create strong city-wide organisations.

Characteristic of the situation in Le Havre was the political dominance of the Republicans, representing essentially the import–export merchants, but not unfavourable to workers' demands, because they believed that both groups had to cooperate against the protectionist tendencies of the French government and the competition of rival ports (notably Rouen, Antwerp and Rotterdam). In turn, the port trade union leaders in the 1890s still considered the municipality as a potential ally, capable of intervening on behalf of the port workers. Indeed, during the 1889 strike, the mayor played a mediating role and, a little later, when the 1894–98 recession placed the unions in too weak a position to implement a more confrontational policy, many workers became quite dependent on public assistance dispensed by municipal services.

From 1899 to 1914, a third generation of trade unions appeared, distinguished from its predecessors by a greater propensity to strike (sometimes in the name of solidarity), a very large, though still fluctuating membership; and, above all, by the emergence of a new type of leader who sympathised with the revolutionary–syndicalist majority of the General Confederation of Labour (CGT) and a more revolutionary trade union policy. A major wave of strike action in 1899 and 1900 led to a break with the radical mayor, M. Marais. The D&E workers formally broke with paternalistic customs and founded a trade union (Union of D&E Workers of Le Havre) in November 1899 open to all three categories of workers. Successively, the hauliers, dockers (now including the *magasiniers* of the D&E and other warehouses), coal porters, sailmakers and port day-labourers struck and won major concessions, such as the eight-hour day and wage increases. Their actions coincided with major movements of seamen, ditch diggers and shipyard workers. In August 1900, port workers of all categories stopped work to protest against the use of police and troops against the general seamen's strike. In 1901 Le Havre port unions helped to create a National Federation of Port and Dock Workers; they hosted its founding congress and offered their leader as the first national secretary of the federation.

The same year witnessed the first street demonstrations on May Day accompanied by clashes with the police.

Employers toughened their tactics: they refused to stop paying the workers in tokens, often bypassed the single official hiring site established in 1900 and refused to hire union leaders. They favoured the founding of the Independent Union of Day-Labourers of the Port, affiliated to the national 'yellow' union. During strikes, they recruited blacklegs in Brittany and Lower Normandy, turned to the sub-prefect or even the prefect when they felt that the mayor did not support their cause, and obtained the massive and repeated deployment of gendarmes and troops. After creating funds to resist strikes, they regrouped in 1910 in the Union of Employers of Labour of the Port of Le Havre.

In turn, the dockers' unions strengthened their links with the city-wide labour movement led by the Labour Council of Le Havre. As a result, when the leader of the 1910 coal porters' strike was framed and sentenced to death, all the city's unions held protest strikes. Likewise, dockers and their wives played a prominent role in the 'Housewives Crusade' against high prices in 1911. And in 1912 dockers struck for six days in solidarity with a seamen's strike and against police and troop brutality. Six port unions – the port day-labourers, sailmakers, coal porters, hauliers, tally clerks and dockers – amalgamated into the General Union of Port Workers, affiliated to the CGT in 1913.

In accordance with the CGT majority's Charter of Amiens, the port unions were officially pledged to abstain from party politics. Their leaders viewed the union as the main vehicle of workers' emancipation: those who described themselves as socialists considered parliamentary politics a mere auxiliary to union organisation, cooperatives and municipal action; those who considered themselves libertarians either actively participated in anarcho-syndicalist networks, or found ways to support the election campaigns of the rising Radical politicians in Le Havre. The Socialist Party therefore remained quite weak among the Havrais port unions.

Like London, Le Havre had developed its harbour in the sail-ship era, but unlike the Thames port, it converted to steam more slowly. Some port trades that originated in cargo-handling on sail-ships survived into the new era (carmen or hauliers, stevedores, sailmakers, tally clerks and coal porters) whereas other trades gradually disappeared (rope towers, ballast heavers and sail riggers). New professions were the crane-drivers, tugboatmen, linemen, pilots, train drivers and a general category labelled *dockers*, including the old trades (carmen, tally clerks and so on) and the new ones engaged in the physical transport of cargo from ship to warehouse or other ships, or vice versa. At times port traffic grew faster than the port was extended (with more basins and quays) and mechanised (with cranes, electric light, rail, conveyors and new warehouses), and the ensuing congestion created opportunities for workers' actions. Other factors affecting labour's relative strength included high tides (up to eight metres in Le Havre), which created opportunities for tactical surprise attacks by the port workers, until the new tidal basin was completed in 1914. In addition, Le Havre has always been a port dealing with the regular transportation of general small-volume and high-specific value cargo: cotton, coffee, spices, leather and exotic wood were imported and expensive Parisian manufactured goods exported. In contrast, the handling of bulk goods was rather insignificant and the port authorities strongly objected to the ranking of ports by tonnage rather than value. However, this could not conceal a steady deterioration of its relative position prior to 1900; after that year a recovery set in.

The division of labour was very similar to that in London, albeit on a much smaller scale. Many distinct trades, originating from the sail-ship era, survived alongside an emerging category of many types of nondescript worker who were termed as 'dockers'. In the D&E sharp divisions existed between the original 'skilled' workers organised in the Mutual Aid Society and the newer ones, considered unskilled, who created a day-labourers' union. Evidence suggests that Le Havre port workers were occasionally capable of collective action at the port level between 1900 and 1912, but often resorted to struggles on the municipal level, as an alternative framework of collective action.

Among the employers, the import–export merchants were originally the dominant group in the port, as well as in the municipality. Later on, new associations were organised in a wide variety of trades for their own particular interests, initially with little coordination. Only during strikes was some temporary unity achieved, and then mainly on the municipal level. In January 1914 the employers' union finally established a port Labour Office with a policy of partial decasualisation and central hiring under employer control; however, it was aggressively challenged by the CGT port affiliates, and made redundant by the shortage of labour during the First World War. It seemed that for the employers, too, the municipal scene was most appropriate for their collective action.

Rotterdam

Unionism in Rotterdam made its way very late and slowly. The anti-socialist tendency in the port was strengthened by a massive influx of immigrant workers from the islands of Zeeland and South-Holland, who were staunch orthodox Protestants. The explosive expansion of the port traffic in the 1880s led to such an intensive exploitation of labour that in 1889, when solidarity with the London strike was requested, these people went on strike for their own demands: restriction of night and Sunday working, no payments in pubs and higher wages. During the strike an organisation with the English name 'The Rotterdam Branch of the Dockers' Union' was established. As a reaction, after the strike a new union was founded called 'The Dutch Flag' stressing its loyalty to Dutch law and aversion to British unionism. Both of them waned, and were succeeded by two other ephemeral unions, of which the most important was the New Dutch Dockers' Union with a peak membership of 6000 casual workers (about 50 per cent of all dockers) in 1897. However, it mysteriously collapsed during the same year. In 1896 the introduction of electric ore-cranes, causing a reduction in the size of the teams, met with vehement opposition from the workers involved. The conflict was resolved when the firm engaged 150 regular dockers. This caused a general strike for similar conditions elsewhere, but the cause was lost owing to a lack of clear demands. The 1900 strike against night-work, also a failure, was the reason why the Amsterdam-centred Dutch Seamen's and Dockers' Union made serious efforts to gain a hold in Rotterdam. As a result, it became the first union of a certain stability in the port of Rotterdam: leaving aside the usual oscillations in membership, it counted some hundreds of members. The years 1905 and 1907 witnessed two strikes against the introduction of the corn elevator, initiated by the elite of corn-weighers. These were interesting, because of the result (the first strike was won, and the introduction, carefully prepared by the employers, was only possible after a second strike) and the debates in the unions on the problem of employment and technical innovation, with the small and newly founded social-democratic union opposing the elevator, and the Dutch Seamen's and Dockers' Union, often labelled syndicalist, taking a more realistic position (accept it, in exchange for concessions).

Both unions grew steadily, favoured by the booming economy of the port. But this upward trend in membership was interrupted again by a protracted strike that failed: that of 1911, initially proclaimed in the name of international solidarity with the seamen, and extended by dockers by raising their own demands. By 1912, after the strike, only some 1500 dockers were organised – that is, about 10 per cent, of which 800 were in the social-democratic union and 300 in the Dockers' Union. However, despite this weakness, the dockers' poor labour conditions had become part of the public and political agenda. Consequently, in 1907 collective labour contracts were recognised by law, followed by the first experimental contract in the port of Rotterdam in 1908. In 1914 the Stevedoring Act regulated dock work, with provisions for minimal rest, working hours, safety, hiring sites, restrictions on the use of alcohol and inspection to enforce its implementation.

As a port of international importance, Rotterdam was rather new: it grew along with the German Ruhr region, the cargo handled rising from 1.7 million tons in 1880 to 3.6 million in 1900, and 13 million in 1913. It was not influenced by tides, as access to the sea was not through the estuary but through a canal dug between 1866 and 1872 (the New Waterway). However, the dominance of tramp traffic over regular lines made heavy reliance on casual labour inescapable. Rotterdam did not have more industries than other average towns without a port, nor was the Dutch home market very important at that time: in essence it was a transit port for the Ruhr, in that 80 per cent of its trade constituted handling bulk goods such as corn, coal, ore and wood, through the Rhine and, as such, it had no serious rivals. Hamburg and Antwerp had to rely on small canals or railways that enabled only the transport of general cargo with high specific value and small size, for their connections with the Ruhr. Rotterdam was very sensitive to the business cycle, but except during the depression of the 1880s and short recessions (1907–08 being the most serious) the port boomed. Sail-ships disappeared rather quickly.

The port's rapid expansion essentially created a very new branch of industry in which labour relations could be structured without taking into account existing conditions; only the corn trade had older divisions of labour that continued to function, at least until the introduction of the corn elevator. An individual docker's work could vary widely according to his preference or, more importantly, to the priorities assigned to various cargoes, and was not influenced by traditional demarcation lines. Of course, many (semi-)regular workers became specialised in some trades, but there were no institutional barriers to switching to other trades. The ultimate know-how on the handling of specific cargoes was provided by the foremen in regular service of the harbour companies.

For the employers the picture was different. The shipowners were the oldest group and constituted, as in Amsterdam, an elite, but their position was challenged by the emergence of a group of ship-brokers and, later on, master stevedores developed out of the foremen who constantly hired roughly the same men and started to work on their own account. The latter group had to fight for recognition in the port; a provisional unity was only reached in 1907, as a reaction to the second strike against the corn elevator. But internal differences and conflicting interests prevented a more coherent employers' policy when the unifying threat of strike action was absent; thus the 1908 collective labour contract, the first in Dutch history, collapsed.

At first sight, the existence of a huge body of dockers not divided by impermeable sectional partitions, all operating in a rather fluid labour market and facing the same groups of employers, might be very favourable to the development of a common consciousness and strong unions. Moreover, although, due to differences in status and lifestyle, some neighbourhoods housed more casual workers than others, dockers lived scattered throughout the city, among other workers, and changed jobs from trade to trade, inside and outside the port. Yet the absence of sectional demarcation lines did not give rise to a feeling of solidarity among the port workers. First and most important, the structural oversupply of casual workers who could be employed anywhere – in the port as well as in other sectors – prevented the development of a common consciousness of being dockers: only a small fringe of overseers (in 1900 about 1000) and regulars (2500) and a somewhat broader fringe of semi-regulars (3500) had that feeling, but as they faced constant competition from the vast hordes of casuals (8000), their first reaction was not towards solidarity or unionism but to maintain their privileged position in relation to the master stevedores, the foremen or the companies in general. Strikes took place only if this group felt mistreated, and furthermore their position was anything but secure, as the rapidly expanding port was characterised by a lack of established labour relations and of informal rules regulating port work. A further barrier to union action was the orthodox Protestant background of the vast majority of Zeeland and South Holland islander immigrants, who were very hostile to any signs of socialism; they were staunch workers with austere lifestyles.

Hamburg

In Hamburg, the first union, the Dockers' Union, was founded in 1886 and organised all categories of harbour workers. Over the next four years, 30 small-scale strikes and lockouts took place, for higher wages and limited working hours (36-hour shifts and longer were not unusual), mainly financed by voluntary donations by workers throughout the country. By 1890 union density exceeded 50 per cent, with a peak of 80 per cent among lightermen and 75 per cent among workers of the state quays. On May Day 1890 work was stopped in response to a call from the Second International, which was followed by a number of strikes by different categories of workers with the lightermen at the centre. The defeat of this strike for better wages and a ten-hour day, was followed by a counteroffensive by the employers: they centralised the labour supply, only hiring dockers who were labelled as reliable.

After some smaller strikes, a new confrontation occurred in November 1896, when traffic reached a peak and many categories of port workers raised various demands. In December the number of strikers culminated at 16 000. The most determined group were the casual workers, who drew the more hesitant regulars into the struggle. The strike attracted nationwide sympathy, partly because of the intransigence of the port employers who refused to make even the smallest concessions and would accept only unconditional surrender, and who were supported, though reluctantly, by the municipal authorities. When in February 1897 the strikers had to give up the struggle, they vented their fury upon the newly recruited blacklegs: these fled the working-class neighbourhoods as well as the port.

The three actors involved in this confrontation drew widely divergent conclusions from its outcome. For the next ten years, the dockers refrained from any large-scale action, and developed a tactic of small-scale partial strikes, gaining some incidental advantages. Under the influence of its socialist leadership, the Dockers' Union concluded that it had to get a firmer grip on workers' actions and should no longer be drawn into spontaneous strikes with which it did not agree; it embarked, as a result, on a process of centralisation and bureaucratisation. The employers concluded that casual workers were more likely to strike and engaged a broader nucleus of regulars pledged to strict loyalty.

During the years 1905–1907, the dynamic of small-scale action developed its own momentum with some 50 open conflicts that led to a steep rise in union membership, and putting the closed shop on the agenda in some sectors. The employers countered with a demand for a written declaration of willingness to accept any night or overtime work, which was refused by 5000 dockers who were sacked and replaced by British strikebreakers. The employers won and extended the number of regular contracts with compulsory insurance. The union lost half of its membership and merged with other transport workers' unions of a social-democratic tendency to form the German Transport Workers' Union which introduced unemployment insurance against the dockers' will. The 1910–14 economic upturn strengthened its position, enabling it to obtain wage increases and a nine-hour day. It abstained from further confrontation with the employers.

Hamburg was also an old tidal port (dating from 1189), with a long tradition of merchants dominating the municipality of this independent city-state. It grew spectacularly after 1850 as the port of departure for the millions of emigrants to the New World, as a transit port for Central and Eastern European goods and, after 1888, also as an industrial centre (coffee, beer, machinery, shipbuilding); in this era steamships became totally dominant, giving rise to a strong new elite of wealthy shipowners with economic interests far outside the city. In 1900 it was the leading port on the Continent, handling 8 million tons; in 1914, 14 million tons were transhipped, mostly general cargo supplied by regular lines.

Harbour work was performed by distinct trades with long histories:

- *On-board shipworkers* (1895: 9800, of which only 1600 were regularly employed; 1913: 5000 on average). These were divided into hourly-wage (general cargo) and piece-wage (distinct groups in bulk goods such as corn, coal and ore, each earning higher wages as a bonus for unusually long, heavy and unhealthy tasks).
- *Quay workers*. These were divided first into those employed by shipowners (1913: 2700 on average) and those employed by the State of Hamburg, owner of the quays (1913: 3500 on average). Second, and more importantly, they were divided by payment method: piece-work for the regular fringe paid by the state and the largest shipowner, HAPAG, and hourly for the casuals. This gave the first group an interest in speeding up the latter, and thus created immense mutual tensions between them: the regulars were responsible for the speed of work and paid fairly well. In turn, however, they were subjected to intense supervision by the police and overseers which impeded nearly all political or union activities.
- *Lightermen* (1913: 2400). This group took over the cargo from vessels anchored in midstream, or at the waterside of boats being discharged at the quay (for the sake of a quick dispatch), and transported it to the many warehouses in the free port built after 1880. As they had to creep between ships in the river and through small canals with a punting-pole, and perform custom formalities, their trade was considered skilled; it had an apprenticeship of four, and later three, years. After the customs union with the German Empire in 1881, cargo had to be transported in a closed lighter rather than being exposed to the air, if it was charged custom duties, and had to be permanently supervised by a bargeman who was, therefore, obliged to live on board. Because the traditional lightermen with their privileged position refused to do so, lighterage companies recruited former fishermen and river bargemen to fill this gap, and these made up to 25 per cent of this group of workers, their presence being strongly resented by the lightermen as an invasion of newcomers. The lightermen were the most steadily employed group in the port, earning equal wages to the unskilled workers who had longer working days.
- *Machinists*. These played a crucial role in the port that far exceeded their small nurnber (not mentioned in statistics) as they steered the rising number of tugboats that were replacing the lighters, and also operated the steam-driven cranes. They, too, were considered skilled

and worked in isolation, considering themselves to be far above the ordinary workers and quite close to the company foremen.
- *Warehouse-workers* (1913: 1000). These could hardly be considered a single group: warehouse companies employed casual workers earning low wages and working under very harsh conditions, whereas smaller and more specialised firms, which rented storage facilities, employed a rather large fringe of regular workers.

So we see a labour force that was not only divided between different sectors of port work, but perhaps even more sharply divided within each sector between regular and casual workers. The same division was reproduced in living conditions: if they were to find daily employment, the casuals had to live in the immediate vicinity of the docks where the houses were of extremely poor quality, overcrowded with lodgers, and more expensive. After the 1892 cholera epidemic and the 1906 strike, these old neighbourhoods were gradually demolished and their inhabitants moved to new housing areas in the outskirts that were more socially heterogeneous.

In addition, industrial relations were characterised by the intermediate position of bosses and the overwhelming power of employers. Bosses constituted an intermediate stratum between the workers and employers operating in the stevedoring, lighterage and warehouse sectors in a dense network of small enterprises. They were of working-class origin and were normally ex-port workers themselves, but after 1880, with the expansion of port operations, they tended to become full-time entrepreneurs who entrusted the recruitment of workers to the foremen. Bosses were distrusted by the workers and were often in a delicate position between the port workers and big employers. The latter group mainly consisted of shipowners and warehouse companies with strong (inter)national connections and a decisive influence on city government. In 1906 they constituted the Port Union to combat strikes and create a centralised placement body. In combination with the policy of employing a broader fringe of regular workers, these measures proved highly effective in curbing trade union power and in disciplining the dockers who, to a considerable extent, clung to the casual lifestyle.

Comparing the struggles

The outstanding common feature of all the ports was the extreme instability of the dockers' unions. The casual workers were harder to unionise, but more strike-prone than the regulars. Small-scale strikes of limited sectional groups offered better results than massive confrontations which, as a rule, failed, but sometimes had a far bigger impact on public opinion. Periods of heavy port traffic proved favourable for gaining improvements and helped to raise membership of the dockers' unions as is clearly demonstrated in London between 1889 and 1890 and betwen 1911 and 1912; large-scale confrontations that failed caused severe setbacks, sometimes even temporarily destroying the organisations. In all ports, extremely sharp membership fluctuations cannot obscure the fact that non-unionism was the rule. But there are also clear differences between these ports.

In London many rival sectional interests, stemming from the past, caused organisational fragmentation that was overcome only partially in 1914. Party politics played no significant role. In Le Havre sectional divisions comparable to London's, were visible, weakening the power of unionism there as well. Municipal politics were very important; at least some Radicals were allies but the Socialist Party was virtually absent. In Rotterdam the rapid expansion of the port and massive influx of immigrants created almost a *tabula rasa* situation that allowed exploitation free rein; the weak position of the unions was – at least partially – compensated by legal protection. In Hamburg the unions were stronger and less divided and the influence of (moderate) socialism was considerable, but the combined forces and the counterstrategy of the employers proved very effective.

Comparing the structures

Comparing the structural characteristics of labour relations in our four ports can yield additional explanations (for the definition of these factors, see the Appendix).

Sectional divisions were characteristic of the *old ports* of London, Hamburg and Le Havre and were almost absent in the *new port* of Rotterdam. The divisions were not identical, however: the distinction between loading and unloading was only made in London, where all divisions are extremely ramified, creating an endlessly subdivided labour force. However, even these divisions turned out to be a major source of unionism: the first to unionise were small professional groups, like the London stevedores and lightermen or the Hamburg regular warehouse workers, State quay workers and lightermen, who enjoyed a certain status, had regular employment, might have boasted some skill, and had to defend themselves against employers' measures, technical innovations or the claims of less privileged workers. When the unions also organised the less privileged sectors and were not deaf to their demands for equality, the first sectors tended to break away, like the London stevedores. However, if some privileged sectors felt strong enough to move without the unions, they often did so, like the Rotterdam corn weighers or the Hamburg machinists: such groups did not refrain from striking if that seemed appropriate to their interests, whereas the unionised regulars demonstrated cautious behaviour. However, the big port strikes were generally initiated by the casual workers, who preferred well-timed direct action as they lacked long-term perspectives. Union membership seemed to be a part of sectional workers' strategies, in which the definition of group identity and group interests was based on the existing sectional divisions, rather than the notion of being part of a greater community of underprivileged proletarians.

Seen in this light, it may seem remarkable that there were any great port strikes at all but this would be to neglect the only great mobilising force that was able, on occasion, to overcome all these sectional interests: *solidarity*. When employers tried to force dockers to take over the work of their striking colleagues – whether these were more privileged or casual workers of the lowest esteem, foreign workers or fellow-countrymen of a competing port – they refused to obey, especially when the employers started to recruit blacklegs from outside the existing groups of dockers which were already too extended to be guaranteed employment. This was the way in which partial strikes could expand rapidly into a general strike and was also the mechanism some radical unions tried to exploit, in order to gain a grip on the dockers who were so difficult to unionise. It also gave port strikes the specific dynamics that made them so unpredictable and so difficult to handle and that brought the dockers a reputation of being unresponsible, impulsive and strike-prone workers (which they were not). The structure of dock work and the peculiarities of the labour market imposed solidarity as the ultimate defensive strategy against employer dominance – not so much to gain immediate results (though these sometimes were gained too), but to show that the workers were no mere tools of cargo-handling. If they were treated as a mass of interchangeable workers, they would behave accordingly from time to time, striking massively.

Tidal ports created opportunities for short-term tactics, as the example of Le Havre shows. These ports also favour casual employment, but this influence does not seem to have been decisive in comparison with other factors. The dominance of trampships in Rotterdam, for instance, created a need for casual labour that far outweighed the lack of tidal movement. A regular stream of the same goods, notably general cargo, and the presence of local shipowners favoured regular lines, a major condition for decasualisation, and these conditions were met in London and Hamburg, and certainly not in Rotterdam.

As for skill, sail-ships kept their position best in London and Le Havre; steampower (ships, winches, cranes) made rapid progress in

Rotterdam and Hamburg, outdating some skilled trades but creating new ones like machinists, the more so when this coincided with a growing importance of bulk goods, as happened in Rotterdam (80 per cent) and Hamburg (50 per cent).

Competitiveness was greatest in Hamburg, which expanded enormously after 1860, and in Rotterdam which started its spurt later but tended to catch up after 1900; London retained its first position and Le Havre suffered a relative setback.

The labour market everywhere had a structural oversupply of unskilled labour, which could be made worse by a lack of alternative employment in other trades outside the port, as was certainly the case in Rotterdam which lacked industrial plants, and was less so in London with its extended small-scale seasonal industries of luxury goods, or Hamburg with its considerable port-tied industrial development. Contrary to many too rash and easy generalisations of the Kerr and Siegel type, nowhere did the dockers constitute a socially or professionally coherent group: they were scarcely capable of collective action affecting all port activities as they were constantly split up and eagerly cultivated differences which they reproduced in their living conditions. London was archetypical in this sense, and Rotterdam was perhaps an exception; with everything still new and chaotic, industrial relations, as well as patterns of social organisation and social struggle, still had to crystallise, and, in the end, this happened only after 1945. In all ports, differences in regional origin and social background played a negative and retarding role in unionisation.

On the other hand, the cohesion of different sectors of the employers was not too strong either: interest groups might clash with each other, to the benefit of the dockers. But as is clearly demonstrated by the Hamburg shipowners, when one group with political and economic power was able to dominate the others, it could mould the industrial relations at its will, exert outright repression, curb the unions and create a relatively large fringe of disciplined regular workers. In the London and Le Havre docks employers also had considerable influence, but their power was more restricted to the docks themselves.

Ports and the national framework

Many differences in the development of trade unions in the four ports compared here can be explained satisfactorily by the structural branch characteristics of these ports. Local or national influences were not absent, but adapted themselves to their environment. The London port unions were part of the British trade union system, but did not fit well under the heading of 'new unionism' as they were, for one thing, not strongly centralised and went their own specific way, with the exception of the Dockers' Union which did, in fact, adopt a centralised model. Perhaps this was also the case with other British trade unions for whom new unionism might have been more a programme than a reality. Nevertheless, the dockers' unions were distinctive on account of their extreme sectionalism and instability, which essentially derived from port characteristics.

In Le Havre syndicalism was predominant as in the rest of France, but this also fitted perfectly into the pattern of direct and short-term action so characteristic for any port at that time and the more so for a tidal port such as Le Havre.

We find the same preferences in Rotterdam where unionisation was very slow and could be introduced with very limited success from outside the port. Quite exceptionally for the Dutch situation, Catholic and Protestant unions were virtually absent and the Radical tendency remained rather strong, despite the social-democratic crusades against them.

Only in the port of Hamburg did a tendency for a well-organised union of port workers, operating as part of a national, disciplined army under social-democratic command, become dominant, but this was only possible after some crushing defeats against a supreme enemy operating like a Prussian army. The social-democratic strategy seemed the only effective counterweapon, and it was only half-willingly and after long internal struggles that Hamburg dockers embraced this kind of unionism. In the meantime, the dockers seemed to follow their own preferences for sectional, short-term action and were not very interested in more sophisticated models of unionism which they considered more inconvenient than useful. Nevertheless, by 1914 their union reflected the national pattern.

The national state was an additional actor influencing but not determining labour relations in ports. Free trade was the official policy, except for Hamburg after its economic incorporation into the German Empire (which implied the construction of an extensive warehouse district). Everywhere local authorities intervened in strikes by protecting blacklegs; national governments did very little. The Port of London Authority Act (1908) did not reach any results in the field of decasualisation before 1914, and further legislation (the 1909 Labour Exchange Act and the 1911 Insurance Act) had no impact on the waterfront. The Dutch Stevedoring Act of 1914 was certainly important as a compensation for the impotence of the parties in the port to structure labour relations and to improve the situation of the docker, but not in our period. Even in highly centralised France local politics and the municipality were more important than Paris for the waterfront of Le Havre.

Everywhere in western Europe, national states were busily integrating heterogeneous elements into a national framework. Like some distant regions with their own language and traditions, the ports had a semi-autonomous status with their own rules and customs. The differences in their responses to a national pattern might be interpreted as differences in the phases of the process of integration. Seen in this light, Hamburg had proceeded furthest on this road, thanks to the overwhelming position of the shipowners, who paved the way for the state and provoked similar responses from the national trade union. Rotterdam followed, because the port did not have old and deviant traditions and could be integrated by law (the Stevedoring Act of 1914), whereas the ports of Le Havre and especially London remained, for a long time, a world of their own.

Appendix: structural factors

If we want to compare structural factors, we must determine what factors are to be compared and why. Our analyses suggest that the following factors are important:

1. **Old ports, new ports.** In old ports traditional divisions of labour and job demarcations are important determinants for professional identities and union organisation.
2. **Tidal ports** have short-term fluctuations of traffic that preclude normal working-days.
3. A dominance of **trampships** over **regular lines** creates a larger fringe of casual labour.
4. **General cargo** requires many experienced workers; by comparison, **bulk goods** require fewer and unskilled dockers but also more mechanisation and skilled machine-operators; a similar contrast exists between **seasonal goods** (with high and low periods) and a **continuous flow.**
5. The replacement of **sail-ships** by **steamers** implies a larger scale of operation, new labour conditions, higher speed and deskilling.
6. **Technical innovations** reduce the numbers of workers involved but may place the remaining workers who operate machines in a better bargaining position; an increase of ships in and out without a simultaneous lengthening of the available quays has the opposite effect.

7. The **competitiveness** of the port, in combination with **business cycles**.
8. The **labour market** of the dockers: supply and demand of labour of different categories.
9. **Social homogeneity of the dockers**: origins, beliefs, life-style, residential quarters.
10. **Cohesion of the employers**: different interest groups and traditions, local concentration, origins, beliefs.

Bibliography

The lists for London and Hamburg are shorter, because there exist very exhaustive monographs on these ports.

London

Lovell, J. (1969), *Stevedores and Dockers. A Study of Trade Unionism in the Port of London. 1870–1914*, London.
Lovell, J. (1985), 'The Significance of the Great Dock Strike of 1889 in British Labour History', in W. Mommsen and H. Husung (eds), *The Development of Trade Unionism in Great Britain and Germany*, London.
Lovell, J. (1987), 'Sail, Steam and Emergent Dockers' Unionism in Britain, 1850–1914', *International Review of Social History*, 32 (3).
McIvor, A. (1984), 'Employers' Organisation and Strike Breaking in Britain, 1880–1914', *International Review of Social History*, 29.
Matthews, D. (1991), '1889 and All That: New Views on the New Unionism', *International Review of Social History*, 36 (1).
Phillips, G. and N. Whiteside (1985), *Casual Labour. The Unemployment Question in the Port Transport Industry, 1880–1970*, Oxford.
Schneer, J. (1994), 'London's Docks in 1900: Nexus of Empire', *Labour History Review*, 59 (3).

Rotterdam

Enquête 1890, Eindverslag der Commissie, Derde Afdeling der Staatscommissie van Arbeids-enquête, zie Ook: Schriftelijke Inlichtingen.
Harmsen, G. en F. van Gelder (1986), *Onderweg. Uit een eeuw actie- en organisatiegeschiedenis van de Vervoersbonden*, Baarn.

Jansen, T. (1979), '"De wil der bazen regelt het werk". Havenarbeiders rond 1900 in Rotterdam en Amsterdam', *Jaarboek 1979 voor de geschiedenis van socialisme en vakbeweging in Nederland*, Nijmegen, pp. 7–88.
Laan, R. (1956), *Jaren van principiële strijd. Geschiedenis van de Centrale Bond 1918–1955*, Rotterdam.
Mol, H. (1980), *Memoires van een havenarbeider*, Nijmegen.
Staatscommissie over de Werkloosheid, dl. 3, Tweede Subcommissie, Den Haag, 1913.
Teychiné Stakenburg, A. J. (1957), *Stand Van Zaken. Een halve eeuw arbeidsverhoudingen in de Rotterdamse haven, 1907–1957*, Rotterdam.
Tijn, Th. van (1978), 'Het sociale leven in Nederland', *Algemene Geschiedenis der Nederlanden*, 13, pp. 295–327.

Le Havre

Annuaire du commerce et de l'industrie de la Ville et du Port du Havre, 1889 à 1914, Le Havre, 1888 et seq.
Geffre, J. (1934), *Les manutentions dans les ports maritimes français*, Bordeaux.
Gillès de Pélichy, (Baron) C. (1899), *Le régime du travail dans les principaux ports de mer de l'Europe*, Louvain.
Hérubel, M. (1910), *La France au travail. En suivant les côtes de Dunkerque à Saint-Nazaire*, Paris.
Legoy, J. (1982), *Le peuple du Havre et son histoire. Volumes 2 et 3. Du négoce à l'industrie 1800–1914*, St-Etienne du Rouvray.
Lemarchand, A. (1994), 'La structuration des marchés du travail portuaire', unpublished dissertation, Paris X.
Vigarié, A. (1964), *Les grands ports de commerce de la Seine au Rhin. Leur évolution devant l'évolution de l'arrière-pays*, Aubenas, Ardèche.

Hamburg

Grüttner, M. (1984), *Arbeitswelt an der Wasserkante. Sozialgeschichte der Hamburger Hafenarbeiter, 1886–1914*, Göttingen.
Weinhauer, K. (1994), *Alltag und Arbeitskampf im Hamburger Hafen, 1914–1933*, Paderborn.

CHAPTER THREE

Trade unionism in textile towns and areas

Jean-Claude Daumas, Rémy Cazals, Marlene Ellerkamp and Alan Fowler*

A comparative study of different types of trade unionism in the textile industry is fraught with difficulties. First, the label 'textile towns and areas' is reductionist because nowhere other than in Elbeuf was textiles the sole industry and, moreover, in Mazamet fellmongery had, in part, taken over from textiles. The complexity of the industrial fabric means, then, that we cannot *a priori* disregard the theory that the type of organisation and militancy of workers in other sectors did influence that of the textile workers. The example of Mazamet, which is in no way unique, is especially revealing in this respect: building workers played a big role here in perpetuating tradition and it was the fellmongers' union which took over the movement. Moreover, the concept of textile industry did not mean the same thing everywhere: in Elbeuf as in Mazamet, wool products were manufactured, whilst Lancashire specialised in spinning and weaving cotton and the Bremen region had eight businesses working different types of fibre (wool, cotton, jute and hemp). As for fellmongery, as carried out in Mazamet, this was obviously not part of the textile industry.

Furthermore, distinct geographical realities are subsumed under the same label. On the one hand, with Lancashire and the Bremen region, we have industrial areas with the textile industry present in several towns. This is why, towards the end of the Victorian era, the cotton region of Lancashire was more of a heterogeneous grouping in which Oldham, Bolton, Blackburn and Burnley played the major roles. The Bremen region included five rural localities (Delmenhorst, Grohn, Blumenthal, Lesum and Hemelingen) situated within a 25-kilometre (15 mile) radius of the city-state of Bremen itself. Conversely, Elbeuf and Mazamet were

---

*Translated by David Hand MA, Department of Languages, Manchester Metropolitan University

small, relatively isolated industrial centres with a distinctly limited sphere of influence.

Finally, the three countries under consideration cannot be contrasted in a simple way – concept by concept as it were – because as much from the point of view of socioeconomic structures as from that of the workers' movements, there were great differences within each country: the Lancashire towns, like those of the Bremen region, each had their own special qualities whilst the French towns, Elbeuf and Mazamet, were total opposites. We should therefore ask ourselves whether or not we are comparing like with like.

Additionally, the four case studies here are unevenly documented. The picture will obviously vary depending on whether trade union archives still exist, as is the case in Mazamet. Indeed, trade union archives allow daily activities to be researched whereas the local press and official sources concentrated only on the most high-profile aspects of union life. Moreover, if the history of trade unionism in Mazamet, Lancashire, and the Bremen region is well-known, this is not the case, by contrast, with Elbeuf on which no comparable research has been done.

Bremen, Lancashire, Mazamet and Elbeuf display quite contrasting characteristics, then, which we have tried to describe clearly in order to underline their unique natures before attempting to highlight and explain similarities and differences between them. The comparative method followed here seeks both to underline similarities between the three countries studied – similarities which typological models tend to underestimate – and to pick out domestic differences – which demonstrate that 'national models' are less consistent than generally supposed. However, we should bear in mind that each variable is not always significant in itself because each case is made up of a particular combination of factors: it is therefore this combination which is significant and which should be examined.

Four different types of trade unionism

Lancashire

In Lancashire, trade unionism is an old phenomenon, going back to the start of the nineteenth century for spinners and to the 1850s for weavers, but it became a permanent mass movement only in the 1880s. Numbers rose greatly between 1890 and 1913, but it was after 1900 that growth was strongest. If in spinning the number of trade unionists rose only by 30 per cent (from 18 145 to 23 713), by contrast there was a threefold increase in carding (from 15 598 to 52 113) and a fourfold one in weaving (from 46102 to 179391). Consequently, the density of union membership rose greatly, from 23.8 per cent in 1890 to 28.8 per cent in 1901, before climbing to 55.5 per cent in 1913. We have here, then, a powerful and dynamic mass trade unionism.

Cotton workers were grouped together in three federations reflecting the industry's sectional divisions according to stages of production – carding, spinning, and weaving. Membership of a trade union was based on the district. The federation was concerned solely with wages issues and, consequently, district organisations had a great deal of power. Unlike unskilled workers' trade unions, the cotton unions' structures were hardly centralised at all, which is one of the explanations for the absence of unofficial strike movements in Lancashire. Forming the majority of the workforce in textile factories, women were also more numerous than men in trade unions – except in the spinners' federation which barred them – but they were totally absent from positions of leadership. The trade unions were, in fact, led by a small group of highly qualified and well-paid male workers.

Trade union activities and workers' disputes were dominated by the question of wages. Trade unions were organised to lobby for wage increases. The end of the Victorian era saw the introduction of collective bargaining at county level. In weaving, collective bargaining was introduced in the 1880s. However, it was during the strikes of 1889–93 in which the cotton workers participated massively that this method of resolving industrial disputes became widespread in the regional cotton industry. The Brookland Agreement of 1893 ended a 20-week lockout of spinners and set up a system of collective bargaining which was to become a model for the whole of British industry. It provided for negotiations at local and county level between the trade unions and the employers before a strike or lockout could take place. The introduction of collective bargaining in weaving and spinning was followed by nearly 20 years of relative industrial peace, unprecedented in the history of British cotton industry, which were ended only by the great disputes of 1908–12. Moreover, unofficial strikes quickly dropped in number because, in this case, the strikers had no access to sustenance funds.

The nature of trade unionism in the cotton industry was strongly influenced by the method of payment of the workers – the wage list. Each town had its own list for all types of work. Cotton workers were paid on piece-work rates but as different quality fabrics were paid at different rates, calculating wages was very complicated and workers suspected their bosses of underpaying them. The local scale was first established in Blackburn in the 1850s. It would be an exaggeration to say that it had been formally negotiated between employers and workers but there had been a sort of collective forum with the most important employers contributing to the discussions.

Calculating wages was one of the main jobs of the trade union officers in Lancashire. So, to guarantee that they could do it correctly, the trade unions devised an examination based on wage calculation problems, and trade union officers were henceforth elected from those who had passed this examination with flying colours. This union bureaucracy emerged in the 1860s and it was the weavers who were the first to select their leaders by this method. The spinners adopted it in the 1870s, before it spread to the whole of the cotton industry during the 1880s and 1890s. Before 1850 the leaders were usually former workers who had set up their own small businesses, often public houses. The growth of trade unionism and the emergence of wage scales subsequently made this system impractical and forced unions to employ permanent officers. These officers were essentially self-made men; they were also as much products of the mechanics' institutes, evening classes and technical education as of the trade union movement. They were, though, totally focused on local or work questions and had no vision of any class-based alternative solutions.

Shortly after being founded, the cotton industry unions joined the Labour Representation Committee, set up in London in 1900. Several factors led to this move, notably the *Taff Vale* case of 1901 which, in effect, limited the right to strike by making trade unions responsible for employers' losses during strikes – Blackburn's weavers' union being the first casualty – and the absence of intermediaries in Parliament to defend workers' interests. Bolton and Blackburn elected Labour MPs from as early as 1906 (they were part of the first group of 29 'workers' MPs elected to the House of Commons), Burnley followed suit in 1918, and more conservative Oldham in 1922. Even if all the first Labour candidates did not come from the cotton unions, the latter, by voting for them, sought both to have themselves defended in Parliament by skilled operatives familiar with workers' problems and to obtain general legislation applicable to all workers.

The Bremen region

In Germany the start of the 1890s witnessed a new wave of unionisation but, in the Bremen region, it was not until the end of the decade that textile workers' unions were founded and their expansion only really started at the beginning of the next century.

Like the other federations, the textile federation, the Deutscher Textilarbeiterverband (DTAV), simultaneously housed three hierarchical levels: central leadership, district committees and local sections. These were not trade-based organisations. In fact, they were open to all textile workers, irrespective of the fibre involved (jute, wool, cotton or hemp) or of the trade (carding, spinning, weaving and rope-making). Grouping members by industrial sector gave great strength to trade unionism here, all the more so because men and women were accepted equally.

The local organisation of unions reflected the complicated politico-administrative structure of the region: textile workers in the Bremen region belonged to four local branches of the DTAV. The Delmenhorst branch was founded in 1900 and recruited its members mainly from a jute factory (Hanseatische Jutespinnerei und weberei AG) where, in 1910, the rate of union membership was 80 per cent, nearly 100 per cent in the weaving section. By contrast, workers in the 'industrial giant' NWK (Norddeutsche Wollkämmerei und Kammgarnspinnerei AG) which employed 3100 people in 1913, remained outside the union. The Vegesack branch, which was founded in 1896 and which recruited its members from four textile factories, numbered in its ranks no more than 10 per cent of the local workforce. It recruited its members mostly from the smallest textile factory in the region, the Bremer Wollwäscherei AG (a wool treatment factory in Lesum) which employed only 130 people (89 per cent of whom were union members in 1906) but it never succeeded in winning over members from the other 'industrial giant' of the region, the BWK (Bremer Wollkämmerei AG – which employed 3600 workers in 1913). The Hemelingen branch was founded in 1897 and the rate of union membership was very high since 52 per cent of workers were members of the union in 1913. In Bremen city, the branch was founded in 1897; numbers fluctuated there but rose steadily over time as, in 1913, the rate of union membership had reached 44 per cent. Women were, overall, less numerous than men in unions but the rate of union membership of women varied from branch to branch: it was low in Delmenhorst (17 per cent against 28 per cent for men in 1913); very low even in Vegesack (1 per cent against 9 per cent); but it was high, on the other hand, in Bremen (42 per cent against 47 per cent); and especially high in Hemelingen (52 per cent against 56 per cent). Overall, in 1913, in the Bremen region, the DTAV had more members from the textile industry (22.4 per cent) than the national average (16.7 per cent). On the whole, this period was characterised by a huge expansion of numbers: considering only the period 1905–13, numbers increased threefold (from 910 to 2633). However, before 1905, numbers were generally low and fluctuating and, in the end, some 20 years had to pass before trade unionism was firmly rooted.

In 1896 and 1898 the national leadership of the DTAV tried to regulate and centralise protest action. Strikes called in reaction to employers' actions (defensive strikes) and lockouts had to be recorded and strikes initiated by workers (offensive strikes) had to receive prior authorisation. In the textile factories of the Bremen region, there were 38 industrial disputes (strikes and 'negotiated industrial action') between 1897 and 1913, no more than about a quarter of which (11 – that is 29 per cent) were started by the local wing of the DTAV.

In the region, protest action took two main forms: on the one hand, spontaneous strikes or walkouts followed by negotiations between, on the one side, the management and, on the other, the works committee,[1] the local authorities or, occasionally, DTAV officers; and, on the other hand, 'negotiated industrial action' – that is, wage claims mainly tabled by union meetings and works committees followed by negotiations, backed up on occasions with strikes. What is typical of the Bremen region before 1914 is the continuity and interdependence of these two forms of dispute because both forms could follow each other directly in the same factory. At the national level, there was a tendency to pass from strike action to non-strike action to the extent that open disputes rapidly decreased in number. The same tendency was at work in the Bremen region but with much less impact as, although ten strikes (eight of which were spontaneous) were recorded between 1897 and 1905 as opposed to three 'negotiated industrial disputes', there were only 11 strikes (eight spontaneous) as against 14 'negotiated industrial disputes' between 1906 and 1913. Thus, strikes subsequently diminished in importance after 1905, although they still accounted for nearly half (44 per cent) of all industrial action.

The role of local DTAV leaders was to bring pressure to bear, to channel strike movements and to guide workers to the negotiating table. The Bremer Wollwäscherei AG is a perfect example of a high level of organisation and face-to-face negotiation between management and union. By contrast, the jute factory in Bremen was the diametric opposite of this model of modern strike organisation because there were never any face-to-face negotiations there between the local DTAV leadership and the management of the factory. Moreover, because of the absence of contact between the union and the workers, strikes there were almost always spontaneous. In the other factories recognition of the union as a negotiating partner was in no way a permanent feature.

In the 1900s the main aim of the unions' leadership was to strengthen their organisations (their motto was: membership first, strike later). It must be noted, however, that in Bremen, as in the rest of Germany, and in contrast to what was happening in Great Britain, there was never any wages scale applicable to the whole region or even to a given town so the union leaders were not involved in wage calculations. When the trade union was recognised as a full negotiating partner in wage discussions, it was always at the level of a given firm and with the discussions controlled by the employers. Furthermore, there was no move towards negotiating collective agreements. Bremen, mirroring the rest of the German textile industry, remained outside this practice which had nonetheless started to emerge during the 1900s before becoming widespread after the First World War. As for the trade union officials, at the local level they were ordinary workers, with no real education, who had no role at all in society outside their factory or their union executive.

Contacts between the trade unions and the SPD (German Social Democratic Party) were close (in Bremen-city, in 1914, 78 per cent of SPD members belonged to a union and 28 per cent of trade unionists were members of the political party), but the unions tended to agree with the party that they should not enter politics actively but would remain dedicated essentially to defending workers' interests in the workplace. Conversely, most workers voted for the SPD in elections. In Bremen-city, in local elections, SPD candidates would get about 40 per cent of the vote even though the complicated electoral system (with eight categories of voter) disenfranchised ordinary workers. In the Reichstag elections, conducted by universal (male) suffrage, workers' votes were split between socialists and left-wing liberals who, between them, would get more than 80 per cent of the vote. For the SPD, Bremen was an electoral bastion: in 1912, it won 53.4 per cent of the vote as opposed to only 34.8 per cent nationally. The results obtained in Delmenhorst and Blumenthal were even better. However, we should remember that the SPD represented only one part of the workforce because neither women nor, of course, immigrants were enfranchised.

Mazamet

In Mazamet trade unionism emerged slowly. A first attempt occurred in 1886 with the founding of a federation for wool and building workers. This soon collapsed, though, under a dual assault by employers and churchmen. So, by 1900 the only trade union in existence was the joiners' union, founded in 1894 and numbering only 30 members, even though there were 6000 workers in the industrial region of Mazamet. It was the successful strike action of 1903, which spread to all trades, that was instrumental in the creation of several unions. The fellmongers' union, the most important and active, was the driving force behind the movement. In 1904 it had 1300 members, all men, and a federation for all the trade unions in Mazamet was founded. The drawing up of a left-wing workers list for the local elections of 1904 (under a proportional representation system) caused a split between right-wing members – the Fédération des Syndicats de Mazamet, flying the tricolour flag – and the left – the Union des Syndicats de Mazamet, which had affiliated to the

CGT (Confédération Générale du Travail) and adopted the red flag. However, after a period of mutual hostility, the two organisations came closer together and took part in joint strike action. By 1908, there were 1800 trade unionists, all men for the moment, although there was talk of opening the door to women.

It was the great fellmongers' strike, which was four months long, backed strongly by the CGT, and a real face-to-face conflict with the employers, that led to the reunification of the workers' movement and the affiliation of all trade unions, including the textile and fellmongers' unions, to the CGT. This was also the starting point for the unionisation of women. By 1910 there were 2800 trade unionists. The victorious workers imposed fines on non-strikers and, soon, the closed shop came into operation. By 1912 there were 4500 members, 2000 of whom were women. The rate of union membership reached 65 per cent in the whole of the region but was close to 100 per cent in Mazamet itself.

In 1910, strengthened by their victory of the previous year, the trade unions obtained, without even going on strike, collective agreements negotiated for three years which made provision for large wage rises and increases in tariffs (rates) for the following year, 1911. However, between 1912 and 1914, signs of a crisis began to loom – reduced attendance at meetings, criticisms levelled at the unions, lack of militancy and failed action. This was all linked to the candidacy of the main union leaders (including Isidore Barthès,[2] the General Secretary of the fellmongers' union) in the local elections of 1912 on a right-wing list whose real ideology, barely hidden by a demagogic stance, was profoundly hostile to the workers' movement. This manoeuvre by the right wing caused disarray amongst workers and led to a further split on the left with the minority Union des Syndicats Libres (Federation of Free Unions) being disowned by the CGT.

The principle of the closed shop made the Trade Union Centre of Mazamet the strongest of the whole county (*département*) of the Tarn in terms of membership. Of 4500 trade unionists in 1912, 2000 were fellmongers and 1600 textile workers. The workers' movement in Mazamet was dominated by the strong, eloquent and ambitious figure of Isidore Barthès.

Without the strong backing of the CGT, the strike of 1909 would not have been successful, hence the affiliation and loyalty of Mazamet trade unionists, Catholic and conservative, to the CGT, led by revolutionary syndicalists. After the 1909 strike, Mazamet sent aid to strikers throughout France and took part in the CGT campaigns against the high cost of living but, conversely, always refused to join in overtly political campaigns.

A minority of workers voted for the left whilst the majority distinguished between protest action and voting and returned to Parliament stout opponents of strikes and trade unions in the shape of successive members of the Reille-Soult family.[3] This lack of interest in Parliament paralleled that of the revolutionary syndicalists, notably Griffuelhes,[4] who played a big part in the 1909 strike and who favoured the autonomy of the trade union through direct action.

Elbeuf

Trade unionism was born in Elbeuf during the crucial years of the 1870s and 1880s: the spinners' union was founded in 1879, the masons' and joiners' in 1880, the boilermakers' in 1882, and the weavers' in 1883. These were trade-based unions with low memberships: no more than 350 members in total in 1886. This was trade unionism which was pacifist in nature, erring on the side of caution, preferring arbitration to strikes and whose main demand was the regulation of the working day. The most active was the Weavers' Union (Union des Tisseurs) which worked hard to preserve its independence from the socialist groups and which was dedicated above all to the study of labour law and the education of the workforce. This union was at the conference which founded the CGT in 1895 and was the first to demand the setting up of a Trade Union Centre.

The 1890s were characterised by a growth in numbers (2015 members by 1900) and a first attempt to found umbrella organisations in the shape of the rival federations La Fourmi ('The Busy Bees') in 1892, and the Fédération Elbeuvienne (The Elbeuf Federation) in 1897. Both were reformist in nature, but differed on the question of their relationship with politics: La Fourmi favoured an overt workers' candidacy in elections whilst the Elbeuf Federation preferred to confine its demands to trade union activity and support for the Republicans. The organisation of the textile trade unions in Elbeuf reflected the division of labour in the wool industry to the extent that each union corresponded to a distinct stage in the production process. This derived from the strength of the traditions associated with each trade and also explains the permanent fragmentation of trade unionism in the textile industry.

The wave of strikes at the start of the 1900s was followed by the founding of many trade unions: a dozen were in existence in 1914. By 1900 the Elbeuf unions were beginning to overcome their divisions and were seeking to form organisations for a collective struggle; this led to the founding of the Trade Union Centre in 1899 and, in 1901, of the Federation of Elbeuf Unions (Union Fédérative des Syndicats Elbeuviens), an umbrella organisation for ten trade unions with 2888 members. The three textile trade unions alone accounted for some 88 per cent of the total membership of the Federation. The Federation, dominated by mainstream united socialists, was linked to the Socialist Party and backed socialist candidates in elections against the independent socialists (whose best-known representative was Emile Martin[5]) who favoured union independence from politics and supported Republicans where necessary. The textile unions were affiliated to the CGT and to the National Textile Federation (La Fédération Nationale du Textile) led by mainstream united socialists. In 1910 all the textile unions joined together in the General Textile Union (Syndicat Général du Textile) the founding of which was evidence of the desire to overcome trade-based professional divisions: this was a genuine organisational transformation which tended to replace trade-based structures with industry-wide ones. Trade unionism amongst textile workers became much stronger during the 1900s, benefiting from its effective intervention into strikes, its gradual unification and the support of the CGT. Based on the figures declared by the unions, the growth in numbers is impressive: from 2015 in 1900 to 3462 in 1912 – that is, a rate of membership of 40 per cent, but the figures were, no doubt, hugely inflated and many indicators lead us to think that it would be wise to halve them. Trade unionism was primarily a male preserve: women represented only 20–30 per cent of the membership and held no positions of power in unions before the war.

From 1890 to 1914 the main demands of Elbeuf workers were for wage increases and the application of the legislation on working hours. They resorted to strikes only as an exception to the rule: there were sporadic outbreaks of unrest rather than a constant use of this particular weapon. Indeed, strikes were infrequent, short and always involved a small number of workers – generally, only workers from a given group (weavers, press operators, decatisers and invisible menders) and never the whole of the workforce in a given firm. Moreover, it was exceptional for a strike to spread from the confines of a single factory floor. So, the strike of 1914, it would seem, heralded something new. It was one month long and hard. A high number of weavers and invisible menders took part (although the 530 strikers represented only 6 per cent of textile workers) and they were led by Inghels, General Secretary of the National Textile Federation. The strike spread to several factories and was characterised by the total commitment of the unions at national and local levels. The strikers remained solid and were eventually victorious, the employers granting the wage rise asked for. From 1890 to 1914, trade union intervention came on the back of strikes but was never their inspiration. However, by the end of our period, it had become systematic with the victorious strike of 1914 bearing witness to its success. A dialectical relationship emerged, then, between strike developments and the strengthening of the trade unions.

Overall, the Elbeuf workers' movement was characterised by twin developments: the move from trade-based to industry sector-based unionism and the move from independent socialism to mainstream united socialism.

By way of explanation

The nature of industrialisation

The conditions in which the textile industry evolved – from the triple viewpoint of the urban environment, the technology in use, and the size of businesses involved – are an important factor in distinguishing between different models of trade unionism. We may, initially at least, contrast, on the one hand, the big industrial complexes of Bremen and Lancashire with, on the other hand, the two French centres whose nature was much more complicated.

Lancashire: where industry was long-established, strong and concentrated

Lancashire is a long-established industrial region with a cotton industry which was continuing to expand rapidly and becoming very prosperous at the end of the nineteenth century and the beginning of the twentieth. Even if they did not evolve at the same rate (Burnley took off, for example, only after 1870), the four towns under consideration all saw huge rises in their populations. Blackburn's population rose from 46 536 inhabitants in 1851 to 133 052 in 1911, Bolton's rose from 60 291 to 180 851, Burnley's from 14 706 to 106 322, and Oldham's from 52 800 to 147 483.

However, if the four towns were more or less comparable in terms of the size of their populations, then, conversely, their social and economic structures readily distinguished them. Oldham and Bolton, which specialised in spinning, in fact boasted a variety of activities because part of the workforce worked in the engineering industry and in the coalmines, with the result that cotton workers there accounted for only 42.9 per cent and 35.5 per cent of the total respective populations, as opposed to 48.8 per cent in Blackburn and 52.2 per cent in Burnley, both of which specialised in weaving and where the importance of the textile industry was much greater. We can see, especially in spinning, a strong tendency towards a concentration of large firms with limited company status although smaller family firms continued to exist nonetheless. Oldham is a particularly good example of this tendency with its 'Oldham Limiteds'. This type of development was slower to occur in Bolton, though, where it started really only after 1900. Conversely, production, in spinning as well as in weaving, was based everywhere on the modern factory unit, and machines were all driven by steam. This was true even in Burnley where small employers rented workshops and engine power. The changes in firms' legal and financial structures naturally reduced mobility between supervisors and workers which, originally, was considerable in small businesses. Towards 1900 this situation obtained only in Burnley. As for the workers, they were mainly concentrated in towns,[6] only a small minority continuing to live in small industrial villages as at the time of the Industrial Revolution. So workers' experience of cotton in Lancashire was essentially an urban one.

Bremen: where industrialisation came late

By contrast, the Bremen region which had no textile tradition saw a late industrialisation. The city-state of Bremen, which was a commercial centre, was totally devoid of industry and of an industrial proletariat until the end of the 1880s, and the five localities making up the region were villages where industry was either small-scale or totally non-existent. Even after the textile industry took off after 1870, the region retained a strongly rural character: out of eight textile factories, six were located in rural areas. Moreover, even though it had become the principal activity, textiles coexisted in Bremen-city with other industries: shipbuilding, foundries, food, engineering and tobacco.

All the textile businesses were established between 1870 and 1888. They grew swiftly since, out of eight firms, only three had fewer than 1000 workers at the start of the twentieth century: the wool treatment factory in Lesum had only 130 workers, and, in Grohn, rope-making and the cotton spinning and weaving factory had 350 and 430 employees respectively. Two of them, specialising in wool, were even true giants: the NWK employed 3100 workers in 1913, and the BWK 3600. The factories were very modern and, apart from wool sorting, all the work was mechanised.

The consequences of this concentration of businesses were further underlined by the concentration of housing because at least half of all textile workers were housed by the firm in the immediate vicinity of the factory. The proximity of workers' dwellings and factories was, then, one of the characteristics of the textile workforce of the Bremen region. Overall, this concentration of housing and of labour could only encourage the workforce to become aware of the fact that they had common interests to defend.

This swift but late industrialisation was based on systematic recourse to immigrant labour. Indeed, with the exception of the wool treatment factory in Lesum and rope-making in Grohn whose workforce were all native to the region, businesses here brought in workers from Poland, Galicia, Croatia and Czechoslovakia earlier and in greater numbers than the old textile regions. Immigrants accounted for between 50 per cent (BWK) and 75 per cent (NWK) of workers in the wool industry and 75 per cent in the jute industry where working conditions were harsher and wages lower.

Mazamet: where a unique industrial revolution took place

The conditions in which textiles developed in Mazamet were quite different. Located on the edge of the Aquitaine Basin and the Massif Central, Mazamet is a small town locked in by mountains and far away from big centres and ports. The first industrial town of the Tarn in 1914, Mazamet nevertheless retained a strong rural character: a large part of the industrial area (25 000 inhabitants) and even the district (*commune*) of Mazamet itself (14 300 inhabitants with 11 400 in the conurbation) were located in the mountains.

Wool had a long history there. The Industrial Revolution took place without steam engines, without huge injections of capital, and without local technological innovations. It was in the middle of the nineteenth century that fellmongery[7] was added to a textile industry which was by then in full expansion. Despite the town's geographical isolation and associated transport problems (the railways came only in 1886), this new industry developed swiftly thanks to hydraulic power and an excellent trading network, with Mazamet soon becoming the world centre for fellmongery. Expansion took place to the detriment of textiles which many industrialists abandoned because it was less profitable. So, by 1900, against 2500 textile workers, 3000 people worked in fellmongery and 300 in tanning, so that hide and sheep workers accounted for 47 per cent of the working class in Mazamet.

In textiles, as in fellmongery, capital was usually family-based and concentration was at a low level. There were about 100 factories and workshops in the Mazamet area. The numbers employed remained low in fellmongery where, out of 41 businesses, only three had more than 100 workers, the biggest having 190: numbers were higher in textiles where 12 businesses employed more than 100 workers; the biggest, Alba-Lasource, established in 1860 and staying loyal to textiles whilst so many others converted to fellmongery, employed 500 people. In the town itself, there were no fellmongery factories, only textile concerns. Factories formed a dense nework only in the immediate surroundings of Mazamet; elsewhere, they were spread thinly throughout the rural area.

Elbeuf: where the transition to modern industry was incomplete

Elbeuf was an old wool town where cloth manufacturing went back to the Middle Ages.[8] The town was at the centre of an industrial conurbation which influenced the neighbouring countryside from where it drew part of its workforce. It was severely hit by the decline in the wool industry and, in 30 years, lost 20 per cent of its population which fell to 18290 by 1911. Elbeuf's prosperity came from a proto-industrial environment which was still strong in 1870: possession of the means of production was extremely divided, the majority of manufacturers having neither a workshop nor employees and having all their work made to order. Manufacturing was split into a large number of distinct specialisms which could be found together under one roof only in a very few establishments. The next 20 years saw the transition towards a modern industry but the process was slow. The concentration of production increased but remained limited: whilst in 1876 there was only one concern with more than 300 workers, there were four in 1889 and seven in 1900, but there were still only two factories – Blin and Fraenckel – with more than 1000 workers.

Mechanisation of weaving came late: power looms became more popular only after 1895. Moreover, not all stages of production were mechanised: in 1904 only two-thirds of factory workers worked with the aid of a motor. The Alsatian transplant of 1871 – in which a handful of industrialists from Bischwiller injected capital, workers, and factories into Elbeuf – was responsible for the duality of industrial structures there: alongside the small Elbeuf establishments, the two Alsatian concerns grew to become distinctive by the scale of their operation (Blin: 1600 workers in 1900; Fraenckel: 1400), their integration of all production, the complete mechanisation of weaving and the automation of spinning.

On the whole, the transition towards a modern capitalist industry was incomplete: despite the disappearance of the smallest manufacturers and the growth in size of a handful of the largest, the production sites remained small (in 1905, on average, Elbeuf spinning factories were three times smaller than those in Roubaix and weaving sites six times smaller). In particular, the large majority continued to depend heavily on having work made to order because they did not have the equipment necessary to perform all the stages of the cloth manufacturing process themselves. The incomplete nature of this transition went hand-in-hand with an unstoppable decline: indeed, Elbeuf industry which had seen a strong expansion up to 1873 saw its sales figures drop from 93 million francs in 1873 to 45.2 million in 1913 and the numbers making up its workforce fell by two-thirds (from 22 000 workers in 1870 to 8–9000 in 1904).

Industrial concentration and trade union power: a complex relationship

The comparison of the industrial structures in Lancashire, Bremen, Mazamet and Elbeuf leads us to a very simple conclusion: the more it was organised within a modern, concentrated industry, the more powerful trade unionism was. Bremen and Lancashire where industry took a more modern form were characterised by their highly organised and powerful mass trade unionism. On the other hand, in Elbeuf and Mazamet the growth of trade unionism was slow and involved relatively low numbers (except in Mazamet from 1909 when the closed shop was brought in). We might think, in part at least, that this slow and weak development was a consequence of the nature of the transition towards modern industry there and, particularly, of the scarcity of concentration and mechanisation.

The earliness of industrialisation nevertheless readily differentiates Lancashire, where the Industrial Revolution and the creation of a proletariat came very early, with the result that trade unionism there already had a long history before 1900. On the other hand, in Bremen, it was not only the growth of the textile industry which was slow but also that of trade unionism, as we have to wait until the end of the century for the founding of textile trade unions.

Moreover, there is no automatic, simple or direct relationship between concentration of manufacturing and trade union power. In fact, it is other factors which intervene in, on the one hand, industrial structures and, on the other, in the level of organisation and militancy of the workers' movement. These factors are to be found in two areas: staffing structures and the history of the workers' movement itself. This is why the large, integrated businesses established in Elbeuf by the Alsatians were no different in terms of the growth of trade unionism and level of militancy from the smaller, less mechanised Elbeuf concerns. Their staff profile may explain this: in 1891, at Blin, a third of the workers came from Alsace. The Alsatian workers, as a group, displayed specific characteristics which distinguished them from the body of workers native to the area – strong sense of identity, close links with the bosses, use of the Alsatian dialect, Protestantism, membership of mutual aid societies and sport and music clubs which reminded them of their proud Alsatian origins, marriages within the group, higher qualifications, more permanent, and forming the backbone of supervisory staff. Within Elbeuf society, they were truly isolated and they developed an ethnically-based sense of community. The Blins depended for the management of their workforce on the Alsatian workers who made up the nucleus of their staff. This division doubtless explains the relative pacifism of the workers in the Alsatian concerns.

The example of Bremen also demonstrates that big business is not always synonymous with a high level of union membership. At the Bremer Wollwäscherei AG, the smallest firm in the region with 130 workers but all of German origin, nearly all the workers belonged to a union (89 per cent in 1906; 78 per cent in 1912). Conversely, the DTAV never gained a real foothold in the NWK – no more than 20 per cent of workers were members of a union in 1913 – a real 'industrial giant' whose numbers had risen from 1600 employees in 1890 to 3100 in 1913 but which recruited most of its staff (75 per cent) from unqualified, highly mobile immigrants. It might therefore be considered that analysis by national origin of staff in textile factories is of great importance: in the Bremen region, trade unionism primarily concerned permanent workers native to the area. Even if the rate of union membership of immigrants was, of course, lower at the start than that of German workers, it could only rise subsequently, the DTAV succeeding on the eve of the First World War in recruiting immigrants who had by then a longer experience of working life and factories and who had also become much more settled. This is partly the reason why we can observe a high level of union membership in certain factories in 1913 especially in the jute factories of Bremen (44 per cent) and Hemelingen (52 per cent), which employed a large proportion of immigrants (75 per cent).

Conversely, Mazamet, despite the dispersal of its businesses and a very compelling rural environment, saw a real explosion in numbers in its trade unions towards the end of our period. This paradox is related, in fact, to the history of trade unionism itself – namely, the successful strike of 1909 which led to the imposition of the closed shop with the tacit agreement of the defeated employers who were threatened with further strike action if they employed non-union members. This strong tendency to demand that only union members be employed and which presupposed that the union would cater for the whole of the workforce in a given trade (to refuse to join would be to marginalise oneself amongst the working class) formed part of a long tradition in the Mazamet workers' movement: patrols and pickets, fines and blacklists all obliged paper-workers to join the clandestine union in 1788, textile workers to join during the strike of 1845, and workers of all trades to join unions from 1903, with this obligation even being formally written into the constitution of the Federation founded in early 1904 to represent all the local trade unions. It was, however, the success of the 1909 strike and the unification of the movement that followed which, by changing the dynamics of the relationships involved, allowed the closed shop to be implemented on a large scale.

The impact of paternalism

Workforce management policies strongly differentiate businesses to the extent that, by seeking to attract, keep and stabilise staff and transform them to adapt them to the needs of the firm by setting up of a more or less complete system of social welfare measures, they created a close dependency between the workers and the benefactor business as well as a feeling of belonging to the same community. We should ask, then, to what extent the existence – or absence – of social welfare measures inspired by paternalism influenced the growth of the trade union movement. From this perspective, a comparative study of textile towns reveals very diverse situations.

In Mazamet paternalism had hardly developed at all: welfare and retirement offices were few and far between, workers' friendly societies only appeared after 1913 and then numbered only 14 in total. On the whole, charity was the order of the day. In Elbeuf the situation was characterised by the clear-cut division between the employers of old Elbeuf origins, indifferent to social policy, and the employers of Alsatian origin, desirous of protecting their workers from poverty and insecurity by implementing generous social policies. Loyal to the traditions of the proto-industrial period in which the wool industry evolved, the Elbeuf manufacturers were happy to subsidise the mutual aid societies founded by the workers, to support charitable organisations, and to help workers in need. By contrast, the Alsatian industrialists whose aim was to stabilise their workforce and adapt it to the demands of the firm, established a complete system of insurance and welfare benefits. In Bremen businesses widely developed, but to different degrees, social policies aiming to mitigate against the shortage of labour. This social policy evolved along two main lines: housing (about 50 per cent of workers were housed by the firms themselves) and welfare benefits (for births, deaths, sickness, Christmas and length of service). The NWK, for its part, had set up dense network of social welfare provision covering almost every aspect of life, from birth to death, to the extent that the factory was almost a town within a town. We must add, though, that, within the German textile industry, the large scale of institutions set up by the businesses was a peculiarity of the Bremen region. In Lancashire, paternalism was a major feature of the style of workforce management. By offering their workers housing and recreational activities, the employers had succeeded in stabilising their workforce and in inculcating a sense of discipline and restraint. However, the big limited companies which had appeared at the end of the Victorian era in spinning (Oldham) and the small weaving firms which rented workshops and engine power and did not have the financial means to implement social welfare policies (Burnley) remained totally outside this type of workforce management. Additionally, the influence that the bosses could exert on their staff was dealt a heavy blow by the rival systems set up by the ever expanding trade union movement.

On the whole, with the exception of Mazamet, paternalism was an important feature of personnel management in the European textile industry at the turn of the century. We might expect that, by fostering loyalty and attachment to the firm, social policy succeeded in stifling workers' class-consciousness and protest action. However, there are no unequivocal, clear or direct links between the existence of paternalistic policies and the propensity of workers to organise and be militant.

In Elbeuf, strikes were no more numerous in factories deprived of social welfare policies than at Blin or Fraenckel where paternalism was particularly well-developed. In terms of protest action, the behaviour of workers in paternalistic establishments does not seem to have been much different either from that of workers in the rest of the Elbeuf wool industry. Moreover, by joining forces with workers from other factories, the workers at Blin during the 1900 strike and at Fraenckel during that of 1914 demonstrated that they were not prisoners of paternalism and that they felt they had the same interests to defend and demands to make as the rest of the Elbeuf working class – a feeling which was ultimately stronger than that of loyalty to any particular firm. Similarly, in Bremen, no clear and simple relationship existed between paternalism and peace on the factory floor. Comparing the NWK and the BWK is especially revealing from this point of view. The NWK which was a family firm (legally, it was a limited company but all the shares were owned by the Lahusen family) implemented the widest set of social policies in the region, whilst the BWK was a limited company in which such policies were almost absent. If, in both cases, trade unionism had hardly taken off at all, the propensity of workers to go on strike was very different: at the NWK, the workforce was quite militant and strikes were frequent whilst the BWK saw only one strike in 30 years!

It was only in Lancashire that paternalism seems to have exerted a strong influence on the workers' behaviour. Oldham, where paternalism was in decline thanks to the disappearance of family businesses, had a very militant working class which, towards the end of the Victorian era – and especially during the disputes of 1885, 1891 and 1893 – constituted the heart of the workers' movement in Lancashire. On the other hand, Bolton like Blackburn, where paternalism was a social and political force to be reckoned with, saw a long period of relative social stability. Even if it obviously did not prevent the emergence of trade unions and industrial disputes, paternalism nonetheless encouraged a particular way of expressing discontent. It was in this way that, in Blackburn especially, after the lockout of 1878 in which the house of an employer had been set on fire, there were only infrequent strikes which never spread to the whole town and the workers' leaders always displayed great moderation.

From local working communities to the specificities of organisation and protest

The skilled community such as it was in each of the four cases studied – nature of the work, hierarchies based on qualifications, wage levels, organisation of labour and staff profiles in the factories – seems to have played a major role in the development of trade unionism and protest movements.

Lancashire: where hierarchies based on qualifications and wages were important

In Lancashire, trade unionism in the cotton industry was partly characterised by the structure of the local working class and the behaviour exhibited by it. Only a very small minority of workers had taken an apprenticeship and, in this sense, could be considered skilled workers. However, this approach is far too simplistic and fails to take into account contemporary realities: many cotton workers were skilled workers even if they had not taken an apprenticeship because, in spinning as in weaving (where the machine had triumphantly totally taken over, however), the mechanisation of labour had not uniformly replaced the skill of the trade with labour merely involving repetitive movements. Having become the servant of the machine, the worker, of course, had to power it and supervise it but the execution of this type of work still depended on the skill, speed and safety of his or her movements. To perform his or her work properly, a worker had to have a thorough knowledge of the properties of the material being worked, of the functioning of the machine, and of the characteristics of the product being manufactured. This was especially true in spinning. Spinners who formed more than a quarter of the male workforce of the cotton industry were often known by their contemporaries as the 'Barefoot Aristocrats' because they worked barefoot so as not to slip on the oil covering the factory floor. In 1906 they received, on average, a wage of £2 per week

– a wage normally associated with the top of the working hierarchy. Other groups of workers also earned high wages. In carding, the best qualified workers, such as strippers and grinders, who were few in number and well-paid (their wages being as high as 75 per cent of those of spinners), had as their ambition the emulation of this privileged group. As for weavers on power looms who accounted for the largest single part of the textile workforce – that is, about one-third – they were largely considered as semi-skilled.

These circumstances explain why the Lancashire unions which were not true craft-based unions often behaved as if they were. This was especially true of the spinners who were as closed and exclusive as a craft trade union. This is why they refused to welcome women into their ranks, women being largely excluded from spinning work because the spinners argued that a spinning mill was not a fit place for a woman and that working on a mule was physically too demanding for them. In weaving, similar circumstances obtained because men had a virtual monopoly over the better-paid work on the six looms whilst the majority of women worked on four looms where basic wages were lower. If the unions always defended the principle of equal rates of pay for men and women, male trade unionists, on the other hand, would state that they wanted to protect women by claiming that certain fabrics were too heavy for them, with the sole aim of keeping for themselves the best-paid jobs. Overall, if the practice of the closed shop which excluded women both from the union and the job itself was peculiar to spinners, we can say that, in general, the trade union movement in Lancashire sought to control the labour market through the process of collective bargaining and the setting up of wage lists. This policy obviously owed its origins to the status of the best-qualified workers in the production process and translated into relatively high wages.

Bremen: staff profiles and the circumstances of industrialisation

In Bremen it was the best-qualified and best-paid workers – that is, sorters, weavers and spinners – who formed the main body of troops in the textile unions and who were behind strikes, whether these were spontaneous or organised. These circumstances are undoubtedly linked to the staff profile of the textile factories where a nucleus of skilled workers was surrounded by younger colleagues of both sexes, aged between 14 and 18, from whom were recruited spinners' and weavers' assistants who found themselves at the bottom of the hierarchy but with the hope of becoming spinners or weavers in turn themselves, and by workers of foreign origin with no real qualifications who were highly mobile. Workers without qualifications were more numerous in jute where working conditions were very poor and wages lower than in wool. There was, however, in all the textile businesses of the region an opposition between a nucleus of permanent, qualified workers and the rest of the staff with no qualifications and a high turnover. It was this opposition, partly reflecting moreover that between workers native to the region and immigrants, which explains the basic characteristics of the trade union movement in the textile region of Bremen.

As for recourse to spontaneous strike action or walkouts, which seems to be one of the defining features of industrial disputes in the Bremen textile industry as opposed to the rest of Germany, if employers' intransigence was not unheard of, at least at the BWK and in the jute factory of Bremen, it would seem that the circumstances in which the local working class evolved played the decisive role. We must, in fact, remember that the textile industry evolved very quickly and from scratch so to speak, in rural areas, with no textile tradition, and in the framework of big modern factories which were totally mechanised. So much so that, for the majority of workers, being taken on by a textile factory was a dramatic and painful experience. Uprooted from their home region, they came to boost the local populations of Hemelingen, Blumenthal and Delmenhorst which, between 1870 and 1910, rose rapidly (by 276 per cent, 441 per cent, and 460 per cent respectively). Moreover, they had to bow to the strict discipline of the factory, get used to working the whole year long, and accept being mere accessories of a machine. This process was all the more dramatic for being quick as it took only two decades to complete. It was, then, a particular type of working community, born of a swift industrialisation, which got involved in many head-on disputes with employers and which conducted them most stridently.

Moreover, the role of women in the textile factories should also be taken into account. Female labour was extensively developed and women accounted for about 40 per cent of the workforce in textiles, the proportion reaching even 60–70 per cent in the jute and cotton factories where the spinning departments were almost entirely female. We have already noted that the feminisation of the factory workforce did not automatically translate into a feminisation of the trade unions, the female membership of which was, additionally, ever changing. We can, therefore, advance the hypothesis that it is because women had so little experience of trade unions that spontaneous strike action was so very important in industrial disputes in textiles. Doubtless, spontaneous strikes were not always called by female workers but it must be noted that, more often than not, it was the departments where they were in the majority – sorting at the NWK and spinning at the jute factory of

Bremen – which took the initiative in calling strikes outside the trade union's framework and against its advice.

Elbeuf: luxury products and the division of labour

In Elbeuf the nature of the trade union movement – late birth, relatively low membership and persistence of trade-based divisions – as well as of protest action – infrequent strikes which only ever involved a small number of workers, never involved a whole factory and, with the exception of 1914, which never spread from one business to another – were largely determined by the structures of the wool industry. Apart from the widespread nature of the sites of production already discussed, two basic traits need to be emphasised: in an industry like cloth manufacturing which delivered a quality product of great diversity, the technology remained characterised, even in 1900, by incomplete mechanisation because the factory constituted not so much an integrated organism as an assemblage of specialist workshops and the share of manual work there was still large. On the one hand, despite the public face of modernity, the division into workshops reflected the division of labour prior to the machine age. Workers' tools in manufacturing had metamorphosed into as many specialist machines, and the juxtaposition of the separate stages of production performed by different workers had been replaced by a juxtaposition of machines performing these same partial stages of production. The production process, then, involved 24 different and successive operations in cloth manufacturing and the different workshops were independent of each other. This meant that the factory was like a community of trades where the passing on of technical know-how was essential, since only part of the workforce (about a quarter) had been cruelly deskilled by the arrival of machines. On the other hand, machines had not yet completely taken over the manufacturing process, leaving behind small pockets of manual work where the technical skill of the worker remained indispensable. Many operations – wool sorting, assembly, sampling, checking finishing processes and invisible mending – continued to demand intelligence, know-how, speed and safety of movement and even, for some, an eye for beauty, with the apprenticeship (two to three years for an invisible mender) being the standard method of training. For all these workers, work more resembled that of an artisan's workshop than a factory. On the whole, the workforce of the Elbeuf wool industry was very diverse and distinctly hierarchical – so much so that the quality of manufacturing, the considerable division of labour and the importance of skilled work may explain the low propensity of Elbeuf workers to organise themselves and to protest.

Mazamet: workers from rural backgrounds with low qualifications

In Mazamet it was fellmongery workers who displayed the greatest militancy and who led the trade union movement, their strike of 1909 representing a turning point in the history of the local workers' movement. Three factors distinguish fellmongery workers from those in textiles. First, many of them were of rural origin and kept close links with the countryside – many continued to live in hamlets where part of their families worked in agriculture, while others would help with the harvest in summer when their fellmongering work declined owing to the shortage of water. As for the factories, they were dotted about the valleys. Overall, the transition from textiles to fellmongery reinforced the rural nature of the working class. Second, fellmongery work required few qualifications, demanded great physical effort (especially for lifting soaking hides) and was done in harsh conditions (workers operated in constant humidity, ammonia would stain their hands and there was a lot of manual work involved). Last, the workforce in fellmongery was not very varied because the job entailed only two operations – cleaning and extraction of wool from the hide – and, apart from a degree of rivalry in wool extraction, there was no real competition between male and female workers.

This unique working community operated in an environment that was particularly conducive to head-on clashes with the employers. On the one hand, Mazamet workers felt very strongly that they had 'rights' which they were entitled to defend: hence their rejection of the employers' proposal to cut wool cleaners' wages (the highest wages of all) to increase those of other groups of workers, which caused the strike of 1909, and their desire to distribute work equally amongst workers to avoid unemployment should production levels drop off. On the other hand, tying in with old local traditions, fellmongery workers firmly believed that, in order to have their demands met, action had to be taken by the whole of the workforce. This led to strikes becoming compulsory with non-strikers being hounded – the 1909 strike was, therefore, almost a general one – and, after the strike, to unification of the union movement and the closed shop principle. Finally, the 1909 strike brought to the fore a level of militancy and an ability of the workers to hold out which took everyone by surprise. For four months, the fellmongers engaged in practically every form of militancy and protest action (electing a strike committee, having frequent meetings, holding big marches in the streets, organising soup kitchens,[9] evacuating children,[10] sending out pickets on patrol to prevent non-strikers from working, and fighting with employers and the forces of law and order).

Examples of great diversity

The example of Mazamet fellmongery seems radically different from all the others. The reasons for this difference are obvious: even if it was born of the need to supply the textile industry with raw materials, fellmongery was another type of industry, different and autonomous, which did not use the same techniques, did not organise its production processes in the same way, and did not demand the same skills of its workforce as the rest of the wool industry. All this created a unique working community. Moreover, fellmongery workers did not belong to the Textile Federation of the CGT (Fédération du Textile) but rather to the Leather and Hide Federation (Fédération des Cuirs et Peaux). Conversely, in the textile industry, despite the diversity of materials worked and products manufactured, the work nonetheless called for similar techniques and knowledge. In all the centres under consideration, the work involved was either skilled or semi-skilled.

If we can identify four different types of trade unionism, this is because the relationship of workers to their work was not enough to create a specific working-class identity characterised by identical trade union organisations and practices across the three countries. Other factors have to be taken into consideration to explain the contrasts found. In the Lancashire towns, the hierarchy based on occupations and wages explains why the cotton workers' unions tended to behave as craft unions seeking to control the labour market and regulate wages. In the Bremen region, the unionisation of the best-qualified and most permanent workers and the preponderance of spontaneous strikes or walkouts were rooted in the nature of industrialisation there, as well as in the characteristics of staff structures and the role of women both in the workplace and in trade unions. In Mazamet if, despite everything that separated cloth-making from fellmongery, the textile workers, emulating the fellmongers as well as all the other trades, applied the principle of the closed shop, this was first because they all belonged to a single working community, but also because they came under the strong influence of the fellmongers whose domination of the Mazamet workers' movement is explained by their weight of numbers, the militancy of their strikes, their recent victory and the decisive role of Isidore Barthès in whom the body of workers placed great confidence. Finally, in Elbeuf, the relative weakness and moderation of trade unionism, as well as the paucity of protest movements, owed its origins to the division of labour characterising the luxury industry that cloth manufacturing remained despite the technological changes which it had experienced. All things considered, it is these factors which allow us to differentiate between the four cases studied and explain the great diversity we have observed.

The role of women

Significant differences in a male preserve

In textiles, as in other sectors of industry, trade unionism was initially a male preserve. This imbalance is all the more striking because, with the exception of Elbeuf, women accounted for at least half of the wage-earners of this sector, and often more. In the Bremen region they made up 60–70 per cent of the staff in the jute industry and 40–50 per cent of that in wool. In Lancashire women made up 62 per cent of the workforce in textiles in 1906. In Mazamet women were in the majority in textiles, although in fellmongery there was parity with women working in wool extraction and men in wool cleaning. Finally, in Elbeuf, the figure did not exceed 40 per cent. Although rising, it was even noticeably lower in the big Alsatian concerns (30 per cent at Blin in 1889; 37 per cent in 1909).

However, significant differences are apparent in the unionisation of women. In Elbeuf the number of women in unions was always very low: in 1906, fewer than 20 per cent of women held a membership card. In Mazamet trade unions did not even consider admitting women until 1908, although wage claims involved them as well and they did take part in strikes. It was the tanners' union which was the first, in 1908, to amend its constitution to allow women members into its ranks. However, the unionisation of women started only after the strike of 1909 in which they were very active – fellmongers and unskilled female factory workers going on strike from day one – and even heroic – lying down in the snow to block the path of police horses – although, on the whole, fewer in number than men on marches and at meetings. Their membership of trade unions became substantial only when it became compulsory. In Bremen the proportion of women in trade unions was lower than that in the workforce but numbers varied greatly from place to place: in 1913 the number of women trade unionists was high in Bremen (42 per cent) and in Hemelingen (52 per cent) but low in Delmenhorst (17 per cent), and almost non-existent in Vegesack (1 per cent). Moreover, if women were very active in protest movements – it was the workshops containing high numbers of women (sorting in wool, spinning in jute) which would take the initiative in this respect – their commitment to the struggle, conversely, did not result in their joining a union. This led to big fluctuations in numbers: in the Hemelingen branch, for example, the proportion of women members went from 15 per cent in 1900 to 8 per cent in 1902 and from 67 per cent in 1911 to 52 per cent in 1913.

How can we explain both the fluctuations in women's membership and the startlingly low figures in the Delmenhorst and Vegesack branches? Without doubt, this is due both to the dual role of women in the workforce and in the family and to the stance adopted by the unions towards them. If, nationally, the DTAV had eloquently put the case for women (equal pay, eight-hour working day, better maternity cover, Saturday afternoon off), then, conversely, local organisations never defended them nor, in practice, did they do anything about the inequality of wages between the sexes (women earned one-third less than men). It was 1910 before conferences for women workers were organised at regional level and 1912 before action committees for women were set up at local level. Moreover, at local level, women had no positions of power in trade unions.

The example of Lancashire is unique from this point of view, for two reasons. First, spinners were totally opposed to women working in spinning and refused to allow them to join the trade unions with the result that, when women started to work in spinning because of the introduction of ring spinning, they had to join the cardroom workers' union. Second, in carding and weaving, women members were in the majority in trade unions even if the latter remained dominated by the best-qualified and best-paid male workers. Not only were their wages and union dues lower than men's, but they also received fewer benefits from membership (we should note that the situation in Mazamet was the same). However, despite the discrimination to which they were subjected, they played a considerable role in the development of trade unionism in Lancashire. While there were no female union officials, there were, conversely, significant numbers of women on committees, especially in weaving, notably in Oldham. On the other hand, their active participation in the Pankhursts' campaigns supporting the advancement of women placed them in an eminent position in the social and political life of their working communities. Moreover, the Independent Labour Party encouraged them to participate in local elections. The reputation for independence enjoyed by the women workers of Lancashire reflected their greater economic independence: the size of their families was smaller and their wages were not merely a supplement to those of their husbands.

The four cases studied display obvious differences. There are many factors that may explain these differences but it is difficult to place them in order of importance. Do these contrasts derive from anthropological family structures which obviously differed from country to country? Are they due to industrial structures? Do they derive from the structure of the workforce and from employers' wages policies? Or, as the example of Lancashire suggests, are they due to the cultural and political traditions of each country? We must be satisfied with asking the question without finding an answer because we are not yet in a position to expand on the information provided in the above analysis.

Gender and trade union policy: a new approach

Beyond the differences we have just outlined, the experiences of Lancashire, Bremen, Mazamet and Elbeuf have in common the fact that trade unionism there was primarily a male preserve. Indeed, if female workers took part in protest action when their economic interests were at stake, then they were rarely at the forefront of such action and their participation in trade union life was always less active than that of the men who, moreover, monopolised the positions of power. Certainly there were many obstacles to a fuller participation in union life, the double shift (at factory and at home) being obviously not the least but also not the only one. On the one hand, even when the job done (workers of both sexes often worked on the same machines) and the rhythms of life brought them together (in many cases, in Lancashire as in Elbeuf and Bremen, women did not stop work on the birth of their first child but left when their children started work), men's and women's experience of factory work was very different. More lightweight and less well-paid jobs, greater job uncertainty and sexual harassment effectively defined the women operatives' working lives. On the other hand, within the family, sharing of jobs and responsibilities was absolutely uneven. Moreover, even though every member of the family had to work to balance the family budget, the dominant model remained that of the male bread-winner. Finally, the lack of interest shown by union leaders in the specific position and claims of women workers – clearly attested in the Bremen region and which could go as far as reflecting and perpetuating the discrimination women workers suffered, as was the case in Lancashire – explains why the unions had so much difficulty in recruiting women and in mobilising them on a permanent basis.

However, these difficulties would be better understood if we remembered that trade union rhetoric appealed primarily to men, spoke the language of masculinity, exalted a model of the family – that of the woman as housewife – which women workers in textiles were quite incapable of fulfilling and which, in the area of representation, excluded them from leadership and protest action, and also had a patriarchal tone which was so strongly pronounced that it made men the only real actors in the workers' movement. The example of Mazamet is highly revealing from this perspective because, at the height of the 1909 fellmongers' strike, during a general meeting of all workers' trade unions, open to non-members and called in solidarity with the striking fellmongers, Isidore Barthès, the General Secretary of the fellmongers,

... encouraged women in the shops [wool warehouses] to stop work without delay before they could be threatened with forceful expulsion, and, as wage rises were being requested on their behalf, their duty was to support those taking action to get those demands met by encouraging all men to keep their wives at home.

This suppression in union discourse of everything that constituted the specificity of working women's experiences was not, and could not be, without consequence for the development of the structures and practices of the trade union movement because workers identified with their class in a different way and more or less closely depending on their gender. However, either because the sources hardly lend themselves to it or, indeed, are absent (especially in the case of Elbeuf for which there are no textile union archives nor even a collection of speeches by the leaders), or because this issue forms in some cases only a small part of the research on which our comparative study is based, this dimension could not be thoroughly explored. It does seem, though, that an analysis of the way in which language and symbolic codes operate to construct gender differences in a social class is likely to be useful in bringing to light the basic structural principles of trade union experience. This, however, is a requirement which is not specific to the textile industry.

The importance of the local political climate

Some of the characteristics of the four cases studied can be explained only with reference to the local political climate which was itself the result of a specific history. In the case of Bremen, though, this is not well-known; we have only a few indications of the relationship between the local sections of the DTAV and the town councils, and with the SPD, which do not allow a full and detailed picture to be painted. The three other cases are better documented.

Lancashire: political conservatism and trade union activism

The four cotton towns are characterised by the absence of any combination of trade union activism and political radicalism. Oldham, which did not have a Labour MP until 1922, is a veritable caricature of this situation. The causes of conservatism in the workforce are the subject of lively debate. The traditional explanation is that the workers chose to oppose the liberal politics of their bosses by supporting the conservatives who presented themselves as being in favour of the state controlling working conditions and, notably, of limiting the length of the working day. More recently, it has been stated that the workers were conservative because they voted as their bosses did, paternalism favouring workers' loyalty towards the industrialist family. Finally, it has also been said that hostility towards the Irish, who accepted low wages and at times willingly played the part of strike-breakers, played a role in this phenomenon. Indeed, the tension between workers native to the region and Irish immigrants rose from the 1850s onwards, following the Great Famine in Ireland. The Conservative Party, whose anti-Catholicism was part of a long tradition, skilfully exploited the popular anti-Irish prejudices in order to extend its own influence.

Mazamet: trade unionism distinct from politics

The position of the workers' movement in Mazamet is an unexpected one: on the one hand, the workers engaged in solid protest action against the employers, with a keen sense of belonging to the working class and, on the other, the majority of them voted for the right in general and local elections. How can this apparent contradiction be explained? Four factors must be taken into account. First, the workers, especially the fellmongers, were locked into a traditionalist conservative rural environment – 75 per cent of fellmongers and 45 per cent of textile workers lived in the country; some of them occasionally participated in agricultural work; they spoke the *langue d'oc* (southern dialect distinct from French) and were suspicious of novelties brought by the 'gentlemen' from town. Second, most of the workers were practising Catholics whilst the majority of the employers were Protestants and on the centre-left. Third, there was strong religious bonding in the rural working community, given shape throughout history by a militant Church which looked after the faithful well. Fourth, the family of Baron Reille-Soult was able to personify the defence of a persecuted religion and of a regional identity, and used their newspaper to contribute to the perpetuation and strengthening of traditional ways of thinking. This meant that, in the eyes of the workers, there was no contradiction between going on strike against Protestant employers and voting for the religious and conservative right. In these circumstances, transferring to the revolutionary syndicalist CGT is explained essentially by the efficient practicality of its militants during strikes – in the first instance, Griffuelhes who was a very well respected adviser – and the distinction that they encouraged workers to make between strike action and electoral behaviour, returning side-by-side Republicans and partisans of the Baron. If, in the case of the fellmongers' strike, we can speak of revolutionary syndicalism, then it is because the strike developed within an autonomous union movement outside the influence of any political party (in fact, the Socialist Party was not a serious contender), rallied large numbers of women and was characterised by recourse to violence.

However, this revolutionary syndicalism was more the expression of a local working environment and the necessities of protest action there rather than of a preconceived theory. So the 'revolutionary syndicalism' of Mazamet workers only extended to the practicalities of striking.[11]

Elbeuf: no class autonomy

In Elbeuf, where the influence of revolutionary syndicalism was non-existent, the history of the workers' movement was characterised by the opposition between independent socialists and mainstream united socialists. Right up until 1900 the independents were the dominant force: they wanted to keep the trade unions apart from the Socialist Party and Emile Martin, their leader, always defended the principle of the socialist candidate standing down in favour of a better-placed Republican. The 1900s saw the mainstream united socialists take over from the independents: links between the party and trade unions started to develop and, if they joined the team of the Radical Party mayor Mouchel (1908–1912) whose programme of 'municipal socialism' they supported, then, conversely, in the general elections of 1912 and 1914, the Socialist Party, appearing as the main force on the left and presenting itself as the defender of Mouchel's legacy and of better retirement pensions for workers, picked up in the second round all the Republicans' votes. All in all, whether on the Radicals' coat tails or as the dominant force on the side of progress in a camp uniting all republican voices, the Elbeuf workers' movement did not plan its action on a strict class basis but rather claimed to integrate it into a larger whole which went beyond it. The local political situation was without doubt not divorced from this stance: the majority of Elbeuf employers, Catholic and conservative, supported the parties of the right;[12] hence the solidarity on the electoral battleground between workers and Republicans. All things considered, the trade unions found themselves gradually subordinated to the Socialist Party which supplied them with their most high-profile leaders as well as supporting strikes but which, moderately and pragmatically, advocated parliamentary action rather than involving itself in a class conflict.

One cannot fail to be struck by the fact that, in France, the relationship of the workers' movement to politics and the nature of the relationship between the trade unions and the Socialist Party derived from unique and complex local political situations which were diametrically opposed: in Mazamet, where the bosses were on the left, the workers voted for the right; in Elbeuf, conversely, where the majority of the employers were pillars of the conservative political party, the workers gave their votes to the left!

Are traditional models valid after all?

The comparative analysis of the types of trade unionism in the textile industry has not brought to light any common trends. If there was, in this industry, no one single type of trade unionism, then this is because there was no homogeneous work community. Admittedly, there are similarities between the cases studied but they are more superficial than profound. The practice of the closed shop attested in Lancashire is similar to the strong tendency found in Mazamet to demand that only union members be employed but, in the former case, we are dealing with a region which industrialised early creating the world's first ever factory-based proletariat where skilled workers defended jobs and wages by seeking to control the labour market, whilst, in the latter case, we are looking at workers barely separated from the surrounding rural environment whose behaviour was an expression of the traditionalist ways of thinking of an isolated and very tightly-knit working community. Moreover, in Elbeuf, as in Bremen, the trade unions were closely linked with the respective Socialist Party but, in everything else, the two towns were diametrically opposed. On the one hand, there was a weak trade unionism, strongly influenced by the traditions of the trades, the organisation of which long bore the hallmarks of protest action, with no overall strategy, in support of that started by the workers but without ever really initiating any of its own. On the other hand, we see a mass highly-organised trade unionism which preferred negotiation to strike action. In Lancashire and in Bremen, the trade unions increasingly came to regard strikes as a means of bringing employers to the negotiating table and influencing the outcome of those discussions, but if, in the British cotton industry, they were a real weapon in the hands of the trade unions, in the Bremen region, despite the efforts of the DTAV to exercise leadership over workers' protests, strikes remained largely out of their control.

Indeed, a practical analysis of the types of trade unionism in textiles reveals a great variety of strategies, types of protest action and organisation. As soon as the differences are seen to be more important, we are brought back to our three 'national models', but we should ask whether the above analyses merely allow a more complex and more qualified picture to be drawn than that offered by traditional historiography or whether, on the contrary, they call this model into question.

In Lancashire textile trade unionism was powerful and bureaucratic, lacking in ideology, organised to defend wages through collective bargaining with the employers, and sought to extend its influence into the political arena. However, on the one hand, the move towards industrial trade unionism desired by the 'new unionism' had not even started on the eve of the First World War and, on the other hand, the political conservatism of the workers acted as a brake on the development of the Labour Party. In this sense, Lancashire seems totally representative of the 'old' trade unions whose traditions had formed before the birth of the Labour Party. Conversely, though, it must be remembered that nowhere else in Great Britain – not even in the geographically close wool region of Yorkshire – did union leaders have the job of calculating wages. It is this, as Sidney and Beatrice Webb have shown in *Industrial Democracy*, which gives the Lancashire 'model' its unique appearance when compared to all the other trade union phenomena in Great Britain.

In the Bremen region we have a mass trade unionism, recruiting its members primarily from skilled male workers of German nationality, which wanted to instil discipline into workers' protest movements and to set up a system of regular talks with employers, the whole closely linked to a reformist Socialist Party. However, the textile trade unionism of this region is distinguished by a rate of membership which was higher than the national average and, above all, by the greater numbers of spontaneous strikes or walkouts, organised outside, and even against the advice of, the local sections of the DTAV. It might be thought that this particularity was the product of a modern, swift, and late industrialisation.

In the two examples above, then, the 'national models' seem quite valid, but the divergences from them are nonetheless considerable. As for the experiences of Mazamet and Elbeuf, both strangers to the revolutionary syndicalist model, they appear to be the products of quite singular histories. The two French examples are very different: we can, in fact, contrast a relatively weak and moderate trade unionism, closely linked to the socialists who played a decisive role in its birth and development, with a 'hard' exclusive trade unionism which, by dint of a deep political and religious conservatism, kept itself resolutely apart from the Socialist Party. These two brands of trade unionism are both equally non-typical of France before 1914. The key to these circumstances is obviously to be found in the profoundly different characteristics of the two working communities, in the contrasting political climates and in the history of the trade union movement.

Overall, then, our comparative study of trade unionism in textile towns and areas shows that the differences brought to light are not necessarily national ones and force a re-evaluation of the importance of local factors which blur models that are too simplistic or even, as is the case in France, destroy them altogether. Conclusions are, however, difficult to draw. Indeed, two factors suggest that we should suspend judgement: first, it is difficult to compare the phenomena studied; and, second, the validity of any comparison is diluted by the fact that some of the cases examined are simply not representative at all, Mazamet being, it would seem, quite unique. So we are forced to leave unanswered the crucial question which this comparative study poses: are the cases studied divergent from truly existing 'national models' or is there a multiplicity of 'models' because, on close examination, the 'national models' prove to be nothing more than a dated historiographical construct? This discovery by our practical analysis of the local regional differences leads us to ask if a re-evaluation of the ideal of the three models would not be better effected by interregional comparisons which, after having brought to light the different forms taken by the trade union movement and by workers' protest action in each country, would allow much more finely tuned points to be made about any common features and dissimilarities.

Notes

1. This committee, elected by an assembly of workers from the factory in case of action or strike, had the name of *Lohnkommission* (wages committee). It was this committee which, in most factories, negotiated with the employer. Most often, it had contacts with the local section of the DTAV before or during the preparation for action and at least whenever action turned into a strike. Often, members of the DTAV would sit on this committee.
2. Isidore Barthès (1874–1936): General Secretary of the fellmongers' union and main leader of the Mazamet trade union movement from 1903 to 1922. A Catholic conservative and loyal to the CGT after the 1909 strike, his behaviour was typical of that of the majority of workers in the town. See the biographical note in Maitron, Vol. 10, pp. 213–14.
3. A marshal under Napoleon and a minister under Louis-Philippe, Soult was born (and later built a chateau) in a village close to Mazamet. His granddaughter married Baron René Reille. Father to son and uncle to nephew, the Reille-Soults were MPs for the Mazamet constituency from 1869–70, from 1876–1924 and from 1928–58.
4. Victor Griffuelhes (1874–1922): revolutionary syndicalist, General Secretary of the CGT from 1901 to 1909 and author of the Charter of Amiens of 1906. See biographical note in Maitron, Vol. 12, pp. 331–33.
5. Emile Martin: weaver, founder member of the union organisation, La Fourmi, in 1892; elected to the industrial tribunal from 1896 to 1910; General Secretary of the Union Fédérative des Syndicats Elbeuviens on its founding in 1901; Elbeuf union delegate to the Conseil Supérieur du Travail (High Council of Labour) in 1903; and Secretary of the Trade Union Centre in 1906. Also General Secretary of the Socialist Union, he was a candidate at several general elections. A moderate, he approved of Viviani's participation in the government and, in 1910, supported the Radical Party mayor Mouchel against the socialist candidate in the general elections. His influence waned from then on.

6. The five largest cotton towns of Lancashire – Blackburn, Bolton, Burnley, Oldham, and Preston – each numbered more than 100 000 inhabitants while the smallest had about 30 000.
7. Unlike shearing done on a live animal, fellmongery is performed on the skin of a dead sheep. The job involves two distinct processes: first, cleaning rids the wool, while still on the skin, of foreign bodies like soil, droppings and plant matter; then, for a few days, the skins are left to soak in steamrooms where the process of decaying starts, allowing the extraction of the wool without damage to the hide.
8. The Elbeuf wool industry specialised in the manufacture of thick and heavy carded wool cloth. After weaving, the fabric was finished – that is, subjected to a whole series of operations (fulling, combing, cutting, pressing, decatising) with the aim of giving it its final qualities and appearance. Of fine quality and highly priced, these fabrics were sold to wealthy customers.
9. Soup kitchens: union practice which consisted of organising meals for strikers, often on the premises of the Trade Union Centre, with the kitchens being stocked by gifts in kind or of money collected by the strike committee.
10. Union practice which consisted, during strikes, of sending strikers' children to neighbouring towns where they were welcomed, housed and fed by sympathising families.
11. The example of Mazamet also throws light on the relationship between revolutionary syndicalists and socialists. Their hostility on the ideological level did not prevent their action on the ground from being mutually beneficial: on the one hand, the socialists encouraged local unions to join the CGT; on the other, direct action in the strike of 1909 favoured the socialists who got more votes in the 1910 general elections.
12. On the contrary, the active commitment of Jewish employers of Alsatian origin to the Republic was longstanding and well-known. At town council level, they were on the lists of the Union Républicaine from 1874 to 1896, as well as in 1912 and, in all other elections, they always supported the Republican candidate.

Bibliography

Lancashire

Beattie, D. (1992), *Blackburn: The Development of a Lancashire Cotton Town*, Halifax.
Bullen, A. (1984), *The Lancashire Weavers' Union*, Rochdale.
Bullen, A. and A. Fowler (1986), *The Cardroom Workers' Union*, Rochdale.
Burgess, K. (1975), *The Origins of British Industrial Relations*, London.
Clarke, P. F. (1971), *Lancashire and New Liberalism*, London.
Clegg, H. A., A. Fox and A. F. Thompson (1964), *A History of British Trade Unions since 1889, Vol. 1 1889-1910*, Oxford.

Farnie, D. A. (1979), *The English Cotton Industry and the World Market, 1815–1896*, Oxford.

Farnie, D. A. (1992), 'The Cotton Towns of Greater Manchester', in M. Williams and D. A. Farnie (eds), *Cotton Mills in Greater Manchester*, Preston, pp. 13–47.

Fowler, A. (1999), 'Lancashire to Westminster: A Study of Cotton Trade Union Officials and British Labour 1910–39', *Labour History Review*, vol. 64, no. 1, pp. 1–22.

Fowler, A. and T. Wyke (eds) (1987), *The Barefoot Aristocrats*, Littleborough.

Joyce, P. (1980), *Work, Society and Politics: The Culture of the Factory in Late Victorian England*, London.

Jewkes, J. and E. M. Gray (1935), *Wages and Labour in the Lancashire Cotton Spinning Industries*, Manchester.

McIvor, A. J. (1988), 'Cotton Employers' Organisation and Labour Relations, 1890–1939', in J. A. Jowett and A. J. McIvor (eds), *Employers and Labour in English Textile Industry, 1850–1939*, London, pp. 1–26.

Rose, S. O. (1991), 'Frères et soeurs en détresse. Ouvriers du tissage mécanique et syndicats dans le Lancashire au XIXe siècle', *Genèses*, 6, pp. 53–72.

Trodd, G. (1978), *Political Change and Working Class in Blackburn and Burnley 1880–1914*, unpublished PhD thesis, University of Lancaster.

Turner, H. A. (1962), *Trade Union Growth, Structure and Policy*, London.

Webb, S. and B. Webb (1982), *Industrial Democracy*, London.

White, J. (1978), *The Limits of Trade Union Militancy*, London.

Wood, G. H. (1910), *The History of Wages in the Cotton Trade during the Past Hundred Years*, Manchester.

Bremen

Barfuss, K. M. (1986), *'Gastarbeiter' in Nordwestdeutschland, 1884–1918*, Bremen.

Boll, F. (1992), *Arbeitskämpfe und Gewerkschaften in Deutschland, England und Frankreich. Ihre Entwicklung vom 19. zum 20. Jahrhundert*, Bonn.

Dehnkamp, W. (1986), *Von unten auf. Die sozialistische Arbeiterbewegung in Blumenthal-Vegesack (Bremen-Nord)*, Bonn.

Düwel, K. (1958), *Die industrielle und kommunale Entwicklung des Fabrikortes Hemelingen. Ein Kapitel der Industrialisierung des bremischen Randgebietes*, Diss., Göttingen.

Ellerkamp, M. (1991), *Industriearbeit, Krankheit und Geschlecht. Zu den sozialen Kosten der Industrialisierung: Bremer Textilarbeiterinnen 1870–1914*, Göttingen.
Grundig, E. (1960), *Geschichte der Stadt Delmenhorst von 1848 bis 1945*, Vol. 4, Delmenhorst.
Mommsen, W. J. and H. G. Husung (eds) (1984), *Auf dem Wege zur Massengewerkschaft. Die Entwicklung der Gewerkschaften in Deutschland und Großbritannien 1880–1914*, Stuttgart.
Schönhoven, K. (1980), 'Selbsthilfe als Form der Solidarität. Das gewerkschaftliche Unterstützungs-wesen im Deutschen Kaiserreich bis 1914', *Archiv für Sozialgeschichte*, 20, pp. 147–93.
Schönhoven, K. (1987), *Expansion und Konzentration. Studien zur Entwicklung der freien Gewerkschaften im Wilhelminischen Deutschland*, Stuttgart.
Schwarzwälder, H. (1987), *Geschichte der freien Hansestadt Bremen*, Vol. 2 (1810–1918), Hamburg.

Mazamet

Cazals, R. (1983), 'Le Mouvement ouvrier à Mazamet au début du XXe siècle', thesis supervised by R. Trempe, University of Toulouse.
Cazals, R. (1983), *Les Révolutions industrielles à Mazamet (1750–1900)*, Paris and Toulouse.
Cazals, R. (1995), *Avec les ouvriers de Mazamet, dans la grève et l'action quotidienne, 1900–1914*, rev. and exp. 2nd edn, Carcassonne.
Maitron, J. (ed.), *Dictionnaire biographique du mouvement ouvrier français*: vol. 10, Paris, 1972; vol. 12, Paris, 1974.
Vidal, A. and R. Cazals (1985), *Le jeune homme qui voulait devenir écrivain*, Toulouse.

Elbeuf

Boivin, M. (1989), *Le mouvement ouvrier dans la région de Rouen, 1851–1876*, 2 vols, Rouen.
Daumas, J. C. (1990), 'Recrutement et gestion du personnel dans la draperie elbeuvienne à la fin du XIXe siècle: le cas des etablissements Blin et Blin', in D. Woronoff (ed.), *L'homme et l'industrie en Normandie*, Alençon, pp. 101–11.
Daumas, J. C. (1993), 'Des politiques paternalistes dans la draperie elbeuvienne à la fin du XIXe siècle', in S. Schweitzer (ed.), *Logiques d'entreprises et politiques sociales*, Lyons, pp. 209–53.
Daumas, J. C. (1993), 'Paternalisme et sociabilité ouvrière dans la draperie elbeuvienne: le cas de Blin et Blin', *Bulletin spécial de la Société de l'Histoire d'Elbeuf*, pp. 71–82.

Daumas, J. C. (1995), 'L'amour du drap. Blin et Blin, 1827–1975. Histoire d'une entreprise lainière familiale', 5 vols, thesis supervised by J. P. Chaline, University of the Sorbonne-Paris IV.

Largesse, P. (1994), 'La Naissance du syndicalisme à Elbeuf', unpublished paper, Archivistes de France conference, Elbeuf.

Largesse, P. (1996), *La bourse du travail et les luttes ouvrières, Elbeuf, 1892–1927*, Elbeuf.

Majorel, J. P. (1979), 'Le mouvement ouvrier à Elbeuf de 1890 à 1914', Masters thesis, University of Rouen.

CHAPTER FOUR

Trade unions in medium-sized textile and machine-building cities: Ghent, Bielefeld and Monza, 1890–1914

Karl Ditt, Giuseppe M. Longoni and Peter Scholliers

Introduction

Immediately before the First World War membership of trade unions in Western Europe reached a first peak; they organised about 20 per cent of the artisanal and industrial labour force in England and Germany, 15–20 per cent in Belgium, and 10–15 per cent in Italy.[1] These numbers reflect very heterogeneous local and regional situations which had confronted trade unions with difficult problems of organisation. To explain trade union growth in cities as the most important places of trade unionism it seems to typify their broad spectrum in the nineteenth century according to their main economic branches: semi-rural cities, monostructural industrial cities whose economy was based mainly on mining, iron, glass or textiles, mixed industrial cities, and service-sector cities (governmental, university, pensioner, tourist cities) with a high percentage of administrative and service personnel.

One of the main types of industrial city in the early nineteenth century was the textile city. Industrialisation here usually started with the mechanisation of spinning and weaving. While some textile cities like Krefeld, Prato or Verviers kept a monostructural status for a long time because they produced specific textiles which gave them an almost monopolistic position, most of them differentiated their economy during the first Industrial Revolution and made the step to the so-called second Industrial Revolution at the end of the nineteenth century. At first, the demands of the textile industry usually attracted machine-building factories which developed dynamics of their own; in addition, workshops and factories were built, which manufactured products on the basis of the textile industry; finally, the diversification of machine-building into electrotechnical factories and the development of a chemical or pharmaceutical industry led the local economy into a new stage. These and other products and branches were usually locally interrelated, and depended on and fostered each other by generating economic spread effects. The success of this industrial diversification essentially determined the growth of the labour force and population in the city; most, but not all, of the textile and machine-building cities remained medium-sized for, in the first and second phases of industrialisation, they lacked booming industrial branches and, in the third phase, a highly expanding (public) service sector. Examples of this type of city and different economic development can be found in England (Leeds, Bradford), Germany (Augsburg, Mönchengladbach, Wuppertal, Bielefeld), Belgium (Ghent), Italy (Monza) or France (St Etienne, Lille).

With regard to trade union growth in this type of city two conflicting expectations arise. On the one hand, textile and machine-building cities were among the cities which industrialised first; thus unions had a rather long time to become experienced, grow, and stabilise. Strong unions could be expected here. At the end of the nineteenth century, living in such a city would have been advantageous for the labour force. On the other hand, the labour force in textile and machine-building cities was highly differentiated in origins, skills and material conditions. While the textile labour force often had many ties to the countryside and a large share of female workers, the skilled artisans in machine-building factories and other branches represented a completely different type of worker. Moreover, the workers were employed in industrial branches with different rates of growth, factory size and managerial policies. This could have meant deep divisions within the labour force and considerable obstacles to trade union organisation.

To deal with these conflicting expectations we have chosen three examples of textile and machine-building cities: Ghent, Bielefeld and Monza – medium-sized cities with common features and well-known to the authors. After a short survey of their economic structure and trade union development at the transition from the nineteenth to the twentieth century we investigate the significance of the type of city, of the strategy of the unions and national circumstances in order to explain the organisation of the workers. Did trade unions face common organisational problems created by this type of city and its labour force? Did they use a common recipe to increase membership or did they choose completely different ways according to national circumstances? Answers to these questions should allow comparisons with trade union organisation in other types of cities.

Ghent

Socioeconomic structure

Modern industry was introduced in Ghent around 1800 when merchants and cotton printers set up cotton spinning mills. Some 20 years later, modern weaving was developed by the cotton manufacturers. From the 1820s onwards a machine-building industry developed, which manufactured textile machinery and highly specialised engines. During the crisis of the 1830s the cotton entrepreneurs helped to set up huge mechanical linen factories. While this industry managed to win and hold a part of the international market, the cotton and linen industries competed on a much wider market of plain, mass-produced goods and were much more sensitive to international market conditions.

The cotton industry was self-financed and, even when limited liability companies spread in this industry around 1875, most companies remained under the control of the founding families. The machine-building industry was gradually, but only partly, put under control of banks, while many linen mills were set up through bank finance. Ties between the cotton and linen industries were close. The cotton and metal industries were family-based, which may explain the paternalistic attitude of some Ghent entrepreneurs. Other entrepreneurs might be characterised as stubborn hard-liners. Most entrepreneurs abhorred any interference in their business, whether from unions, workers, the state or social reformers.

According to the 1896 census, the total number of wage labourers in the Ghent industry amounted to 33 059, which made Ghent the most proletarianised large city of Belgium.[2] In that year cotton accounted for 25 per cent, linen for 26 per cent and machine-building for 5 per cent of the industrial labour force. Just over another quarter of employment was divided between building (8 per cent), food (5 per cent), clothing (5 per cent), woodwork (5 per cent) and the small metal trade (4 per cent), while the remainder of industrial employment was provided by transport and many small, often artisan, workshops in diverse industries.[3]

The labour force of the textile industry was far from homogeneous. There were significant differences between the cotton and linen industries, and large differences between spinning and weaving within the cotton industry.[4] Mechanisation was much more developed in the linen than in the cotton industry, and linen mills were much bigger than cotton factories.[5] The workforce differed with respect to its geographical origins. In linen mills 40 per cent of the workers were born outside Ghent as against 20 per cent in cotton and 23 per cent in machine-building.[6] Even more decisive were the different shares of women. The cotton industry employed 46.5 per cent and the linen industry 61.1 per cent women. Finally, in the linen industry workers were generally younger than in cotton and especially in engineering: 20 per cent of the workforce was younger than 16 years, as against 15 per cent in cotton and only 5 per cent in the machine-building industry.

The differences within the Ghent textile industries were only small in comparison to those between the textile and the (all-male) machine-building workers. Generally, the latter worked in rather small workshops which were relatively moderately mechanised and where skill was important. Job training was of long duration, and young workers were a small minority. According to the industrial census of 1896, the Ghent machine-builders earned an average daily wage of 3.5 francs, the cotton workers 3 francs and the linen workers only 2.5 francs.[7] The machine-builders formed a very specific layer within the Ghent working class, but they should *not* be characterised as a 'labour aristocracy' in the Leninist sense of a bourgeois group of workers leading the labour movement to reformism.[8] Yet, the characteristics of this small group of workers marked the whole of the Ghent workers' movement.

In general, between 1880 and 1914 the Ghent working class had a low standard of living, characterised by poor housing conditions, coarse diets and high mortality. The low wage level – compared to other large cities and the Walloon area of Belgium – were the main reasons. The high labour participation of children (between the ages of 12 and 16) and women (also after giving birth to their first and second children) allowed the entrepreneurs to pay low wages to both sexes. Because, in order to survive, working-class families needed the wages brought in by children and women, a vicious circle was formed which persisted until the end of the century. Only from the 1900s onwards did real wages rise, caused by increases in work effort (work on four looms instead of two, for example), a stagnation of rents, and occasional rises in wage rates; thus, after 1900, the standard of living improved in general.[9]

The development of trade unions and reasons for their growth

By 1913 the Ghent labour movement was admired by Belgian and foreign observers for its many achievements. Most admired was Vooruit, the socialist cooperative which had grown out of the cooperative Vrije Bakkers in 1880. The Vooruit shops offered discounts for members, pension and maternity funds after 1898, and a hotel in Ostend after 1903; before the First World War the organisation owned 29 buildings all over the town, numerous stores and three factories, a very impressive leisure facility (including a cinema, theatre and café),[10] and a commercial and savings Bank of Labour.[11] In 1884 Vooruit had 1700 members (that is, families), and in 1913 nearly 10 000 in and around Ghent. The cooperative became a genuine financial force, acting as a supporter of cultural activities, the socialist press and sometimes strike activities. The organisation itself and its material facilities became overwhelmingly predominant, whereas revolutionary or radical aspirations were totally swept away.[12] Liberal and Christian-democrat workers' organisations tried to imitate the socialists, but only partly succeeded.

Reformism may be found in all the activities of the Ghent socialist labour movement, but is particularly characteristic of the sick fund, Bond Moyson. Founded in 1875 by socialist unions and community circles, the sick fund collaborated with the chemists' stores of Vooruit after 1885, installed a free medical service in 1887 and set up a People's Hospital in 1904. Bond Moyson had some 400 members in 1887, 3300 in 1895, but 15 000 in 1903 and no less than 33 200 in 1913.[13] However, the sick fund soon restricted itself to medical aid, and began to care more about increasing its membership and its finances and less about its connections with trade unions or the social-democratic party. Consequently after 1890 the sick fund accepted members who had joined a liberal or Christian-democratic cooperative or union.[14]

The ideology of Ghent and Belgian reformism may be found in the writings and actions of the socialist party. In 1877 the Vlaamsche Socialistische Arbeiderspartij (VSAP or Flemish socialist workers' party) was set up; its programme showed much in common with the Gotha programme of the German social democrats. In 1885 the Belgische Werkliedenpartij (BWP or Belgian Workers' Party) replaced the VSAP. The new party coordinated political actions of various types of (socialist and 'neutral') labour organisations, grouped in local and regional federations. The Ghent organisations Vooruit, Bond Moyson, unions, workers' cultural societies and others formed a single federation which was coordinated by the *Middencomiteit*. Regional federations formed the BWP. Members of the unions and the cooperative automatically became members of the party too. The *Comiteit* met mostly before elections and functioned as a discussion platform, but was dominated by the party. It put practical demands to the fore, such as social security, free education or limitation of child labour which, it believed, should be accomplished by state regulation.[15] Therefore the leaders put immense weight on the demand for universal suffrage, organisation of general, national strikes (1887, 1891, 1893, 1902 and 1913)[16] and collaboration with progressive liberals. They viewed their party as the organisation of all workers and the guide to great achievements; if workers should become 'angry' and strike, it was the party's duty to control, channel and, finally, abort the movement.[17]

Compared with other regions represented in the young Belgian

Workers' Party, the Ghent *Middencomiteit* was very active. Undeniably, this was caused by the presence of the Ghent unions marking programmes and activities in many other regions of the country. Unions had existed in Ghent since the late 1850s, but it was not until the 1870s that modern unions became more active. In 1876 the two existing cotton weavers' unions united, joining the VSAP in 1877. In the same year, the cotton spinners set up a union which was enlarged in 1879 by male and female cotton workers. Linen and metalworkers started unions in 1875, and especially in 1876. However, none of these unions was very successful. Only on the occasion of a strike did membership rise temporarily.

All this changed in 1895. The huge strike wave of that year – when workers in cotton, metal, linen and printing industries went on strike for higher wages and better working conditions – gave modern unionism in Ghent a decisive breakthrough. Although only the cotton workers were relatively successful, and the strikes led to a financial fiasco, the immediate result of the movement was a fast growth of almost all unions: membership of the weavers' union doubled, that of the cotton, linen and metalworkers tripled. Membership of unions which were not directly involved in the 1895 strike also grew two- or threefold. By 1913 workers were organised most in the metal industry – 70 per cent of all workers had joined one of the three unions (that is, socialist, Christian-democrat or liberal), in cotton it was 60 per cent, printing 55 per cent, construction 47 per cent, wood 46 per cent and linen 41 per cent.[18] In all the industries, the socialist unions were by far the strongest.[19] In the metal unions, socialists represented almost 80 per cent of all union members, in cotton 69 per cent, and in linen 61 per cent. In cotton unions, women accounted for almost 30 per cent in both socialist and Christian-democrat organisations – thus showing a low unionisation rate of female workers in this industry – while in linen unions women accounted for 60 per cent in the socialist union and for 86 per cent in the Christian-democrat union.[20] Clearly, female linen workers were more attracted by the Christian-democrat unions than by socialist ones.[21] However, taken together, social democrats dominated the social and economic organisations of the labour class in Ghent. This preponderance of social democrats is also demonstrated by the results of elections for the *Werk- en Nijverheidsraad* (Council for Labour and Industry) which was installed in Ghent in 1890. This *raad* which was built up – as in other Belgian cities – by the city government, functioned as a conciliation board in cases of differences about labour conditions; it united representatives of the entrepreneurs and labourers which were elected directly by these groups. In the elections of the labour side the socialists won 55 per cent of the votes in 1893, but 62–72 per cent from 1896 to

1912.²² However, the influence of the *raad* never became so strong as to substitute for direct negotiations between the organisations. It remained an instrument of conciliation in special cases and became a forerunner of collective agreements and tariffs.

Another outcome of the 1895 strike was the elaboration of the organisation, programmes and strategies of the unions. Immediately after the strike, each of the socialist cotton, linen and metal unions appointed a permanent secretary – the weavers' union followed suit in 1901 – who organised propaganda, conducted inquiries and prepared meetings. The strike fund was reorganised, while the supply of services was increased by offering libraries, insurances against work accidents, old age, and – very significantly – unemployment benefit, travel money in case of migration, professional training and so on. Most importantly, relations with employers were reconsidered. In the machine-building industry, industrial relations were at first extremely poor and, during the 1895 strike, employers refused to negotiate. Despite many attempts to reconcile positions, the conflict in the metal trade was extremely harsh, including the very first lockout in Ghent. After 11 weeks of strike the workers agreed to accept a very small wage rise and resumed work. But the strike had 'opened the eyes of all workers', and the union leaders strove for recognition by the employers and for the creation of a permanent body of conciliation. 'Talks', 'arbitration', 'reconciliation' and 'agreement' became the key concepts of the Ghent metal union, hoping to avoid expensive strikes.²³ An appeal for a joint committee which should be more specialised on professional matters than the *Werk- en Nijverheidsraad* was repeated frequently, but without leading to a permanent body or collective agreements.²⁴ However, the new strategy did not mean that strikes should be avoided in any circumstances; rather that they should be used within the well-defined framework of the union's strategy. Consequently, the 'domestication of the strike' was a fact in Ghent before the First World War,²⁵ and it may be seen as a pragmatic strategy by a union with very stubborn employers.

The other Ghent unions followed the example of the metal union, but did not succeed in installing a permanent body either. The cotton workers' union, for example, proposed to install a joint committee with representatives of workers, employers and MPs to resolve the 1905 conflict over the reduction in working hours. Employers refused to engage in talks with 'foreign' workers. A referendum, which was recognised by the employers, ended the strike after almost three months and led to a reduction in working hours.²⁶ The general efforts of the union leaders to engage in talks rather than start a strike, did not prevent strikes occurring, even at the initiative of unions.²⁷ But, of course, many conflicts occurred outside unions' control.

In general, the Ghent social-democrat labour movement succeeded in obtaining remarkable results. These were situated at various levels and may be characterised by immediate material benefits and recognition of labour and its representatives. The cooperatives, the party, the sick fund, the press, the unions and the many cultural societies were closely interrelated and represented a genuine force in the city of Ghent.[28]

Many reasons explain the success and the specific path of the Ghent social-democratic labour movement. The first explanation is the presence of thousands of factory workers in a relatively small city. They lived in specific districts of Ghent, close to the mills in which they worked. These districts represented a relatively closed world, with intensive contacts, particular languages, leisure patterns and common experiences. A second explanatory factor is the many technological and organisational changes which took place during the 1880s and 1890s. These contributed to incorporate 'elitarian' groups of workers (such as the highly-skilled and well-paid engineers and cotton spinners) into the social-democratic workers' movement. Indeed, in these decades new machinery was installed in the cotton and metal industries to cope with increased international competition. In spinning, ring-spinning frames became widespread, alongside new, sophisticated machines in the preparatory divisions. In the machine-building industry, a new generation of semi-automated tools was installed, putting an end to the relative control of workers over the production process. Even in linen mills, long since populated by many women workers, technological changes increased the rate of automation. Such changes increased the numbers of new types of worker. For the first time in Ghent, spinning could be done by women; in the metal industry semi-skilled, instead of highly-skilled, workers were able to operate the tools; and in the linen industry many more young workers were recruited from the surrounding countryside. Spinners, weavers, machine-builders, linen workers, and many other wage-earners in the printing, food or woodworking industries had one feature in common: they all were factory workers who were primarily interested in obtaining fair wages. Industrial changes, in other words, created more common interests within the Ghent working class, although, of course, differences remained.

Moreover, together with technological innovations, textile manufacturers wanted to reduce wage costs by moving production lines to the countryside of Flanders where the workforce was – compared to Ghent – cheaper, willing to work longer and to supervise four rather than two looms. Eventually, wage rates fell in virtually all Ghent industries during the 1880s and 1890s. In most Ghent industries, technological innovations and reorganisation threatened the position of workers (through deskilling, feminisation, rejuvenation, wage-cutting and extension of the labour market).[29] This provided solid ground for workers to unite.

The downward business cycle of 1873–95 reduced the retail prices of food and clothing, but the economic revival after 1895 led to a general price increase, and therefore a threat to purchasing power. In combination with the above-mentioned factors, this development radicalised the Ghent working class: an observation which was valid in the case of weavers, cotton spinners and, most certainly, machine-builders who were the most threatened and who became very sensitive to the aims of the socialist organisations.

On the other hand, these socialist organisations began to flourish and developed a densely interrelated network by offering material and social advantages for their clientele. A symbol for the connections within the labour movement was Edouard Anseele, a former printer and journalist, who was not only a leading man in Vooruit, but also in the BWP and who became an MP in 1894.[30] The interconnections were further strengthened by the strike of 1895. As a consequence of the vehement reaction of the employers, both union leaders and most workers wanted to extend and improve the organisations. Based on the results of these efforts they started 'joint talks' with the employers to get immediate material benefits (in terms of wages, working time and work effort). The machine-builders were considered forerunners of this policy by many other Ghent and, indeed, Belgian unions.

Broader political aims of the Ghent labour movement were postponed, or rather were hedged in the one main goal of universal suffrage. When in 1883 and 1895 universal plural suffrage for men was introduced at the local level, the number of voters increased and the first socialists could enter the Ghent city council. However, political conditions prevented the labour class from gaining the majority. In 1893 plural universal suffrage for men (depending on wealth, education, sex and age (minimum 25)) was introduced for the National Assembly, leading to the election (in the district of Liège) of Edouard Anseele, the outright leader of the Ghent labour movement.[31] Once this was achieved, Parliament and government would realise workers' demands. The results of the 1894 election was promising, but up to 1914 socialists' votes stagnated at around 21–24000 or 15–16 per cent in the Ghent district. Moderation and drive for respectability of the Ghent labour movement might have attracted workers – witness the relative success of liberal and Christian-democrat unions – but, on the other hand, more radical workers might have rejected reformism. These, however, were a minority in the early 1910s.

Bielefeld

Socio-economic structure

The population of Bielefeld, a pre-industrial linen trade town, rose from 11 000 at the beginning of industrialisation during the 1850s to 83 000 inhabitants before the First World War.[32] The town's economy was mainly structured by textile, garment and machine-building industries. Before the First World War these branches employed about 22 000 workers or nearly 90 per cent of the local industrial labour force.

The textile industry was founded in the 1850s and 1860s. At first, it consisted of two large flax spinning factories and one linen weaving firm. After the 1880s several medium-sized linen, silk and plush weaving factories in the suburbs of Bielefeld and the city itself were added. Although Bielefeld had a long tradition and was one of the most important locations of the German linen industry this branch and its labour force of about 2500 to 3000 workers began to stagnate after the 1880s. The main reasons for the lack of expansion were partly competition from the linen industry in Flanders and Ulster and partly the cheapness of cotton products which began to replace linen.

Initially, the linen industry's labour force had an equivalent share of male and female workers and a 10 per cent share of children. After the 1860s – especially in the spinning factories – textile managers began to substitute women for children and male workers in order to comply with the state laws against child labour and reduce wage costs. The new silk and plush factories of the 1880s and 1890s had already started with a high majority of female workers. Before the First World War, thus, the percentage of women in the textile labour force of Bielefeld amounted to 70–80 per cent. About half of the textile workers commuted from the rural and proto-industrial population in the villages around Bielefeld into the city. Usually they entered the textile factories by a system of recommendation and 'heritage'. Entrepreneurs and managers, representatives of the still dominating textile merchant class who ruled the factories like patriarchs, accepted and favoured these customs for it created a system of dependence. Moreover, in a local labour market where the textile factories offered the worst labour conditions and paid the lowest wages, they needed a permanent and experienced labour force. After the 1890s, however, they had to advertise in the eastern provinces of Germany to recruit whole families, and especially girls, to fill the vacant places at the machines. The flax spinning mills thus became centres of female workers from East and West Prussia or Silesia; and this foreign influx contributed to the breakdown of patriarchialism.[33]

The garment industry had started in Bielefeld in the 1860s with a home-based sewing industry and outwork system. The first products were based exclusively on linen as raw material; they consisted of high-quality handkerchiefs, towels, table covers, collars, front shirts and so on. When, in the 1890s, demand rose and sewing machines became electrically driven, the entrepreneurs began to centralise production in small and medium-sized factories. After this, the number of workers surpassed the textile labour force and grew to about 6000 just before the First World War. Ninety per cent of this labour force was female. The girls and young women mainly stemmed from the working- and middle-class families of the city, less from the nearby villages. To become a seamstress in Bielefeld required a two-year apprenticeship. Work was clean and wages better than in textile factories, thus seamstresses had a higher status than spinners and weavers. These better conditions and status explain why the entrepreneurs of this industry – merchants from all branches, hardly tailors or textile merchants – did not encounter the labour shortage problems which bothered textile entrepreneurs.[34]

The third and most important industrial branch of the city was machine-building. Before the First World War it employed about 12 000 or 50 per cent of the local industrial labour force. The factories of this branch were partly founded to meet the demand for machines by the garment industry – they initially manufactured sewing machines, then diversified by taking up bicycles, bicycle parts, cream separators, cash registers and even automobiles. They also partly rose from local artisanal origins and produced machine tools, steam boilers, lifting appliances and so on. In the 1890s four large factories dominated not only the business cycle of the local machine-building industry but also its labour policy. The attitude of their entrepreneurs was even more rigid than in the textile industry; it can be termed industrial absolutism which did not accept negotiations.

During the second half of the nineteenth century there occurred within the labour force of the metal industry a process which was considered similar to the development in the textile industry. While the spinning and weaving factories became feminised the workers in the machine-building factories became deskilled: due to mechanisation and rationalisation the percentage of qualified workers dropped from 70–80 per cent in the 1860s to about 40 per cent before the First World War.[35]

The development of trade unions and reasons for their growth

The preponderance of large factories, the processes of feminisation and dequalification, and the strong roots of most of the local labour force in a rural, pious society made it very difficult for trade unions to organise workers. But until the First World War, 60–70 per cent of the local labour force of about 25 000 workers was organised – a good deal more than the share of 20 per cent at national level. However, a closer look at the rates of organisation in the main industrial branches of Bielefeld at this time shows considerable differences: the textile and garment workers had an organisational rate of about 20 per cent, while the metalworkers had a rate of about 85 per cent. What can explain these big differences?

A first explanation can be found in the different traditions of organisation. At the end of the nineteenth century most of the metalworkers still undertook their apprenticeship in artisanal trades which had had a tradition of organisation dating from the Middle Ages. This tradition had been taken over and altered in the 1860s by new elements: the introduction of strikes, the establishment of national connections, the openings for semi- and unskilled workers and the cooperation with political parties.[36] By contrast, textile and garment workers had no such traditions of organisation. Seamstresses were a new labour force and proto-industrial spinners and weavers had developed unions neither at the national nor at the local level of Bielefeld. Even when spinning and weaving was centralised in factories – initially in cotton factories in Rhineland and Saxony at the end of the eighteenth century – the founding of a national trade union took several decades, despite the fact England offered a model of organisation and workers had had two or three generations' experience of conflicts and negotiations.

The reasons for this astonishing failure form the second explanation for the differences in trade union organisation. They lay in the gender division of the labour force. In the textile and garment industries the percentage of female workers was high and rising. Most of them remained in the factories between the ages of 14 and 25, then left to marry and to build up a family. Women's return to the factories after childbirth and the extension of the professional life cycle didn't begin until the 1920s. In view of this short period of factory work, for most women membership of a trade union did not offer sufficient benefits to offset the cost of membership or the risks. Moreover, female rural workers were used to working long hours, to low wages and to having hardly any rights; they were trained in moderate expectations, and it took them a long time to acquire the expectations and pretentions, but also the discipline, of artisanal workers. Furthermore, to organise in trade unions meant – in view of the heritage system of the Bielefeld textile factories – not only to risk one's own job, but also those of other family members. Finally, until 1908 the legal system of the German Empire forbade women to organise in political parties, making the possibility of participating and becoming educated by the political labour movement lower for women than for men. These structural conditions constituted disadvantages for female labourers; they help explain why trade unions in the textile and garment industries were founded rather late and why the rate of organisation differed sharply between textile, garment and metalworkers.

But there was another, third main reason explaining the differences: the strategy of the trade unions themselves.[37] Most of the free trade unions in Bielefeld were founded during the end or after the expiry of the *Sozialistengesetz*.[38] Although in 1892 15 of them united themselves in a trades council (*Gewerkschaftskartell*) the trade union movement remained weak. The first successful step in building up strong unions in Bielefeld was made several years later as a result of a big metalworkers' strike in the boom year of 1896 – which was lost once more – and the creation of an association of the entrepreneurs (*Bielefelder Fabrikantenverein*) which was founded as an anti-strike instrument. This reaction of the entrepreneurs and the long defeat led the Deutscher Metallarbeiter-Verband (DMV) and the trades council, which was dominated by the DMV, to radical conclusions. They agreed to fight the workers' 'strike fever' by refusing to strike or to pay strike subsidies only if 75 per cent of the workers were organised. Indeed, in the following years the DMV under the leadership of Carl Severing – later head of the trades council, member of the leading group of the local Social Democratic Party in the city parliament, member of the German Parliament after 1907 and Prussian Minister of Interior[39] in the 1920s – began to curb its members and to refrain from strikes although the economy boomed and the local joint stock companies paid dividends between 10 and 20 per cent.

In compensation the DMV tried to build up a differentiated spectrum of social insurances. In addition, the trades council founded an *Arbeitersekretariat*, an institution which gave legal advice in questions and disputes about insurance and work. Furthermore, the trades council and the local Social Democratic Party made joint efforts to acquaint workers in Bielefeld with the national and bourgeois cultural heritage by creating a visitor organisation to provide cheap tickets for the local theatre and by inviting orchestras to perform. Even stronger were the attempts to stimulate a labour movement culture by founding cultural organisations and libraries. Finally, in 1898 the trade unions gave up distancing themselves from the local cooperative, which was founded in 1892, and encouraged their members to join and take over the leading posts. In 1900 the cooperative had 2818 members and in 1914 17180.[40] In 1909, 60 per cent of the unions' members were organised in the cooperative.[41] Rebates were reduced, the number of shops increased and some trades (such as bakery and the production of lemonade) built up. In 1907 the cooperative finally resolved to found a savings bank, and in

1911, together with the SPD and unions, a building society. These initiatives directly raised the standard of living: they were steps which fitted into the trade unions' programme. The takeover of the cooperative completed in the Kaiserreich the spectrum of material, social and cultural benefits; after the end of the 1890s most of the Bielefeld workers lived in a dense socialist network. Bielefeld was not only one of the cities where the trade unions had taken over the cooperatives, but also one of those where the SPD had advanced most.[42]

This social and cultural network found its political expression in the voting shares of the Social Democratic Party during the national elections (one vote for men over the age of 21). Until 1898 the party could exhaust its voting potential; between 1898 and 1912 it got between 53 and 57 per cent in the elections for the German Parliament – that is, slightly more than half of the voting population of the city chose the social-democratic candidate. When the SPD competed with only one party in the final ballot it could gain up to about 70 per cent of the voters, since parts of the middle classes would vote for it.[43] However, in 1907, combining of the city ballot district with rural ballot districts where the bourgeois or Christian-democrat parties dominated allowed only the victory of Severing and the SPD.[44]

While the methods to strengthen and increase the attraction of the labour organisations by building up material benefits and a social and cultural network ran parallel to the development at the national level, the strategy to fight strike fever and discipline the members anticipated, in Bielefeld, the national policy of the DMV and other free trade unions by about ten years.[45] Although this policy was heavily opposed by many members, in Bielefeld the DMV succeeded in restraining its membership from open action and in organising about 80 per cent of the local metalworkers until 1906. When in this year of a booming economy the trade union finally wanted to negotiate about improvements in wages and working time the entrepreneurs were deeply impressed by the collective force. For the first time they not only accepted the DMV as partner of negotiations but conceded, in 1906 and 1911, material results which put Bielefeld into the front row of cities with a similar machine-building industry.

The unions' strategy in the textile and garment industries was less successful. The linen workers had led and lost two or three big strikes during the 1870s and 1880s; in the silk and plush factories, whose workers came entirely from the proto-industrial population, no strikes are known of until 1894. The first textile trade union in Bielefeld was founded in 1889 when the workers of one of the big flax spinning firms asked the leaders of the social-democratic committee for help in initiating a strike. The chairman of the committee started a trade union organisation and gave advice but once the strike was over and lost, the organisation collapsed. Proposals from the textile workers to build up a culture of social life – for example, to organise coffee circles and dancing – were rejected by the trades council which favoured persuading with ideology and saw itself as a fighting organisation.

When in 1894 the workers of one of the city's silk weaving factories wanted to take advantage of the booming trade cycle they tried to draw on the experience of the trades union council. This council agreed to lead and subsidise the strike because the group of silk weavers seemed to be of strategic importance in conquering the pious labour class in the countryside. Although the strike lasted for 13 weeks and was the most expensive Bielefeld had ever seen, it ended in complete defeat. In contrast to the conclusions of the DMV and to the efforts of the trades council to persuade the textile workers to build up an organisation of their own, the silk weavers stayed apart from any organisation. The reasons for this resistance were not only the particular social and economic conditions – most of the young workers had to hand over their wages to their parents, the professional career seemed to be rather short and the entrepreneurs demanded an obligation of each worker not to join a trade union – but also the socialist character of free trade unions: the socialists were known as inimical to the Christian religion. Workers' distance from socialism and free trade unions was further fostered by the agitation of the clergy in the countryside where most of the textile workers lived. When in 1909 the *Arbeitersekretariat* surveyed trade union membership in the Social Democratic Party it found that 39 per cent of the DMV, but only 22 per cent of the textile union members had joined the party.[46]

The failure to found a union meant that no educational organisation could influence the textile workers; nor could or would the socialist trades council care for them after the efforts and disappointing experiences of the 1894 strike. When, in 1900, the workers in one of the big spinning factories wanted to strike once more the council refused to support them, arguing that the workers failed to reach an organisational level of 75 per cent. The textile workers went on strike nonetheless, but achieved no results.

Not earlier than 1904 Christian trade unions – which had existed in Germany since 1894[47] – tried to organise the textile workers in Bielefeld. Although the spirit of this movement was more congruent with the convictions of the rural textile workers, the organisational rate climbed to no more than 20 per cent. On the one hand, in these years the entrepreneurs anticipated the claims of the workers and voluntarily increased wages; on the other hand, the workers did not want to wait till the organisational rate was high enough for the union to be accepted by the entrepreneurs for negotiations. They either held the opinion that 'We get more without than with the union'⁴⁸ or joined the unions before a strike and left them afterwards. Their attitude to the unions remained strictly instrumental for they achieved partial success when they went on strike, had little professional or political socialisation like the artisanal trades and no perspective of lifelong factory work. The free and Christian trade unions were further weakened by the entrepreneurs' refusing to negotiate with organisations which had only a small number of members. Finally, neither the free nor Christian trade unions could offer the material byproducts and cultural life which attracted many metalworkers into the free trade unions. In contrast to the situation of the male workers, the wages of the female workers were often considered not as main, but as additional, incomes of the family. And in contrast to the machine-building factories the textile factories had a broad spectrum of social welfare institutions. Thus the trade unions' offer of insurances was less attractive than in the metal industry.⁴⁹

Summarising the reasons which can explain the different rates of trade union organisation in Bielefeld we see at first the differences of social origins and structure, traditions and expectations within the working class, but also the varying abilities of the organisations themselves to discipline the workers and to compensate their will to strike by offering material benefits and social culture. While the disciplining strategy of the unions was successful in the metal industry, the social and religious obstacles to unionisation in the textile and garment industries were too large and the benefits of successful strikes failed to materialise. Thus the level of organisation in these branches remained much lower than in the metal industry.⁵⁰

Monza

Socioeconomic structure

Until the seventeenth century the economy of Monza – an old, independent town of Lombardy, about 15 km north of Milan – was based on the woollen trade. When this trade fell into decay, merchants and artisans began to manufacture felt hats, and Monza soon became the most important centre for this article in the Italian states. In addition, the production of silk and cotton cloths replaced the old woollen trade during the eighteenth century.⁵¹

Industrialisation began in Monza and its vicinity after the unification of Italy in 1861. The availability of low-cost rural labourers, who were already well trained in textile manufacturing, the building of a national market and the protectionist laws of 1878 and 1887 favoured the industrial transformation of the traditional manufacturing activities. In 1876 50 factories employed 2400 people, 2000 of whom worked in silk and cotton factories. In 1911 the number of factories had increased to about 700, and the number of employees to about 17 000. The most important branch remained the textile industry which haad 7000 employees, mostly women. Until the First World War the number of cotton workers surpassed the number of silk workers. The second branch was the hat industry which comprised 185 factories with 4000 employees, mostly men, and the third was machine-building which produced machinery for the weaving and the food industries as well as electric batteries; this branch, which had boomed since the 1890s, employed 2300 workers in about 100 factories. During industrialisation the local population increased from 25 000 inhabitants in 1871 to 53 000 in 1911; by then 72 per cent of the working population was employed in the industrial sector.[52]

The development of the labour movement: mutual aid associations, trade unions and the chambers of labour

The first organisations of the Italian labour force developed at the beginning of industrialisation; they consisted of mutual aid associations (*Società di Mutuo Soccorso*) which were founded at the local level towards the mid-nineteenth century. They granted sick and unemployment benefits as well as low pensions to people over 70 and paid funeral expenses. Often, these associations were backed by liberals and philanthropists from the middle classes who disapproved concepts of economic, social and political revolution but favoured social reforms and more political liberty. Although most of these associations were led by representatives of the middle classes they became a kind of organisational laboratory for the workers. Only after the turn of the century did the mutual aid associations unite nationally. Thus the Italian Workers' Party (*Partito Operaio Italiano*), which was set up in Milan, became the first 'national' labour organisation. The party organised members mainly in the industrial triangle between Milan, Turin and Genoa.

The same region was covered by the first 'national' trade unions, the 'leagues of the sons of work' (*Leghe dei Figli del Lavoro*) which were set up by the party. The unions aimed to 'withstand the capitalists' but did not want to provoke the government; instead they concentrated on negotiations with the entrepreneurs, strikes and the founding of educational and cultural organisations for the working class. Their leader, Osvaldo Gnocchi Viani, a non-Marxist socialist, wanted workers to avoid political action and he hoped to exclude left-wing members of the middle classes from leading positions in the organisations as he feared their agitation for class struggle.[53]

In Monza the mutual aid associations of hatters, mechanical workers and bakers were set up together in a general mutual aid association (*Mutual Generale*). The *Mutual Generale* had 300 members in 1864 and 1600 in 1891. A Catholic mutual aid association was established in the earlier 1870s but remained weak; the membership dropped from 300 to 170 in 1893. The next labour organisations to be founded in Monza were sections of the leagues of the hatters, bricklayers, dyers and weavers, which organised in 1886 with 1200 members.

In 1886 the government dissolved, first, the Italian Workers' Party because of its socialist orientation, then the leagues. However, in 1892 a new socialist party was founded in Genova; it took a course independent from the trade unions and the local chambers of labour (CdL). These were founded on the French model of the 'Bourse du Travail'; the first was in Milan in 1891, followed by Pavia in 1892 and Monza, Brescia and Stradella in 1893; by 1900 there were 35 chambers all over Italy. These chambers were local organisations, led by a secretary and a few clerks who managed the finances, ran a library and often edited a bulletin. They were financed by individual workers and mutual aid associations and supported politically by the Socialist Party, until 1894. Weak unions delegated some of their tasks to the chambers which became the advocates of the interests of all professions, and politically represented the social and economic interests of individual members and labour organisations. They tried to safeguard or increase wages by negotiations and strikes, to develop close contacts with the city government to work as an employment agency, and even were active in creating opportunities for recreation and education for the workers. In contrast to the trades councils which were financed by the trade unions and led by their representatives, the chambers had a broader financial base, their own personnel and thus were more independent; they tried to represent all workers, not only members of the trade unions, and negotiated with the city government directly, not via the party. All in all, the chambers became the strongest labour organisations in the cities. At first the chamber of labour in Monza claimed to be apolitical and was supported by the elderly and the Catholic mutual aid associations. However, when it became clear that the chamber had links with the Socialist Party the Catholic members soon resigned.[54]

Monza – though comparatively small – was one of the most industrialised towns in Italy. Its small size seemed to make it a better base for organisation than a city like Milan, where members were principally bricklayers, clerks, bakers and printers and where the percentage of organised labour was rather low. In the three industrial branches of

Monza which could be considered 'modern' – hat manufacturing, mechanical engineering and cotton weaving – it was possible to fight for wage increases, to oppose dismissals, to set rules for factory organisation and to organise a labour exchange. This strictly economic and social policy could be supported by the democratically-oriented liberal middle class whose support was vital because the governments of the 1880s and 1890s considered the labour movement as politically suspect, subversive, backed by republican France and inspired by the Pope. Even the Catholic clergy, who influenced country people and women in particular, were partly critical of such programmes.

Shortly after its foundation, in October 1894, Monza's chamber already had about 2000 members: 1200 hatters, 260 mechanical workers, 150 weavers and 91 dyers. That meant an organisational rate of 30–40 per cent in hat manufacturing and mechanical industries, but only 6 per cent in weaving, especially cotton weaving. The reason for this rather low rate in weaving lies in the gender division of the weaving factories. Male workers made up only 15 per cent of the total labour force. They occupied the higher-qualified positions whereas female workers, mostly 20–25 years old and sometimes even younger, worked in the factories only temporarily before getting married, to 'earn their dowry' or to supplement the agricultural income of the family.

In the 1890s mechanical workers and hatters managed to increase their wages without severe conflicts due to the favourable economic situation. In the textile industry the trade cycle was less favourable and, in 1897, 370 female and 80 male workers of a cotton factory opposed the reduction in wages in a time of reduced activity. When the factory owner dismissed them all, the chamber, supported by local middle-class democrats, intervened and they were hired again. The importance of this event consisted not only in the fact that the absolute control of employers over labour conditions was broken but that the chamber became popular and were recognised by the city government.[55] Consequently, the number of members of the CdL in Monza increased: in 1898, 3700 or about 30 per cent of the whole industrial labour force of the town were organised either as individual members or by labour organisations.

The victory of 1899 followed the 'crisis of 1898'. The unrest against the increase in prices was bloodily repressed in Milan and in Monza, where seven workers were killed. The installation of an authoritarian government headed by a general, led to the restriction of political freedom, especially the freedom of opinion and of association, until 1900. But already in 1899 the coalition of democrats and socialists were able to win the adminstrative elections and, since then, the local authorities had steadily granted an allowance to the CdL. Peace was further strengthened by the following Italian governments, led by Giovanni Giolitti, which gave more freedom to workers' unions until the First World War.

This period of political freedom coincided with a new stage in Italian industry which grew between 1896 and 1908 by a yearly rate of 12 per cent; both conditions fostered the growth of the labour movement. In May 1900, on the initiative of the hatters' union, which was soon joined by other trades, the CdL in Monza restarted its work with about the same number of members as in 1898 (hatters totalled 40 per cent) but including 500 members from neighbouring towns. Even the Catholics developed a more effective and representative association than before: the Catholic Workers' League (*Lega Cattolica del Lavoro*). However, this league could only manage to establish itself in the textile industry of the neighbouring towns, whereas in Monza the CdL played the leading role. The competition between the CdL and the socialist party on the one side and the Catholic party on the other side remained very harsh and without any agreement until the advent of fascism in 1922.

The hatters became the driving force of the CdL and the unions in Monza. Hat-making was an artisanal trade with a long apprenticeship. Hatters were specialists with a wide horizon; in the first half of the nineteenth century they usually travelled seasonally in northern Italy and France. As a consequence of the beginning of mass consumption in the second half of the nineteenth century some artisans established factories, and although they introduced machines and employed female workers, the hatters could defend their status. In 1893 several hatters' mutual aid associations joined the chamber of labour; one year later the hatters founded a trade union (*Unione lavoranti capellai*). In 1901, after a national conference of hatters had taken place in Monza, a national union was founded under the leadership of Ettore Reina who had come from Milan to Monza to lead the local chamber of labour in 1898. The union organised not only one profession, but all kinds of hat-making, setting an example which was followed by other trades some years later. Particularly thanks to the hatters, Monza became a sort of small 'workshop' for reforms of trade union policy and contributed to the setting up of a new socialist General Confederation of Labour (*Confederazione del Lavoro*) – which included Reina in the Board of Directors – which was founded as a national organisation of trade unions in 1906. These activities helped to settle, in Monza, the Italian Federation of Hatters which joined the International Federation of Hatters in Paris.

Furthermore, after the turn of the century the union of hatters, led by Reina, tried to take advantage of the good economic situation in hat manufacturing and started close negotiations with the employers. Mostly former craftsmen, they welcomed this step for they wanted to increase production and exports. In 1902 a joint agreement was signed, which set rules for paying the whole trade, stated regulations valid for all factories and constituted a mixed committee of workers and employers (*Commissione Mista*) to settle work disputes without strikes. This agreement allowed undisturbed production and strengthened the union which could regulate disputes and keep them under control. It was the starting point of further contracts signed not only in Monza by ribbon-makers, metallurgic melters and dyers but also in Piemonte and Lombardia, where the employers and the General Confederation of Labour cooperated. As a consequence of the negotiations the employers organised too: in 1902 they founded the Federation of Monza Industrialists (*Federazione degli Industriali Monzesi*), the first employers' union on the territory which inspired new associations (1906: *Lega Industriale di Torino*; 1910: *Confederazione generale dell' Industria italiana* and so on). The leader of the Federation, the historian Giuseppe Riva from Monza, stressed the similarity between the praxis of the hatters in Monza and the weavers in England, whereas on the workers' side the German example (Karl Legien) influenced Reina's ideas.

The textile industry took another path. In summer 1902 the chamber of labour, supporting the weak textile union, initiated a strike on behalf of non-organised junior cotton factory workers who were asking for a salary increase. The strike lasted two months and led to a general strike, but was not particularly successful. During the strike the chamber came into sharp conflict with the Catholic league who wanted to participate in the negotiations while the socialist organisation wanted to keep their monopoly of bargaining with the entrepreneurs. In the cotton industry the conflicts between the union and the entrepreneurs stopped in 1907 when a number of strkes in country factories were lost and the economic situation deteriorated.

In 1903 a strike of 350 metalworkers who wanted the head of a department to be removed failed after one month. With Reina's help these workers signed an agreement in the same year, even though it was not very favourable. However, this agreement did not increase membership; on the contrary the number of metalworkers who were members of the chamber of labour fell from 500 in 1903 to 120 in 1904. The same process seized the whole membership of the chamber; it fell from 7500 in 1902 to 4000 in 1905, especially after the unions took part in the first general political strike in Italy during September 1904. Until the First World War neither the hatters' union nor the chamber of labour could prevent the workers from joining the labour organisations when strikes were imminent and from leaving them when the goals had been achieved. One reason for the rises and falls in membership was that the chamber of labour remained basically a city organisation and never managed to get more than 2000 members in their neighbourhood. Compared with the chamber, the Catholic league attracted only about 500 members in Monza, but more than 4000 in the neighbouring smaller towns with their textile industry and female labour force. The fluctuation makes it difficult to calculate the shares of organised workers. Before the First World War roughly 70–80 per cent of the hatters and about 20–25 per cent of the mechanical workers and women in the textile industry (40–50 per cent of the men) seemed to be in a union. While in hat-making, the hatters' specialist status favoured organisation,[56] in machine-building the divisions within the workers (skilled, semi-skilled and unskilled) and the stronger position of the entrepreneurs explained the lower rate of organisation.

In sum, the chambers of labour practised socialist–reformist trade unionism which aimed at granting to professional workers organisation, political consciousness, and a steady and certain income, avoiding as much as possible strikes and disputes with the employers – for the chamber was aware of the weakness of the workers' movement. This policy created good preconditions for the development of the socialist party in Monza. In local and national elections their votes went up from 1000 at the beginning of the twentieth century to about 5500 in 1914, while new laws had increased the number of voters from 5000 to about 12 000. After a period of supporting liberal–democratic governments, socialists took over the city government from 1914 to 1917 and from 1920 until 1922 when the fascists came to power.[57]

Conclusions

Comparing, finally, the conflicting expectations of trade union organisation mentioned at the beginning of this chapter and the real situation of unionism in the textile cities of Ghent, Bielefeld and Monza at the turn of the nineteenth and twentieth centuries, no general picture of weak or strong unions can be drawn; instead we find in all three towns the same differentiated scale. Trade union organisation was rather low among the female workers of the linen, silk and garment industry of the three cities. Only the female cotton workers in Ghent had a significantly higher degree of organisation. The trade unions of the machine-builders and hatters were also fairly strong.

Which role did the type of city, trade union strategy, and national circumstances play in explaining this result? The type and size of the city influenced trade union growth mainly by the structure of its labour force. The high percentage of female workers generally meant an obstacle to trade union organisation. Female status was partly combined with rural origins or habitation – implying, especially in Monza and Bielefeld, Christian, anti-socialist education and traditional hierarchies – and partly meant a low position on the labour market, a short professional life cycle and family dependence. However, the example of Ghent, where the percentage of organised women differed between cotton and linen factories, shows that, in special circumstances, gender as an obstacle to trade union organisation could be overcome. Women who worked in cotton factories were mainly born and bred in the city; they stayed until their children began to earn money by themselves – that is, until they were 10–12 years old. Thus, female cotton workers in Ghent had a long professional life cycle. Moreover, there already existed a strong male-dominated textile union which facilitated organisation for female workers in cotton factories. In contrast to the cotton industry, female workers of the Ghent linen industry were mostly born outside the city, grew up in Christian rural surroundings, had a somewhat shorter professional life cycle, and hardly ever encountered a union when they entered the factories; therefore their organisational rate was lower than in the cotton factories. Urban socialisation and organisational traditions seemed to be important preconditions of trade union growth; they could overcome the circumstances in which female workers usually lived.

This explanation is further strengthened by the situation and conditions of the machine-builders in Ghent and Bielefeld, and the hatters in Monza. These crafts had long organisational traditions, and the artisans had usually acquired some experience of other jobs and cities where they became acquainted with theories about the emancipation of the labour class and the usual demands; relying on their skills, they had a good position on the labour market and a correspondingly strong self-awareness. When this 'personal capital' became endangered by the processes of deskilling, this self-awareness was strong enough for them not to resign themselves to it but to respond by contesting the issue via organisation. Thus, the rate of trade union organisation in the cotton industry and the skilled industrial branches was rather high.

The second important influence on trade union growth was the strategy of the unions themselves, especially the chambers of labour. It is noteworthy that the understanding of the necessity of organisation and discipline began in all three cities with the start of the trade cycle in 1895–96. Previously, workers and trade unions in Ghent, Bielefeld and Monza had had enough experience to recognise that traditional methods – striking in each case of injustice or giving in when workers wanted to strike – had proved unsuccessful. This realisation usually took place when a big strike was lost, making it evident that further demands and strikes were useless, in view of the history of defeats and the strength of the entrepreneurs, if no strong organisation could back them. These realisations, which were supported by a growing level of class-consciousness and the influence of new, gifted leaders (Anseele, Severing and Reina) often helped the unions find support when they tried to strengthen the organisations by engaging permanent secretaries curbing the workers, avoiding big strikes and negotiating with the entrepreneurs. Only in Monza did workers continue to enter unions before a strike and leave them afterwards. One explanation for this variation could be that it was rather difficult to build up a cultural life and the dense socialist labour movement network which was created by the socialist trade unions and parties in Ghent and Bielefeld and which could control and compensate members for their self-restraint. In Monza there already existed a dense Catholic environment which absorbed many of the workers and made it difficult to establish an alternative ideology. Indeed, in cultural matters – for example, in the running of a popular university – the cooperation between middle classes and workers was quite intense – on the basis of Catholicism. Thus in Monza the stabilising socialist network, which fostered the growth of the labour movement in Ghent and Bielefeld, remained weak.

This difference reveals that trade union development depended not only on the type of city – for example, the social structure of the labour force on the policy of the trade unions – but also on the national political situation. One of its most important consequences for the workers became the different possibilities for cooperation between the socialist and the Christian and liberal labour movements, especially between the socialist labour movement and parts of the middle classes, city governments and the state. In Bielefeld hardly any forms of cooperation between the socialist and the Christian labour movements were developed. In the textile industry no serious efforts to cooperate were made; even in the metal industry conflicts dominated. The relationship of the socialist labour movement with the middle classes, the city and the state government was characterised by deep mistrust and great distance. The ideology of Marxism and the history of these relationships – traditional social discrimination of the labour class, the liberals' restriction on education and savings as means of labour emancipation and the suppression of labour organisations during the time of the *Sozialistengesetz* by the state – prevented real cooperation or joint institutions of greater significance. Only when the labour movement became a real force after the turn of the century were the organisations acknowledged as negotiation partners; thus the metal union could get material results. In the city parliament the results remained weak, for the *Dreiklassenwahlrecht* prevented the Social Democratic Party from having any significant influence and the bourgeois parties avoided any cooperation.⁵⁸ The lack of cooperation, discrimination and repression existed alongside the strategy of discipline and compensation and was the second reason why the labour movement created a broad spectrum of social and cultural organisations separated from the bourgeois sphere – a state within the state – which attracted large parts of the working class.

In Ghent the opportunities for cooperation seemed to be somewhat easier. Although the Belgian Workers' Party, a joint venture of socialist and some non-socialist organisations of workers, adopted large parts of the German, Marxist Erfurt programme, the general attitude of the BWP and the unions was strongly against theory.⁵⁹ Instead, they could cooperate with the (progressive) liberals in questions of liberal rights, mainly before elections. Moreover, although there were big confrontations between socialist and Catholic trade unions about religious, strategic and political issues, both sides could take similar stands in joint committees when strikes were imminent.⁶⁰ And, after 1890, conciliation councils (*Werk- en nijverheidsraad*) were founded, where representatives of the employers and workers of each branch met and negotiated with each other. On rare occasions Ghent's municipality even favoured the workers' demands in order to maintain social peace. For example, the creation of the 'Ghent system' around the turn of the century meant that the city contributed to trade union unemployment insurance – a form of cooperation which set an example for other countries. Before the First World War it was introduced in more than 100 German cities – especially in Southern Germany, but not in Bielefeld.⁶¹

Finally, in Monza the relationship between the socialist and Christian unions was rather strained. Catholic leagues, especially in the textile industry, strongly opposed the irreligious, socialist chamber of labour in order to assert themselves; during local elections, however, Catholic candidates joined the conservative wing of the liberals. Instead, the socialist labour movement, especially the chamber of labour, could cooperate with the democratic wing of the liberals which was prevailingly anti-clerical. They even received subsidies from the city government – a kind of support which took place neither in Belgium nor in Germany. One reason for this cooperation could be that the building of the Italian Kingdom took place rather late, and the centralisation processes in economic, social and political life took a long time. Thus decisions continued to be taken at the local and regional level, which would go a long way in explaining the strong position of the local chambers of labour compared with the centralised trade unions. Moreover, the cooperation between the chambers and the middle classes and city government, on the one hand, and the absence of centralised unions with a strong, levelling economic, social and political programme, on the other hand, could explain why no strong front between workers and middle classes/entrepreneurs emerged. The ties between the classes at the local level remained rather strong, so it was hardly possible or necessary to build up a counterculture which could stabilise membership. In any case, Monza became the only one of the three cities in which the socialist party first participated, then took over municipal administration before the First World War.

Notes

1. England: J. Lovell, *British Trade Unions 1875–1933*, London, 1977, p. 52. Germany: calculated by the number of workers in industry and artisanal trades in W. G. Hoffman, F. Grumbach and H. Hesse, *Das Wachstum der deutschen Wirtschaft seit der Mitte des 19. Jahrhunderts*, Berlin, 1965, pp. 194–9, and G. Hohorst, J. Koka and G. A. Ritter (eds), *Sozialgeschichtliches Arbeitsbuch. Matterialien zu Statistik des Kaiserreichs 1870–1914*, Munich, 1975, pp. 135–6; Italy: I. Barbadoro, *Storia del sindacalismo italiano dalla nascita al fascismo*, Vol. 2, Firenze, 1977, pp. 91, 118, 304–5; V. Zamagni, *Dalla periferia al centro. La seconda rinascita economica dell' Italia (1861–1981)*, Bologna, 1990, pp. 101–43.
2. Total industrial employment (employees and employers) amounted to 42 380 (or 26.6 per cent of total population) in Ghent, 40 416 (or 15.1 per cent) in Antwerp, 37 918 (or 22.9 per cent) in Liège and 36 817 (or 18.9 per cent) in Brussels. See *Recensement genéral, 1896, Analyse des volumes 1 et 2*, Brussels 1900, p. 35.
3. For a survey of Ghent's industrial development, see J. Hannes, 'Industrialization without Development. Some Aspects of the History of Ghent', in P. Kooy and P. Pellenbarg (eds), *Regional Capitals. Past, Present, Prospects*, Assen, 1994, pp. 9–18.
4. Within the cotton industry, differences existed between workers of the weaving and spinning divisions. In 1896 there were more women workers in spinning (52.7 per cent of employees in the Ghent spinning mills) than in weaving (with only 40 per cent women). In cotton spinning, the spinners – who were all male up until then – formed a kind of elite, surrounded by many female and a few male preparatory workers. In weaving, female and male weavers worked alongside each other, men producing in general fewer but larger lengths of cloth than women.
5. In 1880 the average horse power per steam engine amounted to 105 hp in the cotton mills, to 140 hp in the linen mills and to only 18 hp in the machine-building trade; the average numbers of workers per factory amounted to 227 in cotton, 429 in linen and only 54 in engineering.
6. L. Varlez, *Le plan social de Gand*, Vol. I, Ghent, 1897, p. 11. Data refer to the early 1890s.
7. Data refer to the wages of adult male workers. See P. Scholliers, *De Gentse metaalbewerkers in de 19e eeuw*, Brussels, 1985, p. 83.
8. Ibid., pp. 126–32; and G. Vanschoenbeek, 'De wortels van de sociaal-democratie in Vlaanderen. Le "monde socialiste gantois" en de Gentse

socialisten voor de Eerste Wereldoorlog', 5 vols., unpublished PhD thesis, Ghent University, 1992, pp. 851–77.
9. P. Scholliers, *Manufacturers, Wages and Workers in the 19th-century Factory. The Voortman Cotton Mill in Ghent*, Oxford, 1996, pp. 213–14; P. Van den Eeckhout, 'Family Income of Ghent Working-Class Families ca. 1900', *Journal of Family History*, 18, 1993, pp. 87–110.
10. Avanti, *Een terugblik. Bijdrage tot de geschiedenis der Gentsche arbeidersbeweging*, Gent, 1930^2, Vol. II, pp. 397–7.
11. Vooruit was thoroughly studied by Vanschoenbeek, 'De wortels van de sociaaldemocratie', pp. 388–427.
12. Contemporary criticism was made in *Die Neue Zeit* of 1911 by H. De Man and L. De Brouckère, who focused on Anseele's Vooruit. See H. De Man and L. De Brouckère, *Le mouvement ouvrier en Belgique*, Brussels, 1965.
13. The number of members grew by 31 per cent per year from 1895 to 1898, by 9 per cent from 1898 to 1903 and by 8 per cent from 1903 to 1913. See Vanschoenbeek, 'De wortels van de sociaaldemocratie', pp. 459–60.
14. Ibid., pp. 466–7.
15. Avanti, *Een terugblik*, Vol. I, pp. 361–2; D. E. Devreese, 'Belgium', in M. van der Linden and J. Rojahn (eds), *The Formation of Labour Movements 1870–1914. An International Perspective*, Vol. I, Leiden, 1990, pp. 41–3.
16. Universal male suffrage was obtained in 1919; universal suffrage in 1948.
17. See, for example, L. Michielsen, *Geschiedenis van de europese arbeidersbeweging*, Vol. I, 1914, Brussels, 1973, pp. 204–33. There are many examples of Edouard Anseele, the Ghent leader, characterising strikes as 'wild' and 'inopportune'.
18. Scholliers, *De Gentse metaalbewerkers*, p. 65.
19. By 1913 the Ghent socialist unions had about 11 000 members, of which the metal and cotton unions had 20 per cent each, the linen union 17 per cent, and the weavers' union 14 per cent.
20. Vanschoenbeek, 'De wortels van de sociaaldemocratie', p. 70.
21. Regarding these questions, see P. Penn Hilden, *Women, Work, and Politics. Belgium, 1830–1914*, Oxford, 1993, pp. 261–302.
22. The distribution of votes over industries shows remarkable differences: socialist votes were over 70 per cent in the metal, cotton and weaving mills, between 65 and 70 per cent in the transport, linen and food industries, between 45 and 65 per cent in (additional) house building (painting, wood etc.) and clothing industries, and below 45 per cent in the fine arts industry and house-building. Christian democrats had a strong position in the clothing, fine arts and food industries (over 35 per cent of the votes). Vanschoenbeek, 'De wortels van de sociaaldemocratie', pp. 33–6 and 66.
23. J. De Clerck, *De Organizatie der metaalbewerkers te Gent 1872–1912*, Ghent, 1912, p. 51.
24. Ibid., pp. 68, 80; Scholliers, *De Gentse metaalbewerkers*, pp. 122–4. Collective agreements were introduced after 1918.
25. J. Neuville, *L'évolution des relations industrielles. Vol. 1: L'avènement du système de relations collectives*, Brussels, 1976, p. 203.
26. P. Scholliers, 'Grown-ups, Boys and Girls in the Ghent Cotton Industry: The Voortman Mills, 1835–1914', *Social History*, 20, 1995, p. 215.
27. This was the case in the cotton mills after 1900, when the union's strategy tended to concentrate on the wage demands of young girls employed at ring spinning, assuming that, if this was successful, the wages of all cotton

workers would follow the increase. See L. Varlez, *Les salaires dans l'industrie gantoise*, Vol. I: *Industrie cotonnière*, Brussels, 1901, pp. 55–6.
28. Avanti, *Een terugblik*, pp. 242–56, provides a survey of the various achievements of the socialist labour movement before the First World War.
29. Scholliers, *De Gentse metaalbewerkers*, pp. 41–7; Scholliers, 'Grown-ups', p. 215.
30. 'Edouard Anseele', in G. Kurgan-van Hentenrijk et al. (eds), *Dictionnaire des patrons en Belgique*, Brussels, 1996, pp. 20–2.
31. Cf. for the development of universal suffrage Devreese, 'Belgium', pp. 26, 45.
32. Generally, see K. Ditt, *Industrialisierung, Arbeiterschaft und Arbeiterbewegung in Bielefeld 1850–1914*, Dortmund, 1982; K. Ditt, 'Probleme gewerkschaftlicher Organisierung in der Metall- und Textilindustrie Bielefelds 1890–1914', in D. Langewiesche and K. Schönhoven (eds), *Arbeiter in Deutschland. Studien zur Lebensweise der Arbeiterschaft im Zeitalter der Industrialisierung*, Paderborn, 1981, pp. 221–39; K. Ditt, 'Der Weg zur Massenorganisation. Die Gewerkschaftsbewegung in Bielefeld von den Anfängen bis zum Ersten Weltkrieg', in G. Brenneke, A. Klönne, H. Lienker and W. Vogt (eds), *'Es gilt die Arbeit zu befreien'. Geschichte der Bielefelder Gewerkschaftsbewegung*, Köln, 1989, pp. 19–86.
33. K. Ditt, 'Technologischer Wandel und Strukturveränderungen der Fabrikarbeiterschaft in Bielefeld 1860–1914', in W. Conze and U. Engelhardt (eds), *Arbeiter im Industrialisierungsprozeß. Herkunft, Lage und Verhalten*, Stuttgart, 1979, pp. 237–61.
34. K. Ditt, 'Die Wäsche- und Bekleidungsindustrie Minden-Ravensbergs im 19. Jahrhundert', in A. Lassotta and P. Lutum-Lenger (eds), *Textilarbeiter und Textilindustrie. Beiträge zu ihrer Geschichte in Westfalen während der Industrialisierung*, Hagen, 1989, pp. 103–22.
35. Ditt, 'Techologischer Wandel', pp. 244–7.
36. U. Engelhardt, *'Nur vereinigt sind wir stark'. Die Anfänge der deutschen Gewerkschaftsbewegung 1862–1869/70*, Stuttgart, 1977; C. Eisenberg, *Deutsche und englische Gewerkschaften. Entstehung und Entwicklung bis 1878 im Vergleich*, Göttingen, 1986.
37. See generally about the trade union movement in the German Kaiserreich, W. Albrecht, *Fachverein–Berufsgewerkschaft–Zentralverband. Organisationsprobleme der deutschen Gewerkschaft 1870–1890*, Bonn, 1982; K. Schoenhoven, *Expansion und Konzentration. Studien zur Entwicklung der freien Gewerkschaften im Wilhelminischen Deutschland 1890–1914*, Stuttgart, 1980.
38. The *Sozialistengesetz* prohibited labour organisations between 1878 and 1890; only at election times could the Social Democratic Party, which operated from Switzerland, build up committees and participate.
39. C. Severing, *Mein Lebensweg*, 2 vols, Köln, 1950; T. Alexander, *Carl Severing. Sozialdemokrat aus Westfalen mit preußischen Tugenden*, Bielefeld, 1992.
40. *Festschrift zum 25jährigen Bestehen des Bielefelder Konsumvereins e. GmbH 1892–1917*, Bielefeld, 1917.
41. *Jahresbericht des Arbeiter-Sekretariats Bielefeld 1909*, Bielefeld, 1910, p. 29.
42. In 1909, 40 per cent of the 8572 members of the free trade unions were

members of the Social Democratic Party: *Jahresbericht des Arbeiter-Sekretariats Bielefeld 1909*, Bielefeld, 1910, p. 29.
43. See Ditt, *Industrialisierung*, p. 265.
44. K. Ditt, 'Die politische Arbeiterbewegung in Ostwestfalen zwischen der Reichsgründung und dem Beginn der Weimarer Republik', in K. Düwel and W. Köllmann (eds), *Rheinland-Westfalen im Industriezeitalter, Vol. 2: Von der Reichsgründung bis zur Weimarer Republik*, Wuppertal, 1984, pp. 234–56.
45. H. Kaelble and H. Volkmann, 'Konjunktur und Streik während des Übergangs zum organisierten Kapitalismus in Deutschland', *Zeitschrift für Wirtschafts- und Sozialwissenschaften*, 92, 1972, pp. 513–44; F. Boll, *Arbeitskämpfe und Gewerkschaften in Deutschland, England und Frankreich. Ihre Entwicklung vom 19. und 20. Jahrhundert*, Bonn, 1992.
46. *Jahresbericht des Arbeiter-Sekretariats Bielefeld 1909*, Bielefeld, 1910, p. 29.
47. M. Schneider, *Die Christlichen Gewerkschaften 1894–1933*, Bonn, 1982.
48. *Volkswacht*, Bielefeld, 8. November 1912.
49. See, for comparison, the situation of the textile workers in Bremen: M. Ellerkamp, *Industriearbeit, Krankheit und Geschlecht. Zu den sozialen Kosten der Industrialisierung: Bremer Textilarbeiterinnen 1870–1914*, Göttingen, 1991, pp. 223–55.
50. Within Germany the *Deutsche Metallarbeiterverband* organised, in 1914, 539000 members or about 25 per cent of this labour force, the *Deutsche Textilarbeiterverband* 135000 members or about 10 per cent. P. Umbreit, *25 Jahre deutsche Gewerkschaftbewegung 1890–1915*, Berlin, 1915, pp. 164–5.
51. S. Zaninelli, 'Vita economica e sociale', *Storia di Monza e della Brianza*, Vol. 3, Milan, 1969.
52. G. M. Longoni, *Una città de lavoro. Industria, associazionismo imprenditoriale e relazioni sindacali a Monza all'epoca della prima industrializzazione (1870–1930)*, Bologna, 1987.
53. Later, Viani became one of the founders of the chambers of labour in Milan and Monza.
54. I. Granata and G. M. Longoni (eds), *L'armonia dei produttori. Impresa, sindacato, am- ministrazione pubblica a Monza (1893–1963)*, Rome, 1994.
55. The role played in this event by Ettore Reina should be pointed out. A young socialist printer sent to Monza by the Milan chamber of labour, he became in the following years the secretary of the chamber in Monza, leader of the national workers' movement and, finally in 1911, a Member of Parliament for the socialist reformers. From 1902 until 1922 Reina represented Italy in the *Consiglio Superiore del Lavoro* (the Higher Council of Labour), a government board for the study of social law-making. He was involved, among other things, in the achievement of a law on workplace accidents and for the setting up of the Board of Labour, of a corps of labour surveyors and a maternity fund, as well as for a law on work agreements and on the settlement of industrial disputes. G. M. Longoni, *Ettore Reina. La vicenda di un riformista*, Monza, 1983.
56. Longoni, *Una città*, pp. 203–10. See for Brussels, Devreese, 'Belgium', pp. 33–4.

57. M. Punzo, 'L'amministrazione socialista 1914–1922', in I. Granata and G. M. Longoni (eds), *L'armonia dei produttori. Impresa, sindacato, amministrazione pubblica a Monza (1893–1963)*, Rome, 1994, pp. 171–217. The aims of the chamber of labour hardly differed from the aims of the Catholic organisation which had to fight a long time among the workers of the city against its insincere social image.
58. The *Dreiklassenwahlrecht* which was valid for elections at the regional and local levels based on the tripartition of the local personal taxes of the inhabitants: those few who paid the first part of the whole tax sum constituted the first class of voters and could determine one-third of the delegates in the city parliament. The larger group of taxpayers who paid the second third of the whole tax sum could determine the second third of the delegates and the large remainder of taxpayers, mostly workers, determined the last third of the delegates. Thus, even if the SPD won all the delegates in the third class of voters, they still had to win over and secure the cooperation of the delegates representing the second class of voters if they were to determine policy in the city's government.
59. A. Mommen, 'De receptie van het marxisme in de Belgische arbeidersbeweging', in E. Corijn et. al. (eds), *Veelzijdig marxisme*, Vol. 2, Brussels, 1988, pp. 118–56.
60. C. Strikwerda, 'Three Cities, Three Socialisms: Class Relationships in Belgian Working-class Communities, 1870–1914', in S. G. McNall, R. F. Levine and R. Fantasia (eds), *Bringing Class Back in Contemporary and Historical Perspectives*, Oxford, 1991, p. 191; idem, 'The Divided Class: Catholics vs. Socialists in Belgium, 1880–1914', *Comparative Studies in Society and History*, 30, 1988, pp. 333–59.
61. On the '*Genter System*' see L. Varlez, 'Die Kommunalversicherung gegen Arbeitslosigkeit in Gent', *Archiv für Sozialwissenschaft und Sozialpolitik*, 17, 1902, pp. 238–47; H. Henning, 'Arbeitslosenversicherung vor 1914: Das Genter System und seine Übernahme in Deutschland', in H. Kellenbenz (ed.), *Wirtschaftspolitik und Arbeitsmarkt. Bericht über die 4. Arbeitstagung der Gesellschaft für Sozial- und Wirtschaftsgeschichte am 14. und 15. April 1971*, Munich, 1974, pp. 271–87; E. Deslé, *Arbeitersbemiddeling en Werklozencontrole. Het Voorbeeld van de Gentse Arbeitdsbeurs (1891–1914)*, Brussels, 1991. About Bielefeld see Ditt, *Industrialisierung*, pp. 255–7.

CHAPTER FIVE

Large towns: Liverpool, Lyon and Munich

John Belchem, with the assistance of Karl Heinrich Pohl and Vincent Robert

Large provincial cities do not feature prominently in early labour history. Their remarkable demographic growth was accompanied by increasing complexity: *grandes villes* lacked the structural foundations for collective action found in small and single-industry townships where communal loyalty reinforced occupational solidarity. As this chapter shows, however, the size and complexity of large cities did not necessarily impede trade union development. Indeed, workers could take advantage of the metropolitan atmosphere, utilising the facilities of an agitational infrastructure – public venues, the press, the presence of intellectuals, speakers and activists – to coordinate and enhance local neighbourhood and workplace networks. (This metropolitan public political space was also open to the advocates of female emancipation, a cause which attracted considerable early support in large cities.) Furthermore, large cities were keen to assert their own identity and their provincial pre-eminence, a double-aspect cultural process which awaits adequate historical deconstruction. While distinguishing themselves from the capital, *grandes villes* placed themselves at the forefront of wider, more representative national trends. As this chapter suggests, in such proud 'second capitals' as Liverpool, Lyon and Munich, the development of the labour movement tended both to prefigure and accentuate the respective national 'model'.

Although entirely arbitrary, the selection of Liverpool, Lyon and Munich as the *grandes villes* has proved a fortunate choice for comparative labour history. Any other group of cities, it must be admitted, might have produced very different findings. At first sight, the chosen cities seem outside the scope of conventional labour history. None of the three was essentially industrial or 'proletarian': there was an absence of huge factories and large employers. Each city was multi-functional, a pattern emphasised by the inexorable (and complementary) growth of the 'white-collar' lower-middle class and of the 'uniformed' working class ('semi-skilled' workers in public transport and utilities). Traditional urban dwellers, whether artisan craftworkers or the bourgeois professions and patriciate, were steadily outnumbered and/or displaced. In these (and other) respects, Liverpool, Lyon and Munich were altogether more 'modern' and complex than the mono-industrial towns and medium-sized 'polyactive' towns privileged in most accounts of 'labour's turning-point'. As pointers to the future, they surely merit special attention.

This chapter is divided into three sections: first, an introductory analysis of the socioeconomic character and political and cultural identity of each city; second, a brief survey of trade union development within them between 1880 and 1900, focusing on the role of local coordination and intertrade union bodies; and, third, a case study of railway workers and tramway workers – occupations of particular significance to large cities.

The cities: structure and identity

Population

By the end of the nineteenth century, Liverpool, Lyon and Munich were substantial cities: the 1901 census listed Liverpool Borough as having 684 958 inhabitants, while calculations for the greater Lyon area and Munich in 1900 have produced figures of 507 000 and 490 000 respectively. The pace and pattern of demographic growth of each city, however, differed significantly. Liverpool grew inexorably, although by 1880–1900 there was considerable outmigration from increasingly unattractive inner residential areas. The most rapid growth, indeed, was outside the recently enlarged borough boundary: the wider Merseyside conurbation (the whole of Liverpool, West Derby, Birkenhead and Wirral registration districts along with the Huyton, Much Woolton and Hale subdistricts of the Prescot registration district) grew from 817 821 in 1881 to 1 022 748 in 1901. In Lyon, there was a similar expansion and annexation of the built-up area – la Guillotière, la Croix Rousse and Vaise were annexed in 1851 – but the growth rate began to level off towards the end of the century. Population growth (along with modern factory development) was restricted to the outer suburbs and unannexed townships, such as Villeurbanne where the population doubled from around 20 000 in 1896 to about 40 000 in 1911. In Munich, by contrast, long-term population growth accelerated dramatically at this stage: the population more than doubled between 1882 (240 000) and 1900 (490 000), a faster rate than in comparable

German cities. Thereafter, there was a marked deceleration until after the First World War.

Inmigration was the main factor of growth in all three cases, but Liverpool, a major port of entry for migrants and a human entrepôt for transcontinental emigration, was a case apart. In Lyon and Munich, inmigration was preponderantly short-distance, essentially from adjacent rural and out-working areas, from a hinterland of shared culture, religion and regional identity. Figures for newly married members of the working class in Lyon in 1911 show that only 4 per cent of the women and 4.7 per cent of the men were born outside France. However, there was a significant Italian presence in small shops and businesses in working-class areas. Among the working class, in fact, there was a certain reticence towards Italians, even in trade unions. In Munich, where two-thirds of the workforce in 1907 had been born outside the city, some 90 per cent of inmigrants came from Bavaria. Liverpool, by contrast, attracted long-distance migrants, primarily the Irish (22.3 per cent of the population in 1851 was Irish-born), but also significant numbers of Welsh and Scots. Where rural inmigration into Lyon and Munich served to reinforce their culture, character and status as regional capitals, the multi-ethnic, mainly celtic inflow transformed Liverpool, setting it apart from surrounding Lancashire (and from the rest of England). The 'melting-pot' of inmigration gave Liverpool its unique identity, a construction riven with considerable cultural, sectarian and political divisions.

Social and economic structure

Inmigration also accounts for the pronounced pattern of spatial segregation which emerged earlier in Liverpool than in other cities. Residential location was a compromise between proximity to work and a suitable residential area in terms of cost (often linked to position in the family life cycle), social status and ethnic affiliation. The skilled working population, located in inner residential suburbs, was associated with Welsh and Scottish minority groups, while a large proportion of the unskilled and semi-skilled working class, clustered close to the casual labour markets of the city centre and the waterfront, were of Irish origin.

While there were significant changes in the topography of Munich with the development of a commercial and industrial belt to the south and west of the city centre, the extent of spatial segregation was less evident. Unlike Berlin or Hamburg, Munich lacked specific working-class areas with high indices of segregation. With its four-storey 'workers' barracks', rapidly expanding Westend was the most working-class part of the city, separated from the centre by railway lines and industrial development, but even here there was a considerable lower middle-class presence (mainly white-collar workers and state employees) alongside manufacturing, transport, postal and other workers. Commercial development and industrial relocation transformed the topography of Lyon, forcing the working class out of the old central areas into the new industrial areas along the left bank of the Rhone and into outlying districts. The city centre was transformed by commercialisation between 1850 and 1870 as banks, department stores, newspaper and other offices displaced working-class inhabitants. The mechanisation of silk production led to its relocation on the right bank of the Rhone, along with its associated finishing industries, and a variety of metalworking, chemical and glass-making factories. La Croix Rousse, the original centre of Jacquard hand production, became an area inhabited by office workers and self-employed artisans. Lyon was metamorphosed into a largely commercial metropolis with 33 per cent of its workforce in the service and white-collar sectors and its new proletariat dispersed into outlying suburbs. Such structural change, Yves Lequin has argued, accounted for the 'lull' in militancy in the 1870s as the radical culture of the *canuts* was undermined.[1]

Despite the rapid growth of the white-collar sector – the numbers rose from 10 per cent in 1851 to some 30 per cent of the newly married in 1911 – Lyon remained a working-class city, although different in character from the heavy industrial districts of France. There were few large industrial establishments. Small firms flourished in symbiotic relationship with the needs of large primary concerns. Some firms in mechanised silk production and dyeing employed over 100, but most establishments in the textile industry had a workforce of between 25 and 100. Similarly in metalworking and engineering, there were one or two large concerns, but small to medium-sized firms remained preponderant. As a result of technological change, the number of male workers in silk fell dramatically, from 41.5 per cent of the male working-class population in 1876 to 15.4 per cent in 1891. By this time, building accounted for 31 per cent, the largest occupation for working-class males, but here units were small-scale, scattered and transient. In general, most workers in the city worked in medium-sized establishments or small workshops.

In Munich there was greater economic diversification. As a multifunctional city with a weakly developed industrial sector, Munich exemplified the 'South German model'. There were significant numbers in public administration (in 1907, 20 per cent of income was earned in the public services), as well as many scientists, artists, pensioners (rich and poor) and workers associated with tourism. By 1907 only 40 per cent of the working population was employed in industry (most notably in metalworking and engineering, building, clothing, woodworking, printing and brewing), and some 20 per cent in commerce and transport. Even so, Munich was the largest industrial city in Bavaria. Unlike other parts of industrial Germany, however, establishments tended to be small to medium in size. There were 15 firms employing more than 500 workers in 1907, but taken together these accounted for only 6.5 per cent of the working population. About 70 per cent worked in small to medium-sized establishments – in fact 26.4 per cent worked in units employing between one and five workers. Within this industrial structure, skilled male workers and the self-employed retained considerable significance. In social terms, Munich was weighted towards the middle class – in 1906, the upper class comprised 10 per cent of the population, the middle class 45.1 per cent, and the lower class 44.1 per cent – but many of the lower middle class were financially insecure, often on similar incomes to skilled workers.

Liverpool was dominated by the docks and a vast casual labour market, the 'mecca of all British jetsam'. General labour and dock and warehouse labour – in which there was a high proportion of Irish migrant labour – together accounted for 22.3 per cent of all males over 20 in the 1871 census. Not all waterfront labour, however, was casual and unskilled. Alongside labouring work on the docks and in the adjacent processing and refining plants, there was a substantial 'manufacturing' sector associated with iron founding, ship repairing (shipbuilding had crossed the Mersey to Birkenhead) and marine engineering, comprising some 10.3 per cent of all males over 20 in the 1871 census. These trades, with their regular high wages, attracted skilled migrants from Scotland, Wales and the Black Country. Of particular importance for the growth of the labour movement, was the development of the railway sector which provided regular employment for less skilled workers, the 'uniformed' working class.

Given the prominence of casualism and the 'macho' culture of the docks (where employment was exclusively male), the sexual division of labour was particularly pronounced in Liverpool, more so than in Lyon where gender marked the boundary between skilled and unskilled labour in textiles and other industries. In Liverpool there was no textile employment: female factory and warehouse employment was restricted to the lowliest tasks in food and tobacco, sack-making and mending, rag and cotton picking. A few apprenticeships were available in printing and related trades, but in the workshop sector most women were confined to the sweated clothing trades. Restructuring and mechanisation undermined the few areas of skilled and apprenticed women's trades in the factories: even in the tobacco factories, where nimble-fingered women cigar-makers had once been a skilled elite, women's work soon became equated with unskilled work. Along with the retail sector, the expanding office sector offered an alternative for the daughters of the lower middle class, but within the overall deskilling of clerical work, male clerks succeeded in upholding a superior status. By far the largest category of female employment was domestic service.

Identity

From the construction of its innovatory wet-docks system in the early eighteenth century, Liverpool identified its prosperity with commerce, not with manufacture. Not just a great seaport, Liverpool was the leading financial and commercial centre outside London, the northern outpost of 'gentlemanly capitalism'. Aspiring to the status of 'second metropolis', commercial Liverpool defined itself against industrial Manchester and in rivalry with London. The ethos was to endure, preventing a wider and much needed industrial diversification. Eschewing the 'second industrial revolution', Liverpool entered the twentieth century with a distinct (and distorted) economic structure. In the 1920s, when only 37 per cent of Liverpool workers were engaged in production compared with the national average of 67 per cent,[2] the city Corporation still expressed satisfaction in the absence of manufacturing and industrial blight.

Proud of its heritage in the Kingdom of Bavaria, Munich regarded itself as the capital of the liberal south in rivalry with Berlin and the conservative north. Its famous beergardens symbolised social harmony and a democratic culture, providing the context in which progressive reformism could develop in advance of the rest of Germany, aided by the presence of a significant number of intellectuals, writers and artists. Although there were signs of growing social and political conflict, it was the one city where there was substantial Catholic (and middle-class) support for the SPD.

Lyon regarded itself as the guardian or 'capital' of *republican* France, proudly in advance of the rest of the country. As the May Day demonstration of 1891 evinced, the workers took great pride in the city's republican credentials and its primacy in earlier workers' revolutionary struggles (as in 1831 and 1834). It is this proud republican heritage which probably explains why the government regarded the Lyonnais socialists and anarchists with a fear disproportionate to their actual numbers or influence. While socioeconomic differences between Lyon and other parts of France steadily diminished, the city continued to uphold its political heritage and mission, regarding itself as a rival to Paris.

Trade union development

This section begins with a summary overview of developments in each city, pointing to conformity with national models and characteristics. This is followed by more detailed comparative analysis focused on the role of local coordinating bodies, the Liverpool Trades Council, the Lyon Bourse du Travail and the Conseil de la Fédération des Syndicats, and the Munich Gewerkschaftskartell (Union Cartel).

Liverpool exemplifies many of the key features of British 'new unionism'. In the favourable economic climate of 1889–91, labour turbulence was prolonged and severe, more so than in London. There was a major explosion of militancy and union organisation, a classic British 'strike wave' (similar to subsequent events in 1911–13 and 1919–20) which registered a shift towards more inclusive organisation of less skilled workers, a rejection of the cautious advice of established officials, and a renewed emphasis on the efficacy of strike activity. Despite the socialist revival of the 1880s, ideological developments accounted for little in this militant tenor, prompted for the most part by cyclical fluctuations and adverse changes in the labour process – dockers, seamen and other workers fiercely contested employer prerogative as they sought job regulation. Unlike previous attempts to organise the semi-skilled and unskilled, the new unionism of the late 1880s and early 1890s was to endure, although survival was dependent upon amalgamation and/or the abandonment of some distinctive 'new' features. Without supplanting the old craft unions, new unionism broadened the base of organised labour in Liverpool, as reflected in a list of 79 unions operative in the city in 1911.

The leading organisers and activists of new unionism in Liverpool came from a bewildering variety of political backgrounds – J. G. Taggart, a former labourer at Tate's sugar refinery and the first secretary of the Mersey District of the National Union of Gasworkers and General Labourers, was an Irish Nationalist; the cotton porters and carters (occupations traditionally dominated by Protestants) were led by Tories. As the great western seaport, Liverpool was particularly receptive to American (and Irish) influences. From its branch in Bootle, the Knights of Labour pointed the way towards broad and inclusive structures, but rejected strikes in favour of harmony, arbitration and boycotts, tactics which the Catholic Church was prepared to endorse. Within a few months, however, the Knights were ousted from influence by the arrival of a more militant body on the Liverpool waterfront, the National Union of Dock Labourers, whose leaders were not socialists, but radical supporters of the great American radical and land reformer, Henry George.

The dockers' strike and its settlement introduced a new structural dimension to industrial relations with a movement away from autonomous and fragmentary regulation by small groups of employees and individual employers towards a wider coverage of the unit of regulation – one which would be subject to approval of external authority as represented by the union on the one side and the employers' association on the other. Both organisations were to become permanent, but each had teething problems: the union had to restrain and control its members' actions in the union's own long-term interests; employers were not entirely united in response to the challenge of the union as some still refused to join the Employers' Labour Association, and relinquish their self-sufficiency in labour matters.

Limited as it was, socialist influence was more notable among women workers. Assisted by socialists and middle-class critics of the sweating system, such as Jeannie Mole, a Fabian socialist and wife of a wealthy local fruit merchant, women workers were encouraged to form all-female unions. Unlike the men, female unionists were ready to accept middle-class organisers: other women were frequently more sympathetic to their demands than were the unionised menfolk of their own class. In the height of the fervour for new unions, female unions were established (if only briefly) among cigar-makers, book-folders, upholstresses, marine-sorters, coat-makers, laundresses and sack- and bag-makers. Joseph Goodman of the Social Democratic Federation was joint organizer of the Liverpool Tailoresses and Coatmakers Union and chairman of its strike committee, which also received financial support from the Liverpool Socialist Society. The successful outcome of the strike in 1890 sparked off a general recognition of the plight of exploited women in the city. Once the reduction in hours was secured, however, the number of women in the union began to diminish – by 1894 only 100 members remained. More than their male counterparts, female new unions in Liverpool tended to be episodic: women seemed to have joined unions for short-term goals, moving out either when these were achieved or once it became apparent that they were not immediately to be granted.

Trade union development in Lyon in the late nineteenth century exemplifies what have subsequently been considered as national trends in France: numerical and financial weakness; intense ideological and political division – finally resolved at Lyon when the 'apolitical' *blanquistes* (inspired by the memory of the pioneer communist Louis Auguste Blanqui) and anarchists supplanted the *guesdistes* (followers of the Marxist Jules Guesde); and the use of strikes and mass demonstrations, such as May Day. Lyon, however, already had a strong trade union tradition with substantial participation. But towards the end of the century, unions were fragile and membership fluctuated wildly, even among craft workers: the leather-tawers rose from 12 members in 1892 to 340 in 1893, then down to 6 in 1897 and back up to 140 in 1898; the powerful union of glassworkers of Lyon and Oullins, capable of exercising considerable control over the trade, collapsed from a peak of 500 members at the time of a major strike in 1887, and was rendered almost lifeless by defeat in an eight-month strike in 1891 – by 1895 it counted just 56 members. Following the defeats, however, several glassworkers moved elsewhere in the region to swell the numbers of other unions – at Rive de Gier, some 40 kilometres from Lyon, the union grew from 400 members in 1891 to 1100 in 1894 before itself collapsing in a hard-fought strike.

Organised workers in Lyon were to the fore in proposing and promoting a number of national federations in the 1890s – glassworkers, masons, builders, leather workers, and weavers – but none secured institutional permanence. By British and German standards, the degree of organisational mobilisation was low. However, there were high levels of militancy and ideological awareness among the mobilised minority – another 'national' characteristic. The glassworkers were *blanquiste*, while metalworkers and builders were *guesdiste*. Traditionally, weavers' unions were radical–socialist strongholds, but the *guesdistes* led the way in attempts to organise weavers and dyers in the mechanised sector. There was also a Catholic union among the silk weavers, with some 500 members throughout the 1890s, the only 'independent' union in Lyon prior to the later expansion of 'yellow' unionism. The one exclusively female union in Lyon, comprising office workers, the needlework trades and silk-workers, was also organised by the Catholics between 1899 and 1903.

Among the socialists, the *blanquistes* were less numerous but better organised: there were some 200 activists, almost all of whom were based in the city itself. The *guesdistes* had between 250 and 300 activists, mainly located in the suburbs and surrounding industrial areas. Within the Bourse du Travail, as will be shown below, ideological affiliation was of crucial importance. In other arenas, however, socialism proved less schismatic. Both groups cooperated in upholding May Day as a day of socialist protest and demonstration in contradistinction to anarchist aspirations to trigger revolution. Both groups, too, aligned themselves within the large coalition of the left upon which the dominant Republican regime could generally rely – in 1898, an independent socialist in la Croix Rousse and two *blanquistes* in la Guillotière were elected in the municipal elections thanks to an accord with the moderate Republicans. Furthermore, they worked together in the Fédération Lyonnaise des Syndicats, a pioneer attempt at local trade union coordination established in 1881, from which, however, the main textile manufacturing unions kept their distance. Having suggested the formation of a national federation, the Fédération Lyonnaise was reconstituted as the Conseil Local de la Fédération Nationale des Syndicats in 1887, at which point militant *guesdistes*, already in control of the Bourse du Travail, asserted their dominance.

Little influenced by strike waves or ideological division, trade union growth in Munich, as throughout Germany, was steady and secure. In the formative decades at the end of the nineteenth century, Munich set the pace in Germany, with high membership levels, close cooperation between unions and political parties, and the extension of institutionalised collective bargaining. The percentage of the workforce in 'free' or social democratic unions rose from 12.7 per cent in 1894 to 24.7 per cent in 1899 to around 70 per cent in 1907, by which time some 77 different trades were organised, usually linked in a centralised manner to the Generalkommission in Berlin. There were also a number of Christian unions, mainly formed where socialist unions were not allowed, as was the case with the railway workers discussed below. This remarkable expansion can be attributed to two related factors: the crucial role of the Munich Gewerkschaftskartell in coordinating industrial, political and cultural activity (discussed below); and the extension of institutionalised collective bargaining.

Here Munich was in advance of the rest of Germany, setting a pattern of reformist progressivism based on union recognition, state involvement and conciliation. Such collective bargaining agreements extended to 75 per cent of the male workforce (60 per cent of the combined male and female workforce) in 1912, when only 12 per cent of workers elsewhere in Germany were covered by similar arrangements. It should be noted, too, that the Sozialdemokratische Partei Deutschlands (SPD) enjoyed considerable political influence. At state level, Bavaria prided itself on being open to reform. The Bavarian government, confident that the socialists would not acquire majority status, saw no risk in liberal and democratic policies, prompting the socialists to move further in a reformist direction. At community level in Munich itself, the SPD enjoyed greater active participation and strength in the bicameral system, the restrictions of the franchise and the large number of Catholic and middle-class voters notwithstanding. On educational and cultural issues, the SPD cooperated with the Liberals against the Catholic Centre Party, while in matters concerning workers' rights and status the SPD cooperated with the Catholics against the right wing of the Liberals. By 1911 the SPD emerged as the largest single party with 37.9 per cent of the vote and most of the seats in one of the chambers. In no other German city had the socialists yet achieved such political integration.

The presence and involvement of middle-class intellectuals and activists (including Hope Bridges Adams Lehmann, the British wife of the socialist Dr Karl Lehmann, and a leading campaigner for the emancipation of women) ensured against a class-exclusive 'proletarian' image, and encouraged Munich social democracy along the path of social liberalism, a 'modernising' course followed throughout Germany some decades later.

In each city, the character and shape of trade union development was much influenced by the local coordinating body. The Liverpool Trades Council (LTC), established in 1848, was among the first in the country, but membership was restricted to well-established craft organisations in the building industry and waterfront trades. By 1887 the LTC had an affiliated membership of only 3000 and an annual income of just £10 from affiliated trade unions of engineers, printers, tailors, saddlers, bookbinders, railwaymen, gilders, cabinet-makers, sawyers, brush-makers, bootmakers, mast-block makers and upholsterers. By 1891 with the advent of new unionism, the fortunes of the LTC had been transformed: with 47 affiliated trades and over 46 000 members the LTC was the largest and most important provincial trades council.

Throughout the 1890s there was considerable tension between the National Union of Dock Labourers, the most significant of the new unions, and the LTC. Although aggravated by the personality of James Sexton, the new leader of the dockers, these tense relations exposed the social and cultural gulf between the regularly employed, relatively well-paid and time-served craft workers who still dominated the LTC – 'would be aristocratic artisans', to use Sexton's terminology[3] — and the low-paid, casually employed waterfront workers in the surviving new unions. (There were gender tensions as well: when the LTC reluctantly admitted its first woman delegate in 1890, it decided to transfer meetings from its usual public house to a more 'respectable' venue.) The LTC continued to be dominated by skilled craft workers: in 1905 most delegates to the LTC lived in wards near the city centre but some distance uphill from the river, well away from unskilled, Catholic waterfront wards.

Given these divisions in the labour movement, and the strength of sectarian political formations, it is not surprising that Liverpool played a backward role in the next stage of 'labour's turning-point', the slow and pragmatic development from trade unionism to independent (and parliamentary) labour politics. Given the entrenched strength of the city's ethnic–sectarian political formations, there was neither space nor need for independent Labour. There was no working-class Conservative councillor before 1914, but through the interlocking associational network – party, sectarian and popular – local Tory notables were forcibly reminded of the need to protect the 'marginal privilege' of the Protestant worker. As the Irish National Party passed into the hands of second-generation (that is, Liverpool-born) Irish, it displayed less interest in the fate of Ireland than in the immediate needs of the local Catholic community in housing and employment. While the extent of political patronage and welfare benefits at the disposal of these sectarian machines is open to question, both reached deep into their respective constituencies, assisted by pub- and parish-based networks of associational culture and collective mutuality.

Despite valiant efforts to provide a vibrant, non-sectarian counter-culture, socialists secured little influence within the Liverpool labour movement. The LTC resisted proposals for a new political alignment put forward by socialists and others involved in agitation among the unemployed: in 1893, for example, Sexton's attempt to federate the LTC with the Independent Labour Party was rejected. But pressure for labour representation steadily increased. Resolutions in favour of independent labour representation (as well as 'fair-wage' clauses in corporation contracts and an eight-hour day) were a key feature of May Day demonstrations, the first of which was held in Liverpool on 2 May 1891 – May Day in Liverpool, however, was traditionally the occasion of the horse parade by the carters, an exclusively Protestant occupation. In 1900 the LTC eventually joined with the socialist groups – the ILP, Fabians, and the Social Democratic Federation – and the Edge Hill and Garston Labour Clubs (wards with large numbers of railway workers) to form what became, by 1903, the Liverpool Labour Representation Committee, which in turn affiliated to the national Labour Party in 1907. However, there was limited advance until interwar slum clearance gradually destroyed the community base of the old sectarian politics. It was not until 1955 that Labour gained control of the municipal council, a generation later than equivalent triumphs in other major conurbations. In its combination of political and ideological weakness with workplace industrial militancy – a pattern established in the formative decades at the end of the nineteenth century – Liverpool labour history provides an accentuated inflexion of British national characteristics.

During the next great strike wave, 1911–13, when Liverpool was 'close to revolution', syndicalists were able to exploit the structural tensions not only between old craft unions and new unions but within the new unions themselves. As casual labourers lacked the guaranteed time, relevant experience or financial resources for regular involvement, new unions were perforce dominated by full-time officials. These bureaucrats soon sought union incorporation in national agreements with employers, to which end they were prepared both to discipline and decasualise the membership. In so doing, they offended the independence and pride of the Liverpool labourers. For all its ills, casualism was a cherished symbol of independence, the best guarantee of freedom from irksome work discipline, from the tyranny of the factory bell. In protesting against decasualisation, the workers were championed by syndicalist advocates of direct action, but the incidence of subsequent rank and file militancy seems to have been determined less by theory and praxis than by specific grievances and traditional attitudes. Long after the decline of the docks, shipping and casualism, Liverpool workers continued to protest against workplace impositions and innovations – national agreements, bureaucratic structures and new work practices – which denied their residual independence and democratic local autonomy. To unsympathetic observers, 'militant' Merseyside represented the 'British disease' at its worst.[4]

In Lyon, local attempts at coordination foundered on ideological divisions rather than structural tensions. The Conseil Local de la Fédération Nationale des Syndicats secured a temporary dominance of the labour movement from 1889–90, when it assumed responsibility for May Day and other major demonstrations. By 1890, 45 Lyon-based unions were affiliated – building workers and metalworkers were strongly represented, along with glassworkers, leatherworkers and shoemakers – as were 33 weavers' unions in the adjacent Beaujolais region. In Lyon itself, the old weavers' unions, still dominated by radicals, kept apart, but unions in mechanised weaving and dyeing sectors were quick to affiliate. Such coordination, however, did not endure. At the second May Day demonstration, more revolutionary elements came to the fore. Rioting led to repression which in turn prompted the more politically-minded, notably the *guesdistes*, to seek some accommodation with the authorities. This sequence of events led to disillusion and apathy, to the point at which the purpose of the ailing Conseil Local was called into question. There seemed no prospect of its calling a general strike, while more routine administrative matters of local coordination were increasingly undertaken by the Bourse du Travail.

There was no equivalent in Liverpool or Munich of the Bourse du Travail, where workers from different industries could meet in premises provided by the local authorities. At Lyon, the local authority operated a separate employment exchange for women workers, but some women workers in the organised weaving, dyeing and tobacco trades were represented at the local Bourse du Travail, housed in the former *théatre de variétés*. Sponsored by Republican municipalities throughout France in the hope of co-opting a tame labour movement, the Bourses du Travail soon engendered a syndicalist *mentalité* – a general 'workerist' mistrust of both Republican reform and socialist sectarianism. In Lyon, the latter was much in evidence. Ideological divisions were particularly pronounced as the dominant *guesdistes* seemed intent on eradicating any *blanquiste* influence within the Bourse. Indeed, it was this determination which created the impression of fundamental polarisation in Lyon between moderates and revolutionaries, whether *blanquiste*, anarchist or independent. In the event, the *guesdistes* were unable to impose control and gradually lost influence within the Bourse du Travail. Furthermore, they were excluded by *blanquistes* and anarchists from the new committee for May Day which appeared in 1897, along with a new local federation which was ultimately to adhere to the CGT (General Confederation of Labour).

The Munich Gewerkschaftskartell secured a much higher degree of integration and coordination, in both the industrial and political aspects of the local labour movement. A clearing house for all social, cultural and economic questions, the cartel provided the organisational and financial infrastructure – and the overlap of personnel – for coordinated reformist practice by unions and party. The cartel, however, did not construct a workers' counterculture as was the case elsewhere in Germany. In Munich this was unnecessary: by no means proletarian in image and identity, the labour movement developed within the wider framework of Bavarian democratic and 'social–liberal' culture.

Occupational case studies

Given the multifarious nature of economic activity within the cities, it is difficult to select representative occupations for case studies. In the city centres, office and shop-work expanded rapidly, but judging by the Liverpool experience, powerful barriers of status, work practice and culture – a veritable 'collar gap' – kept these white-collar workers apart from the wider labour movement and the working class in general. The development of 'professional' organisations attested to insecurity as the rapid expansion of numbers (and the introduction of new office technology) threatened to diminish traditional status and gender differentials. While work in small shops was long, poorly-paid and ill-regarded, the new multiple and department stores in the city centres were altogether more prestigious. Educational requirements were high, and beyond the reach of most working-class young women.

White-collar workers kept their distance from organised labour. As commercial centres, large cities required efficient transport networks to link with the rest of the country and to serve their own rapidly expanding built-up area – not least to carry clerks and shop assistants from respectable suburbs to central workplaces. Preliminary comparative research has revealed important differences in the organisation of railway workers and tramway workers in the three cities.

Railway workers

As members of the uniformed working class with job security and a regular wage, railway workers occupied an important position in Liverpool labour history. In the 'false dawn' of new unionism in 1871–73, the railwaymen alone managed to secure a permanent form of organisation with the establishment of a Liverpool branch of the Amalgamated Society of Railway Servants. Not dependent on the casual labour market, railwaymen were the one group of non-craft workers with the time and means to devote to trade unionism; to the cooperative movement (in 1891–92, 43 per cent of new male members of the Liverpool Cooperative Society were railway workers); and to the development of independent labour politics. Where most workers moved within the sphere of sectarian associational culture, Liverpool railwaymen developed a more proletarian style and culture.

In Lyon, some 350 railway workers were unionised in 1891. The real strength of the union, however, was outside the city in railway workshops in Oullins where 1000 of the 1500 workers were organised. Like the local metalworkers, they kept apart from the labour movement in Lyon itself. They used a different Bourse du Travail and concentrated their efforts less on local coordination than in spreading unionisation along the Paris–Lyon–Marseille line.

Despite the consensual political atmosphere, railway workers in Munich were prohibited from joining socialist trade unions. There were no such restrictions, however, on membership of the Christian (or Catholic) unions. In 1897, 1500 railway workers belonged to the Christian union, comprising more than 60 per cent of the total membership of all such unions in Munich.

Tramway workers

Efficient local transport was very important for large cities. Tramway workers were constrained in their options for militant action, however, by a complex framework of industrial relations, which included the general public as well as employers and local authorities.

The lengthy tramwaymen's agitation in Liverpool (late June 1889–January 1890) has been described as an abject failure.[5] The United Tramways Company was a notoriously tyrannical employer, but the tramwaymen decided against militant strike action for a number of reasons. Previous attempts at unionisation and strike action in the 1870s had ended in disaster and fiasco. This time it was the Knights of Labour who organised the men into the Liverpool Amalgamated Tramway and Hackney Carriage Employees' Association and advised them not to strike but to rely on public opinion and conciliation. Those activists who favoured a more militant policy lacked support among the workforce, most of whom were reluctant to jeopardise regular employment within the uniformed working class. Take-home pay fluctuated as a result of petty fines imposed by the employer but the advantage of regular work and a regular income, particularly within the context of Liverpool's predominantly casual labour market, was a benefit not lightly to be discarded. As late as the great Liverpool transport strike of 1911, tramwaymen remained weak, apathetic and abused by their employers, municipalisation of the service notwithstanding.

In Lyon, where a private company operated the network under a concession from the local authority, tramway drivers and conductors were not organised until 1896 when Victor Darme, a *guesdiste*, took the lead. Tactical considerations, rather than ideology, accounted for their moderate stance in industrial relations. Given their prominent visibility to the general public, tramway workers sought, above all, to project an image of moderation and respectability. When they took strike action in 1900, they marched silently through the town centre in neat columns, all dressed in uniform, behind the tricolour, not the red flag. The union officials were at the head, followed by the workers ranked according to age and seniority. Similarly in Munich, tramway workers were well organized, but were reluctant to take militant action for fear of jeopardising their job security, particularly as many were elderly and thus unlikely to find alternative employment. Within the Gewerkschaftskartell, the tramway workers were a moderating influence, seeking to pacify more militant workers.

For the uniformed working class, large cities held out the prospect of an early advance into 'public service' or 'municipal' socialism. However, they were often restrained in their industrial tactics, fearful of jeopardising their relative security or of offending public opinion within the city. As providers of essential services, unionised manual workers were conditioned by the discourse of civic pride. The interests of the city could take precedence over those of labour.

The predicament of the tramway workers is an appropriate reminder of the ambivalent identities (complementary, overlapping or competing) on option to workers. Pride in the city did not preclude commitment to wider affiliation, particularly if the city took the lead in constructing national, occupational, confessional, class- or gender-based associations. At times of industrial dispute, however, workers faced the charge of civic disloyalty, alienating public opinion by bringing city services to a halt. To understand the origins of this complex (and increasingly familiar) pattern of industrial relations, more research is urgently required on the *grandes villes* of the late nineteenth century.

Notes

1. Yves Lequin, *Les ouvriers de la région lyonnaise*, 2 vols, Lyon, 1977.
2. P. J. Waller, *Democracy and Sectarianism: A Political and Social History of Liverpool 1868–1939*, Liverpool, 1981, p. 330.
3. James Sexton, *Sir James Sexton, Agitator*, London, 1936, p. 95.
4. Merseyside Socialist Research Group, *Merseyside in Crisis*, Liverpool, 1980.
5. Eric Taplin, 'The Liverpool tramwaymen's agitation of 1889', in H. R. Hikins (ed.), *Building the Union: Studies on the Growth of the Workers' Movement, Merseyside 1756–1967*, Liverpool, 1973, pp. 55–73.

Bibliography

Belchem, J. (ed.) (1992), *Popular Politics, Riot and Labour: Essays in Liverpool History 1790–1940*, Liverpool.

Hikins, H. (ed.) (1973), *Building the Union: Studies on the Growth of the Workers' Movement: Merseyside, 1756–1967*, Liverpool.

Lequin, Y. (1977), *Les ouvriers de la région lyonnaise*, 2 vols, Lyon.

Pohl, K. H. (1992), *Die Münchener Arbeiterbewegung. Sozialdemokratische Partei, freie Gewerkschaften, Staat und Gesellschaft in München 1890–1914*, Munich.

Neumeier, G. (1995), *München um 1900. Wohnen und Arbeiten, Familie und Haushalt, Stadtteile und Sozialstrukturen*, Frankfurt.

PART TWO
Customs and representation

CHAPTER SIX

May Days

Gita Deneckere, Marie-Louise Goergen, Inge Marssolek, Danielle Tartakowsky and Chris Wrigley

Following a proposal by two French militants, Raymond Lavigne and Jean Dormoy, and after consulting French Marxists along with the German delegates Bebel and Liebknecht, the International Socialist Congress of Paris of 14–20 July 1889 decided to organise:

> A major international event on a certain day in order that in all countries and in all cities at the same time on the same day workers could force the authorities to reduce by law the working day to 8 hours and to carry out other resolutions of the Congress of Paris.

From its creation, the First of May was therefore an international movement based upon the two principles of universality and simultanearity in the celebration and making of labour's demands. It was designed to help young movements not yet fully developed to escape from their national isolation and to give them a new impetus. Several years later, Albert Thomas recalled the moral weight which the decision of 1889 had:

> The Socialist parties which were weak minorities still in a number of countries small groups isolated, ridiculed sometimes, often persecuted and hunted down, had need of the comfort which a feeling of universal propaganda could give them and the awareness of the progress which had been accomplished by the stronger parties was very important. The international meetings gave members of the Socialist parties a clear vision of socialist action and situating themselves within the great task which would be accomplished everywhere they took on a new confidence. The establishment by the First International Congress in 1889 of the May Day celebrations devoted to the claim for the eight hour day is a proof of this state of mind. The Socialists wanted to affirm by this celebration the universality of their organisation and it is undeniable that the moral effect obtained henceforth was enormous.

The dates of 18 March or the 14 July which were first of all considered by the Congress seemed in the end to have too much national significance and they went for the 1 May which was linked to the recent American practice of May strikes and therefore presented an external significance valid for each of the states concerned in this study. The international resolution of 1889 was kept sufficiently vague in order to allow certain national sections which were under close surveillance (Russia and Germany) to take measures adapted to the political situation of their country. This resolution left to the different national organisations freedom of action regarding the way in which the day was to be celebrated but would not admit any ambiguity on two points: date – the demonstrations would have to take place on 1 May 1890 – and the character of the day which was to be based on demands and not festive.

Despite this intention clearly expressed in the text and respected to the letter in a number of practices, divergent attitudes towards particularly the date and the form of the May Day demonstrations and related to national realities caused debate. At the same time the desire for unity expressed internationally by the decision to make the eight-hour day *the* major universal demand of the First of May was undercut by the emergence of demands which were exclusively linked to different national contexts, even local ones. An examination of the major figures and the means of action put into effect between 1890 and 1906 in Germany, Belgium, France and Britain provides proof of the diversity which dominated.

A multiple repertory

Chronology

The four countries which concern us here all responded from 1890 to the call of the Congress of Paris and it is therefore easy to compare their first May Day celebrations. The comparison of the average length of time the celebration was widely supported poses more problems as the relevant chronologies for each of the states diverge almost immediately. In Great Britain the First of May brought together huge crowds which were significantly greater than those in neighbouring countries. The May Day demonstrations remained powerful until 1895 then declined; but they grew again after the turn of the century but with a different geographical pattern of strength. In France, after the powerful movement of 1890–91, there was a parallel decline which accompanied a growth of organisers and activities. The revival began from 1901 and especially from 1905 to 1906. In Belgium the movement took off from 1895 but then stabilised at a high level. In Germany it maintained its force acquired from the very beginning then crossed a barrier of still greater growth with, and after, the Russian Revolution of 1905.

Organisers

In France the First of May was a day dominated politically by the *guesdistes* who saw in it a means of transition from the class *in* itself to the class *for* itself. In order to achieve their aims they did not exclude any form of action but preferred warnings. The general organising committee of the First of May, on the contrary, disdained concepts which could be called pedagogic and held on to the First of May as a possible means of its strategy of direct action. This led, until 1894, to diverging calls for mobilisation. This clear division of approaches became more blurred afterwards. The calls for action ceased to be national and the initiative was transferred to the local level, with all the implications for variations. The birth of confederate trade unionism in 1895 did not have any immediate effect. This took until 1900, and more definitely 1904, when the CGT claimed the leadership of the First of May and took control of it. The SFIO (Section Française de l'Internationale Ouvrière), which had just been formed, accepted this transfer of power. Nevertheless, on the ground, the organisers remained diverse and frequently it was socialists and trade unionists who led the action together, notwithstanding the strategies which become antagonistic towards the CGT and the SFIO.

In Belgium the Congress of the POB (Parti Ouvrier Belge) in April 1890 gave to its local sectors and its regional federations entire responsibility for the organisation of the First of May. The tradition of autonomy characterised this party. A manifesto translated into the two official languages and published in Ghent and Brussels under the title *Het Achturenwek* or *Le Travail de huit heures* constituted the sole example of a brochure distributed at national level for this occasion between 1890 and 1906. Only newspapers reproduced national and international calls for action. The multiform structure of this secondary type of organisation, of which the POB was an example, removes the possibility of knowing which organisations were the most involved in the most significant activities carrying out the 1889 decision. Nevertheless, it seems that the trade union movement showed itself to be less active on the ground than the political organisations. This signified less that it abstained than that it adopted a low profile and demonstrated a lack of initiative.

In the German Empire the socialist party's executive committee and various trade union conferences took action in 1890 on distinct bases, then rapidly coordinated and worked together. From 1905 the major divisions were between those in favour and those against the mass political strike and not between the party and the trade unions.

Finally, in London the major organisers of the massive 1890

demonstrations were a committee which had been created especially for the occasion, the Eight Hours Legal Working Day Committee, and the London Trades Council, dominated by the old Lib-Lab generation, and accompanied by the Social Democratic Federation (SDF) of H.M. Hyndman. The Eight Hours Committee was made up of 94 trade union branches and various radical and socialist groups. Eleanor Marx was the pivot of this organisation, supported by the Bloomsbury Socialist Society. The Eight Hours group and the trades council organised separate demonstrations in Hyde Park. The Marxist Socialist League and the SDF established rival demonstrations and the anarchists and certain of the unions did the same. In the provinces the new unions often constituted the major thrust of these movements. Later, the Independent Labour Party (ILP) and the Labour Party took over control of the First of May after several years of discord.

Means of action

Date

In France the *guesdistes* felt that postponing the First of May was quite unacceptable because of the immense international impact of a universal celebration held in various countries at the same time. This orthodox view took little consideration of various problems: the time taken off work when First of May fell during the week, the problem of clashing with certain local celebrations when it coincided with them, and the problem of Sundays and the political timetable when the electoral calendar coincided. With a few local exceptions, however, the First of May was nevertheless celebrated on the date agreed. Elsewhere departures from the actual first of May took place from the beginning of the 'red May Days'.

In Great Britain and Germany the majority organisations chose, from 1890, to postpone the celebration to the Sunday following the 1 May in order to avoid any general strike on that day. This principle was essential in Great Britain but was progressively called into question in Germany. Up until 1894 the SPD called for the organisation of a meeting in the evening of 1 May and for the celebration of the 1 May on the Sunday following. Then, from 1895, it organised both the celebration and the demonstration simultaneously on the date agreed, with possible exceptions. In Belgium, where the decisions for action were the responsibility of local groupings, the two choices coexisted. It was even possible for two demonstrations to be organised both on 1 May and then on the first Sunday in May as in the case of Ghent. Belgium, in addition, was the only country where the party tried to make 1 May a public holiday – but without success.

We see therefore, other than in Britain, a growing respect for the date which had initially been selected.

Celebrations, meetings and processions

In Great Britain the dominant form of action was the mass meeting held in a space recognised as one for public meetings in the heart of the city. The political aspect of the day eclipsed all other forms of parallel or competitive expression, the press rarely giving any indication of any other festivity. This does not, however, exclude the notion of a carnival atmosphere.

In France the warning to the authorities was transmitted by the delivery of petitions to the Chamber or to the local authorities. The demonstrators met earlier to debate questions relating to the day, to vote on the resolutions and to devise petitions with lists of demands. The *guesdistes'* processions which accompanied these events were well-prepared, well-publicised in advance and essentially male-dominated. They deployed demonstrators dressed in workers' overalls or the clothing of their trades and aimed at conveying the image of a working class conscious of its own identity but one with a respect for discipline and legality. These processions were often accompanied by music and singing but gave rise to a less symbolic production than in neighbouring countries. This form of action was opposed by the *allermanistes* and the *blanquistes* and was viewed sceptically by many trade unionists. Henceforth, this action was even less exclusive than strikes which the *guesdistes* never excluded from their principles. From 1890 to 1906 the petitioning and demonstrations in support of their claims diminished without totally disappearing. In contrast demonstrations which raised the identity of the marchers without speakers became more numerous. They were able to be concentrated in suitable working-class spaces (often around the Bourses du Travail) but sometimes came into urban centres where the collective memory of the town or city was concentrated or, in case of the capital, the nation. They therefore bore witness to the desire to appropriate local or national history and to affirm in this way the integration of the working class into society. These different types of demonstrations often opened or closed with an aperitif or a reception (often held at the town hall when the local authority was favourable to the demonstrators), punch, a banquet, a picnic or a dance. An important role was also played by those well-known social gathering places of France, the cafés.

In Germany the processions were based on the guild tradition. Because the workers had not yet taken over control of the street, they moved away from the urban centres which were full of history and moved out to the urban periphery. They expressed workers' aspirations towards sun, fresh air and leisure and not their integration into national history. In Bremen, for example, demonstrators were found at an early hour in various quarters of the city. Their processions reached the Burger Park in the centre of the city and moved around it. They marched on the pavements in order not to disturb the traffic and were clothed in their Sunday black suits with red carnations in their buttonholes. There were few women with them and no bands, no red armbands and no singing. This respectability led to the marches being tolerated by the authorities. In the afternoon a political meeting was organised and games were arranged for children.

In Belgium, on May Days, the procession was the keystone of the day. Due to a greater level of tolerance than in Germany, with the exception of Liège, the procession invaded the centre of the city and marched almost always peacefully under the protection of a security force arranged by the socialist organisations. After the processions, meetings with speeches took place in the Maisons du Peuple. Banquets were organised as well. From 1895 the First of May became an artistic event in the cities, giving rise to an impressive level of creativity. Monumental paintings created for the event were particularly spectacular; they were carried amongst the processions in which numerous carts exalted the triumph of socialist ideals and emphasised what could be possible for workers. The First of May could become a diverse event. At Ghent, in 1897, the celebration lasted for a whole weekend and the people of Ghent profited from this day of freedom to take long walks outside the city, taking picnics. To this was added in Belgium, as in Germany, dances and cultural events.

Strikes

The strike was seen as one of the modes of action in three of the four countries, even though two of the three socialist parties nevertheless rejected it at the outset. Even in Great Britain, strikers engaged in local disputes often showed up in good numbers at May Day meetings. This form of action was adopted because it could take place everywhere, at a predefined time and according to the workers' local custom. In France, as in Germany, in the early 1890s, the month of May remained the month in which there were the most strikes and the most strikers; and that was also true for Belgium in spring. The nature of such class action was locally determined, with notable variations even when identical types of worker, but from different countries, were involved. These workers were groups based at industrial workplaces which traditionally had been the most prone to strike action and which everywhere mobilised the most people on the First of May; strikes organised on that day were not the result of any overall direction. There are no global studies which enable us to give detailed figures for these strikes in detail, or to look at the main proponents and the main demands. However, individual studies show a primacy of local demands directed towards the boss (and not the employers generally). In the mines the demands were often the expression of the entire branch.

Geography

In Great Britain, until 1895, London was the site for demonstrations of a quite extraordinary size with a clearly national significance (between 250000 and 300000 participants at Hyde Park from 1890–94). In contrast, the demonstrations in the provinces were much smaller. This pattern corresponds to the areas of new unionism's strength more than to those of radical socialism and corresponds also to personal factors (such as the direct influence of Eleanor Marx). The London demonstrations declined in size afterwards, while the provincial demonstrations grew in size. But, until 1906, the provincial extension of this mobilisation remained lower than in neighbouring countries.

None of the three other capitals rivalled London and dispersion was the rule in the other countries concerned.

In Belgium the forces and the regions which were mobilised for the events were essentially the same as those which were mobilised to gain universal suffrage, and therefore they present no special characteristics. The strong regional inequalities reflect both the strength of socialist organisations and religious divisions. In the Walloon area – characterised by its industrial power, the strong unity of the proletariat and the decline in Catholic influence – the workers' organisations' eagerness to fight was legendary well before the First of May. The May Days there were constructed in a way which reflected the image of the power of the party. The strike was general in the mines, the steel industry and branches of industry where workers' organisations had acquired power since the riots of 1886. Processions formed in the suburbs to enter the city where the mass demonstration was to be held, as, for example, in Liège in 1890. In Flanders the situation was completely different. Nothing happened on the first May Days, except in Ghent. The Church made its opposition very clear, including in little towns with no industrial development like Alost, and this gave May Day demonstrations no chance whatsoever. However, Flanders soon followed the pattern of neighbouring countries and witnessed organised processions, the natures of which were determined by local conditions. The secondary differentiations from one town to another can also be explained by the POB's strong tradition of autonomy. The local organisations which planned the action coloured their initiatives with important local characteristics and thereby contributed to the success of the celebrations. In Brussels, as in other Flemish towns, the participants from neighbouring communes made their way individually to the central meeting point and the procession was organised subsequently in the centre of the city. On the other hand, strikes remained exceptional (non-existent in Ghent and rare in Brussels).

In Germany regional studies are lacking (it would be interesting to know to what extent the Catholic regions can be distinguished from Protestant ones). Nevertheless, we know that, at the turn of the century, the First of May had succeeded in being instituted as a celebration (in the broadest sense) in all the regions of the German Empire and that, in most of the cities, a minority of workers went on strike, held meetings or took part in processions.

The French situation was different, partly owing to the workers' movements' slowness in structuring themselves and the attitude of the state. Until 1905 the geography of the First of May celebrations partially corresponded to the geography of socialist or trade union strength or the geography of industrial bastions. Paris, and the Parisian region in particular, were areas of relative weakness. Here we can see a paradoxical consequence of Jacobinism. Political centralisation resulted in a control of public order which was much stronger in Paris than elsewhere, making it more difficult for workers to march in procession in public spaces and bringing resulting problems of non-visibility. Ideological tensions between rival workers' organisations, which were much stronger in the capital than elsewhere, constituted an additional impediment to action. Conversely, we can find certain examples of discord between the move to action on the First of May and the first socialist bodies. In certain places the First of May events owed their existence to spontaneous action more than to the role of socialist or trade union militants. The type of trade union branches which were involved often seems pertinent to the level of activity: organisations which mobilised more people than others included mines, the building industry, glass, textiles and steel, then – to a lesser extent and for different reasons – ports and docks and the drinks trade.

The choice of forms of action in France made the situation even more confused. Certain organisations were exclusively in favour of one particular form of action and no other. Socialist local authorities of a *guesdiste* persuasion preferred municipal celebrations, republican circles celebrated the First of May clothed in tricolours and organised social gatherings with punch, while strikes were obviously the major activity of the unions. This correspondence between organisers and means of action was, however, far from being the rule. Meetings, gatherings, demonstrations, punch-drinking and family celebrations could come from any one of a number of different organisations. Certain strikes were spontaneous, while there were some unions which preferred organising dances. Action, and different types of action at local level, therefore stemmed from determinants which were not strictly organisational. In this way such matters as the control of a local authority by socialists, the existence of a Bourse du Travail, the particular nature of local trade union branches or other local circumstances all played their part. That the Departments Nord and Pas-de-Calais, for example, took to celebrations and processions was due in large part to solid local festive traditions, while the glassmakers, strongly mobilised from 1890, traditionally organised their own country walks on the First of May.

Local cultures and industrial cultures can be at the roots of transnational groupings. The north of France, the Walloon area of Belgium and northwest Germany constituted in this way a cultural grouping made up of similar ethnological substrata and with similar industries. For this reason, the First of May celebrated in this geographical triangle presented more similarities than the First of May celebrated in Flanders and Val aux Nis or in the north and the west of France. This coherence was reinforced by a cross-border traffic of workers' groups and cultural developments. Thus at the beginning of the twentieth century the Parti Ouvrier Français (POF) in Lille published a tract, *La chanson premier Mai* (the song of the First of May), the work of a Belgian songwriter, Jacques Gur, set to music by H. Weyts.

We can find, therefore, in each of these countries all types of workers' organisation and, with the exception of Great Britain, all types of an extensive repertory of action. Their weight and their respective place differed, however, from one country to another. So there were clearly distinct types in existence.

National types

The first May Days

The turnabout in the economic situation characterised by the emergence from 'the great depression', a growth of strike action and the development of initiatives which expressed international solidarity contributed to the success of the first May Days and together constituted a unifying factor. In contrast, the nature of each state and the relationship which workers' organisations had with it, the festive system which dominated and, above all, the political situation were factors of national differentiation.

The trade unions and the SPD were organisations which had been constituted much earlier and which had strong resources which they had no intention of sacrificing to symbolic action. In order to satisfy decisions which went against their own strategies they adopted a low profile in the period 1890–91. This was characterised by the movement of the First of May to the Sunday and rejection of the notion of strike.

In Great Britain most trade unionists preferred to achieve their aims through collective negotiations with employers as opposed to relying on legislation by the state. In addition, the memory of the recent bloody demonstrations of the unemployed of 1886 and 1887, initiated by the SDF, increased their mistrust of the principle of powerful mass demonstrations. In contrast, some of the newly born socialist organisations and the new unionism, which included organised sectors which were too weak to undertake direct negotiations with employers, considered the decisions of the Congress of Paris as a golden opportunity. However, the hegemony of the Lib-Lab trade unions was sufficient to force most of these organisations to operate within agreed patterns of activity. The pressure which the socialists and new unionists exerted enabled them to overcome the hesitations and cautiousness of the older trade union leaders who remained anxious, nevertheless, not to dissociate themselves from a movement of international solidarity. In taking such action they benefited from the prevailing political liberalism which accepted the right of people to demonstrate in large numbers in major public spaces. The success of the large London demonstrations was helped by the strong presence of political exiles from all over Europe and so, in this way, helped provide an ideological aspect to the British May Days which was greater than those of neighbouring countries.

In Germany the First of May demonstrations coincided with the completion of a major stage in the development of the workers' movement. The SPD had just adopted a Marxist programme at its Erfurt Congress, the trade union movement was in full growth and professional associations were beginning to unite, thus constituting mass movements based on social reform and a policy of pressure which could be exerted with the help of the proletarian party. The relationship with the state had also simultaneously been transformed (these phenomena are naturally connected). The government of Wilhem II had put an end to the Anti-Socialist Law of 1878 and, soon after, the SPD had obtained 20 per cent of votes at the February 1890 elections. Anxious to not compromise these gains and to guarantee it future progress, the SPD expressed strong reservations regarding any steps which might lead to conflicts. As a result, the SPD initially decided to postpone the May Day activities to the following Sunday and, from 1889 onwards, recognised the First of May as an international labour day. The SPD was even happier to support the festive forms of the event because they were part of the German workers' tradition whereas days of struggle were not, given the absence of revolutionary traditions. But the choice, already mentioned, of modest activities and general festivities was not only linked to the absence of freedom to demonstrate and an exaggerated caution, it was part of the policy of 'cultural disintegration'[1] of the SPD in which the First of May was prominent. Apparently anodyne events like walks in the country ought not be seen as simple copies of a bourgeois festive tradition. They should be seen as part of the emergence of an alternative culture, of which the dominant theme was the humanisation of the working class. May Day provided the occasion for the working class to learn to express new forms of political behaviour, to affirm the strong link between the political demand of the eight-hour day and cultural aspirations (free time for cultural activities, for education and for the emancipatory role of science), all of which were strongly marked symbolically. At the same time these celebrations were a symbolic contradiction of the imperial holidays; they were an anti-imperial Sedan day.[2]

But, in 1890, in Germany the question of the relationship between the unions and the party was not totally resolved, and these choices were not unanimously taken. The resolution of the Congress of Paris came to Germany at a time when the unions were beginning to free themselves from the domination of the party. If the party subordinated the First of May to the repeal of the Anti-Socialist Law and the electoral campaign, the situation was different with the unions, for their congresses from August 1889 to May 1890 all pronounced themselves in favour of a strike. This had the effect of creating a strike fever perceptible in the weeks preceding 1 May. The employers reacted by a countermobilisation which was unprecedented and marked by lockouts, in particular in Bremen and Hamburg. In the latter city the workers responded by striking.

This early integration of the working classes into the nation-state corresponded to the initial characteristics of the French May Day. The political reformism deployed by the republican state and the tradition of universal suffrage determined there the principle of the international May Day quite as much as its characteristics. The *guesdiste* proposal formulated at the Congress of Paris aimed at, among other things, running counter to the practices of political integration instituted by the victorious republicans and which blocked the political autonomy of the working class. But, because of republican hegemony, no separate principle capable of opposing the dominant means of class identification was able to come into being within France without some exterior sign which could constitute a rallying point of another type. The appeal to class, a universal determinant, satisfied such a need. But the First of May was not able automatically to liberate itself from the dominant culture. The parliamentary system responded to the claims made on it. If the First of May portrayed itself as an anti-14 July demonstration, this was not evident in the dominant festive policy nor in republican symbolism (such as the long-lasting presence in a number of provincial towns of the tricolour flag and the *Marseillaise*). To these may be added locally many borrowings from civic celebrations (such as firework displays, processions to cemeteries inspired by homages to the dead) and republican sociability (punch, banquets, and so on).

In Belgium the political situation confused the initial schemes. In December 1889 the Ghent newspaper *Vooruit* wrote 'Thursday, 1 May must not be a day of strikes but a celebration of work'. This definition, similar to the one which simultaneously dominated in Germany, gained the upper hand and became dominant within the POB. In 1890 this party, nevertheless, launched a campaign for universal suffrage, advocating the general strike as a means of action. However, it then retreated and, in April 1891, proposed to postpone this principle until the discussion of the budget on 20 May. The First of May 1891 can, in this context, be seen as constituting a trump card as much as a handicap, becoming a catalyst or risking being a distraction from a major demand. The Federation of Miners which for some months had adopted the principle of the political general strike took an immediate decision and, notwithstanding the reservations of the POB, went on strike on 1 May. This strike, whose object was universal suffrage rather than the eight-hour day, became a general strike and acquired sufficient strength for the Chamber to adopt on 20 May the principle of revising the constitution. This was put into effect in April 1893. It was thus the struggle for universal suffrage which unified the movement, and the First of May was only a secondary aspect.

These initial characteristics had a lifespan which was very unequal between countries.

National evolutionary factors

Great Britain underwent neither a notable change in the relationship between the state and the workers' movement nor a reversal of the balance of power within the workers' movement itself. The trade union movement for the most part was dominated by the ideas of political and economic liberalism. This excluded strikes which had wide-ranging aims, especially political objectives.

Large demonstrations depended on attracting the support of Lib-Lab trade unionists. Successive organisers of May Day events could not escape from this constraint. The main variations recorded in celebration of May Days concerned the size of demonstrations, and these may partly be explained by internal changes within the labour movement, such as the varying strength and enthusiasm of the Workers' Union and other new unions, the decline of the new unions generally, the death of Eleanor Marx and the emergence of the Labour Party. The period 1890–1906 in Britain was also marked by the waxing and waning of May Day events across much of the country.

In Germany internal changes in the workers' movement were similar responses to these changes. In 1890 the SPD saw its dominant position being rivalled and contested both by a grassroots movement and by the general committee of the trade unions. The SPD went back on the offensive and in 1895 defined the First of May as a 'day of celebration and struggle'. Then, in the following year, at the Congress of Gotha, it declared that general leisure was the most dignified form of the First of May. In 1905 May Days were the occasion for general strikes (inspired by the Russian model and not the French one) and, from 1907, the First of May was at the centre of discussions concerning the general strike. This was to such an extent that the party decided, the following year, to set aside funds so as to be able to face widespread lockouts following the First of May. In this way they were going beyond the limits of a trade unionism which could only guarantee economic support to workers on strike when the conflicts were limited to one town, one region or one branch of industry.

In Belgium, on the contrary, it was the reversal of the political situation which led to changes. The parliamentary elections of 1894 gave 20 per cent of the vote to the POB. This party therefore tried to defuse the revolutionary potential of the First of May. Its congress of 1895 decided to ask school, factories and local government to close their doors that day and proposed a law aiming to make May Day a public holiday (with the lack of success already indicated). The POB then adopted the initial choices of the SPD and gave its principal support to the celebratory forms of action which, in Belgium, were an alternative to the great religious celebrations. Structured around the Maisons du Peuple, they owed most to the support of cooperatives which had much stronger resources than the trade union movements until the First World War. Their funds were very important in supporting the blossoming of artistic production which placed the event in the workers' subculture, as in Germany. May Day events spread, often being manifested in processions (at least in Ghent and in Brussels). This evolution did not in any way signify the disappearance of strikes, but the combative element of the First of May was thereafter subordinated to its celebratory aspect.

The prevailing social reformism and the incompleteness of political reform led to the pragmatic and social-democratic model and to the construction of subcultures which were to dominate in Germany and in Belgium. The control which each of the parties exercised over organisations of other sorts, and in particular trade unions, allowed these parties to accept and support the strikes which they had initially rejected in principle, and they did this by integrating them into their own strategies.

In France, these changes resulted from the state's attitude as much from developments within the workers' movement. The *guesdistes'* decisions had been conditioned by their confidence in the state to intervene and by willingness to operate within the framework of democratic liberties (or assumed liberties, such as the right to demonstrate). However, the republican state disappointed them. On one level, its commitment to economic liberalism prevented it from satisfying the demands which were addressed to it. On another level, the First of May 1890, although dominated politically by the *guesdistes*, was the occasion for a powerful strike movement which continued beyond the agreed date. In 1891 May Day, without particular dramatic strengths, reflected the division of French socialism and presented a very large diversity of local situations, but the scale of the strikes at the previous First of May led, for weeks, to fears and worries (even outside France). The employers feared that the strikes would be renewed and called in the troops. The state, which had tolerated the processions in 1890, banned them. It held that such mass processions with petitions were illegal now that each citizen was free to express himself through the ballot box. Thus the state satisfied the bosses' demands.

The French state, which was, in its way, one of the makers of the resolution of 1889, became in practice the archetype of the repressive state until 1905 when the Tsarist regime took up the baton. The workers' movement, which had counted on parliamentary legality, took up a strategy which, at its most radical, constituted the rejection of parliamentary legality; though this was after some time.

The *guesdistes* who had emerged victorious from the elections of 1893, remained alert to the warnings and subordinated the First of May to the needs of electoral campaigns each time that the two calendars coincided (which was frequent). Their position, contested from 1890 and 1891, was damaged when the concept of the general strike was victorious at the fifth congress of the Federation of Trade Unions in

1892. The division of the workers' movement, however, was such that the decision had no effects which were immediately felt on the First of May, which for many years did not have again the connotation which had led to so much strike action in 1890 (strikes organised during the week which preceded or followed the First of May). Perhaps we should see also in the 1892 decision a riposte to the repression at Fourmies (where troops fired salvos at demonstrators, killing nine young people and wounding a further ten, on 1 May 1891).[3]

The change only took place decisively when, in 1905 and 1906, the CGT decided to constitute the day as a test of a general strike, with the effect of returning to a strike environment greater than that of 1890. Simultaneously the CGT accused the Congress of Paris of having perverted the idea of First of May and henceforth aimed to follow the path of the American May Days and the Martyrs of Chicago. It mobilised the memory of Fourmies to a greater degree than that of preceding years and gave its propaganda an anti-militarist connotation. This was nothing less than the hi-jacking of the May Day heritage, facilitated by the fact that the socialist parties, who were perpetually trying to redefine themselves, ceased from 1895 to consider the First of May as a priority and that mobilisation of support for it – certainly neither negligible and multiform – had become the major local initiative within the ranks of the organisers of a number of trade unions. The impetus given to the First of May by the CGT leadership thereafter permitted a better national unification of propaganda and action, and the stabilisation of the forms of the First of May was accompanied by more uniformity between regions.

The Republican state therefore owes to its political reformism both its lack of social reform and its occasional repressive interventions and these in turn helped produce both the petitions and the general strike which were antipathetic to it. The early effects of May Days were at the symbolic level: the will to distance themselves from the dominant symbolism reflected by the repressive forces in France and the early invention of symbols specifying universalist class principles (the red flag and the song, the Internationale).

The characteristics of the First of May depend therefore on the nature of the state and the characteristics of its reformism more than on the relationship between the party and the the trade unions. The dominance of the unions ensured the absence of strikes in Great Britain and, in contrast, the principle of the general strike in France. Conversely, political dominance did not exclude strikes either in Belgium or in Germany. It allowed the political parties to integrate strikes into political strategies to which strikes were subordinate (mass political strikes, general strikes with political aims).

A unifying principle

A diversity of modes of action is recognised today by the historian, but not by contemporaries who had no external means to appreciate a system of representation (in the form of images, songs and so on) which was deliberately unifying. International unification had been attained, at least in the imagination of participants.

This unification was included as a constitutional matter in the directives of the Congress of Paris which aimed to unite all the 'workers of the worlds', thus giving a shape to the working class beyond differing nationalities. The subsequent broadening of the objectives of the First of May to socialism and peace on the same level as the eight-hour day, which was the initial basis, gave a more explicit political character to that day. It set out perspectives which required, and indeed encouraged, the extension of the national framework and constituted the working class as a major subject of international history.

This internationalist message constituted a strong idea everywhere, and workers rarely opposed it in order to remain on a purely national basis. This internationalist will was generally set out in the manifestos of the national sections but it was also obvious in the choice of references. By including in the tragic repertoire of the First of May certain national events or, indeed, local events (the French Revolution, the Commune, the Chicago Martyrs, Fourmies) they highlighted the link between the national and the international.

The same pertains to the cultural practices and productions linked to the First of May. Hence the use of the Red Flag, the presence of internationalism in songs, the adoption of national songs in the international repertory (the *Marseillaise*, the *Carmagnole*), the invitation of foreign militants to national meetings, the reminder of the international character of the First of May in slogans and in speeches, along with the carnival floats which made up part of the processions, are all signs of this determination to underline the international orientation of the day.

This international dimension allowed the participants to increase the power of any action which was associated with the First of May, giving it greater meaning, even if it took on apparently anodyne forms. But this is not the essential point.

Eric Hobsbawm has underlined that the Congress of Paris would have only been one meeting among many if it had been reduced simply to its conclusions and its explicit decisions.[4] What explains the success and the permanence of the day, he has written, are less its officially articulated demands than the fruits of an unplanned evolution: 'The extraordinary thing about the evolution of this institution is that it was unintended and unplanned. To this extent it was not so much an "invented tradition" as a suddenly erupting one.'⁵ The festive elements, as well as the strike, contributed to the transcending of national divisions and to their integration into universal concepts which subsumed them and which they helped to construct.

Eric Hobsbawm admitted the religious connotations of the First of May but considered that the convergences between the two were minimal except where Protestantism took the form of sects which were unofficial and oppositional, rather than part of the established Church, as notably the case in Great Britain.⁶ The question, he asked, was rather to explain why religious models had so little influence even in countries where religion remained dominant. He did emphasise, however, a major borrowing from the religious practices: the idea of having a feast day (implying the equal rights of every individual to have his or her feast). The First of May, he reminded us, was in fact the only successful attempt to create a national holiday outside the religious calendar (being officially recognised in 107 states in 1990), and the opponents of this have regularly tried to subvert this date. It is distinguished from all other such festive days in that it commemorates nothing, and deals with nothing, other than the future.

One could attribute this 'eruption' of the feast to the pre-existence of this social occasion as already inscribed in popular culture as the May of the folklorists. But if the 'multi-coloured custom' really facilitated the transplanting and implanting of the First of May in areas which were barely industrialised and urbanised, it could not play a determining role in the industrial and urban bastions which were the centres of the main thrust of the movement. Moreover, we have found only a few explicit traces (in France) of such underlying feasts and residual practices. In contrast, one can postulate that the image of Maria Blondeau killed at Fourmies while she carried the flowering branch of May contributed to the re-evaluation of practices about to disappear but which nevertheless were present in the collective unconscious of a population that had often only recently been transplanted from a rural milieu. In this way was provoked the reactivation of an imagination which was capable of integrating itself into the image of the First of May. (The direct references to folklore could therefore be expressed in the 1930s, with profound changes to the cultural context.)

It is essential to have recourse to other sources in order to explain this 'eruption' of the popular festival. It was an eruption which was too general even if it did take on diverse forms, to result solely from national determinants, as has previously been shown. Whether the German term, *feiern*, signifies *chômer* (to be employed) as well as *fêter* (to celebrate) in French could well provide a key to the whole problem. The strikes organised on the First of May gave substance to a small piece of freedom won by the workers themselves. The strikes were important as a symbol of emancipation while they permitted the use of a specific time and the possible alternative of a festival invented in order to oppose a comfortless capitalism. It is from this that the day can become 'a principle of hope',[7] the symbol of self-determinism of the worker who has alone appropriated a space of freedom and alone determined the forms of the festivity. This form of action presented the additional advantage of associating women and children, in contrast to many militant practices which excluded them. In particular when the festivity was postponed until Sunday, the family was not there as part of a strike.

The celebration thus understood became the occasion for the gestation of a common consciousness and a common memory. It constituted the emotion coming from politics at a time when scientism dominated everything in all socialist parties. The existence of a common martyrology elevated May Days to the dignity of holy feasts. This emotion gave body to demands which until then had remained abstract, pedagogic and ideological and thus allowed the affirmation of the primacy 'of symbol over practical reason'.[8] In this way the intellectual representation of socialism came into the street, into the hearts of men, and became tangible in this way. Internationalism in the abstract became universalism and sometimes even salvation. The First of May became, therefore, an ideal model which could bypass national frameworks, and be the means of constituting a universal approach outside of the area of intellectual concepts.

As seen by those who celebrated the First of May, the questions of the day, or of the hour and of the form of the celebration had little importance from then on, and was then merely a question of political opportunity. What was important were the social and cultural models which made this a celebration in its own right, a medium for socialist politics.

Because it was the symbolic gesture of ceasing work which transformed the First of May into something more than the initial project, it became a central element of the life of the working class and of the identity of the world of labour. But this happened only where the socialist parties and trade unions adopted the principle of the strike as the symbolism. In Great Britain, between 1890 and 1906, there was never a mass stoppage of work for the First of May, so May Days did not play this role despite a brilliant beginning. In contrast, in the three other countries, the First of May constituted a major period in the construction of a class culture capable of unifying from within each one of the states because it could unify across frontiers. This culture borrowed from the dominant forms of political sociability as much as it did from each of the national cultures.

In France, the French Revolution and its symbols were at one and the same time models and countermodels. In Belgium religion played the same role. The First of May was placed there under the sign of salvation, of renewal and, indeed, of religious ardour. In its songs and its poems, the First of May was represented as a modern Messiah who brings to the suffering man (working man) comfort and hope. People prayed to the God of work. It follows from this that there were considerable similarities between the celebrations of May Day and Catholic celebratory days. The procession served as a model, but the general socialist demonstrations were more combative. The meaning of the First of May had to be acquired from early childhood exactly like the Catholic religion. The socialists also clad themselves on May Days in their Sunday best. The tension was nevertheless permanent between religious ardour and anti-clericalism. Criticisms were formulated against the Church even though the critics utilised its vocabulary to announce the earthly paradise, while Catholic festive days were denounced as days of enforced unemployment with no significance whatsoever. The most criticised festive days were those which, like the carnival, were likely to give rise to excess. In the eyes of the labour movement, these made even more manifest the scandal of the failure to recognise the First of May as a public holiday. This religious dimension is found in Germany, in the vocabulary and in the concepts used. The future (of which the eight-hour day is only one aspect) is there as well, with comparisons to the promised land. Finally, Italian immigrants in France who organised their own festive days, continue to hold the First of May as 'the Passover of the workers'.

In Germany, the language which was used in the cultural and symbolical productions prepared for the occasion often took their source in the lyrical treasures of the nineteenth century and dated back to the French Revolution, to Wormärz and the revolution of 1848–49. The First of May was, in addition, related to the popular feasts and customs of Germany. The German festive tradition and Christianity's attempt to destroy it were compared to the attack made by reactionary forces on the social-democrat festive occasions. While making allusion to the expulsion of the winter feasts in the German May feasts, the social-democratic version found it easy to transform spring into a metaphor for progress which triumphs over the winter of reaction. These Aryan myths are much more rarely present in the Belgian cultural output.

This national ingredient does not constitute an obstacle to the emergence of unificatory images. Because of various conflicts, France took on at an early stage the development of symbolic internationalist expressions from the revolutionary symbolism of 1789, but that very symbolism of 1789 continued to circulate in the three other countries (Marianne, the Phrygian bonnet and the *Marseillaise*). In Belgium, for example, the First of May took on invariably the figure of Marianne, the young, beautiful, woman with blonde hair under a Phrygian bonnet winged and clothed in red, symbolising science, enlightenment and hope of a radiant future. The same phenomenon is seen in Great Britain where the symbols of the American revolution and the Commune of Paris were mobilised simultaneously. As a counterpart, in these countries internationalist symbolism was adopted somewhat later: the international dimension was recognised for the first time in 1898 at Armentières in France whilst the *Marseillaise* remained preponderant in Belgium until 1906.

Religious references circulated similarly and widely throughout Europe, without totally sparing France. Everything was unified by aesthetics. In Belgium artists who participated in the development of May Day cultural productions were linked to art nouveau, to naturalism, to symbolism or to monumental art. In Germany, from 1900 onwards, new contributors to such work all belonged to controversial tendencies – notably the Jugendstil symbolism or German impressionism. In Great Britain the figures of William Morris and especially Walter Crane were deeply important. The works produced by Walter Crane were reproduced in Italy, Germany, Belgium and elsewhere.

But unity came especially from a common symbolic fund of different means of representation. Speeches given in the period were full of references to nature. If, for the most part, it was a question of a simple and naive lyricism, a number of texts at least established a link between the renewal of nature, the rise of the spring sap and the awakening of the proletariat. This comparison allows us also to reach a myth, although it could by hypothesised that this myth was less widespread in France than in other states.

Everywhere and equally, the feminine allegory dominated until the beginning of the twentieth century. At that time it was swept aside in certain countries by masculine figures symbolising liberation. In France from 1902 onwards it gave way to a male worker with naked torso or to the crowd led by its leaders (sometimes with women in small numbers appearing in the riot pictures of the 1890s). In Belgium there emerged, alongside Marianne, the masculine worker symbolising the socialist proletariat. This figure, often a blacksmith with a leather apron and hammer in one hand, spread a calm assurance and a virile force. He stood in opposition to the worker bending under the capitalist yoke.

Work occupied an equally important place. In Belgium it sometimes was represented and exalted as a god, constituted as a factor of nobility and not as a fruit of divine curse. It would not be revealed, however, as a source of all riches except with the arrival of socialism. The system of representation was finally, everywhere, strongly dichotomised. The worker was contrasted with the lazy idler and the capitalist, often presented as a leech, work was contrasted to non-work, the poor person to the rich person, privation to excess, the slave to the master, ignorance to knowledge and so on. There was one nuance which needs to be introduced. If capitalism (the capitalist) and money were everywhere designed as the target, they were more and more systematically associated in France to the state and to its repressive and oppressive apparatus from the beginning of the twentieth century.

The political impact of May Day (understood in the broadest sense), therefore, lay especially in its ability to generate everywhere myths in favour of which the part can affirm itself as an indivisible element of the whole. May Day was therefore the occasion of a unity which could be called mythical and which was attained in imaginary, across even a diversity of, modes of action. The First of May dominated in effect only through unifying in favour of the diversity of symbols and practices which were mobilised from their insertion in national cultures, local cultures and the branches of industry which determined them. This diversity permitted its richness and its meaning, its vivacity, its elasticity and constituted a major trump card. It was only in Britain where homogeneity of forms seemed to be the greatest that this mythical dimension appears to have been the most weak.

With the exception of Britain, the formation of myths took on two principal aspects. In Germany, as in Belgium, the first May Days highlighted one or two major issues and also had an impact on the relationships between socialist parties and the trade unions. In Belgium May Day constituted the catalytic element which unleashed the general strike for the achievement of universal suffrage in 1890. In Germany it favoured the unification of the unions at the national level. The trade unions, although constituted in central societies, did not then have any experience of a generalised action and it was during the preparation of the First of May that workers attempted for the first time to develop identical demands in different places, branches of industry and among workers of different skills. Committees were formed in numerous towns in order to coordinate action, so one notable consequence of the strike was the constitution of general committees of trade unionists. After this date the characteristics of the First of May depended directly on the nature and preferences of the socialist parties, and their autonomy, effectively, was principally cultural. It is through and within the cultural area that myths were constructed.

Here, unification operated above all in eschatology, iconography, songs and pictures. Cultural productions which drew from the utopian and poetic potential of the socialist movement and revealed that potential were probably the best expression of the future to which the workers aspired. The general strike, which was one of the elements of the political arsenal of May Days, could not give identity to myths in the same way as it could in revolutionary syndicalism once it had been subordinated to a political strategy.

In France the autonomy of the First of May in relation to the organisational structures of the workers' movements and its capacity to become an active principle was, for a long time, stronger than elsewhere. This was due to the slow structural development of the workers' movements and their fragmentary character as well as to the small size of their membership.

The First of May released the powerful movement of strikes in favour of the eight-hour day in 1890 and then in 1905 and 1906. It rediscovered this role of a catalyst in 1919. It was also significant as it came to provide training in peaceful demonstrations (with increased tolerance on the part of authorities, with the exception of Paris, from 1896 onwards) and often locally constituted one of the means of constructing unity on the left. Celebrations, meetings, processions of certain Bourses du Travail and of some local authorities became an often unique occasion for bringing together various trade union branches and a variety of socialist bodies. After the institutionalisation of the antagonism between the CGT and the SFIO in 1905–06, a number of May Days still retained this unificatory character at a local level. Given these probable local effects, more local May Day celebrations should be studied.

It was through the practice of May Days that the myth was developed. The image of the glorious future became confused with the myth of the general strike (itself a strategy). Cultural output was less prolific in France than in Belgium and Germany. Is there a link between cause and effect? In this country, where proletarian culture was always a marginal phenomenon, symbolic production took on a characteristic which was clearly more populist. It was based on talented cartoonists who belonged very much to the populist current and not to the *avant garde*. This primacy of practice can throw some light on to one curious feature in the symbolism used: until 1906 red flowers, of whatever type, were dominant and the lily of the valley was a minority phenomenon. In France, at the turn of the century, you could, however, much more easily adopt the lily of the valley – though white – because the First of May was linked to the general strike. By affirming in action one's class and giving symbolic, if not superficial, expression, one responded to the needs of the situation.

Conclusion

The workers' organisations' preferences for taking particular forms of action on May Days determined the characteristics of May Day in each country. However, within countries there were great variations in different towns and cities both of activity and of levels of support. At this level popular and workers' cultures were very important: these involved local culture and the culture of branches of industry or organisations – cultures which, above all, were non-national or, in the case of the strike, transnational. Workers' culture changed into class culture and constituted the myths by which that class affirmed its vocation to emancipate humanity and internationalism became its body, or perhaps its soul. This powerful determinant was only transnational because it was built on the basis of common representations of work and its future. If not class representations, then they were at least social ones. That this emancipation from local determinants was never achieved except in the sphere of the imagination does not signify the uselessness of its external achievements, unless by denying the myths we are at the same time denying the ethical principles as well as the action.

Notes

1. Gottfried Korff, 'Volkskultur und Arbeitkultur. Überlegungen am Beispiel der sozialistischen Maifesttradition', *Geschichte und Gesellschaft*, 5, 1979, pp. 83–102.
2. Emperor Louis Napoleon had been defeated by the Prussians at Sedan in 1870.
3. Madeleine Rebérioux, *Fourmies et les premier mai*, Paris: L'Atelier, 1994.
4. E. J. Hobsbawm, 'Birth of a holiday: the First of May', in C. J. Wrigley and J. Shepherd (eds), *On the Move*, London: Hambledon, 1991, pp. 104–22 (at pp. 106–7).
5. Ibid., p. 106. See also E. J. Hobsbawm, 'Mass producing tradition: Europe, 1870–1914', in E. J. Hobsbawm and T. Ranger (eds), *The Invention of Tradition*, Cambridge: Cambridge University Press, pp. 263–307 (at pp. 283–6).
6. Hobsbawm, 1991, 'Birth of a holiday', pp. 115–18.
7. The title of a book by Ernest Bloch quoted by E. J. Hobsbawm: 'it represents ... The Principle of Hope; the hope of a better future in a better world.' (ibid. p. 122).
8. Ibid., p. 109.

Bibliography

Achten, U. (ed.) (1980), *Zum Lichte empor, Mai-Festzeitungen der Sozialdemokratie, 1891–1914*, Berlin.

Boll, F. (1992), *Arbeitskämpfe und Gewerkschaften in Deutschland, England und Frankreich, Ihre Entwicklung vorn 19 zum 20 Jahrhundert*, Bonn.

Boll, F. (1994), 'Aspects internationaux du premier 1er Mai 1890: le case de l'Allemagne', in M. Rebérioux (ed.), *Fourmies et les premier mai*, Paris, pp. 371–81.

Bouvier, B. W. (1995), 'Es wird kommen der Mai ... Zu Ikonographie des Arbeitermai im Kaiserreich', in I. Marssolek, T. Schelz-Brandenburg, *Demokratischer Sozialismus und sozialistische Theorie*, Bonn.

Brécy, R. (1981), 'Les chansons du 1er Mai', *Revue d'histoire moderne et contemporaine*, 3, pp. 393–432.

Brécy, R. (1994), *Florilège de la chanson révolutionnaire de 1789 au Front Populaire*, Paris.

De Beule, N. (1985), 'Juichen en zingen op grootse wijze', in *De rode verleiding. Een eeuw socialistische affiches*, 2 vols, Ghent.

Dommanget, M. (1953), *Histoire du 1er Mai*, Paris.

Foner, P. S. (1986), *May Day: A Short History of the International Workers' Day*, New York.

Hobsbawm, E. J. (1991), 'Birth of a Holiday: The First of May', in C. J. Wrigley and J. Shepherd (eds), *On the Move*, London.

Hobsbawm, E. J. (1984), *Worlds of Labour*, London.

Korff, G. (1979), 'Volkskultur und Arbeiterkultur. Überlegungen am Beispiel des sozialistischen Maifesttradition', *Geschichte und Gesellschaft*, 5, pp. 83–102.

Fricke, D. (1980), *Kleine Geschichte des Ersten Mai*, Frankfurt.

Liébin, J. (1994), 'La grève générale dans les bassins miniers wallons et les événements de Fourmies', in M. Rebérioux (ed.), *Fourmies et les premier mai*, Paris.

Marssolek, K. (ed.) (1990), *100 Jahre Zukunft. Zur Geschichte des 1 Mai*, Frankfurt.

Panaccione, A. (ed.) (1989), *The Memory of May Day: An Iconographic History of the Origins and Implanting of a Workers' Holiday*, Venice.

Perrot, M. (1984), 'The First of May in France', in G. Crosswick and P. Thane (eds), *The Power of the Past. Essays for Eric Hobsbawm*, Cambridge.

Robert, J. L. (1994), 'Autour des premiers 1er Mai en France', in M. Rebérioux (ed.), *Fourmies et les premier mai*, Paris.

Rodriguez, M. (1990), *Le 1er Mai*, Paris.

Rossel, A. (1990), *Le 1er Mai*, Paris.

Tartakowsky, D. (1994), 'Enjeux et dimensions politiques du 1er mai: Internationales et 1er Mai', in M. Rebérioux (ed.), *Fourmies et les premier mai*, Paris.

Tendfelde, K. (1987), 'Die Entstehung der deutschen Gewerkschaftsbewegung vom Vormirz bis zum Ende des Sozialistengesetzes', in U. Borsdorf (ed.), *Geschichte der Deutschen Gewerkschaften. Von den Anfängen bis 1945*, Cologne.

Van Goethem, G. (1990), *De roos op de revers. Geillustreerde geschiedenis van 1 Mei in België*, Ghent.

Verbruggen, P. (1991), 'Deelaiternatieven voor de traditionele golsdienstbeleving in het Gentse socialisme. Een bijdrage tot de geschiedenis van de arbeiderscultuur', *Tijdschrift voor sociale geschiedenis*, 17, pp. 425–8.

Wrigley, C. J. (1990), 'Il I maggio del 1890 e del 1891 in Gran Bretagna', in A. Panaccione (ed.), *I Luoghi E I Soggetti Del I Maggio*, Venice.

Wrigley, C. J. (1990), 'May Day and After', *History Today*, London.

100 jaar 1 Mei. De geschiedenis van een strjddag, Antwerp, 1990.

CHAPTER SEVEN

Workers, others and the state: a comparison of the discourse of the French, German and British labour movements at the end of the nineteenth century

Antoine Prost and Manfred Bock

Comparisons between trade unionism in the major Western European countries generally emphasise the differences in their attitudes towards the state, and more generally, towards political action. Roughly speaking, we are used to juxtaposing French direct action, independent of political parties and against a dialogue with the state, with British trade unionism, determined to enter Parliament in order to defend its interests, and even more with German trade unionism, so much a part of social democracy as to appear at times as one of the party's dependencies.

These distinctions, while frequently cited, have yet to be explained. To do so requires the examination of as large a set as possible of social and political representations in which attitudes towards the state and a more general trade union discourse are expressed. Certainly, many other factors are relevant to this discussion, notably the legal framework which delimits the space in which trade unionism can operate. But it is essential to investigate the different forms in which British, French and German trade unionism draw upon social and political representations. We need to discover what images and ideas workers constructed about themselves, about their adversaries, their conflicts, their sense of politics. Only through such an investigation can we clarify the assumptions which underlie workers' organisations in these three countries.

The problem is how to identify the social and political representations of trade unionists at the end of the nineteenth century. If we examine their discourse on the surface – that is, if we ask simply what they wanted to say and what they explicitly argued – we will rediscover what we already know about their attitudes towards the state and towards politics more generally. For that reason, we have decided to abjure straightforward reading of trade union texts, in favour of another emphasis – on the words they used and on the constellations of associations and oppositions they created.

Surprisingly, this kind of 'linguistic turn' is rather infrequent. The interest in a linguistic approach has led American historians to deal with historians' writings and criticise their claim to objectivity.[1] They did not consider historical sources as linguistic material. Some social historians of the British working class paid attention to languages and words. Careful analysis of what people had actually said drew new perspectives on this history that replaced previous interpretations. But, although pointing at 'the materiality of language itself',[2] they did not investigate the linguistic structure of historical documents with linguistic methods.

Is it possible to study languages without linguistics? It is clear that any sentence, any discourse, is preformed and predetermined by the structures of language. These structures are *prefigurative*, as White would say: once given a vocabulary, with all its relations of opposition/substitution, with its semantical structure, grammar rules and so on, the set of sentences one can form is defined. Linguistic framework defines the limits of representations; words prefigure wordings. Hence, to explore this lexicon or to enter these semantic fields are ways of reconstructing mental universes, of drawing into the political and social arena precise pictures of representations which are at stake. Such methods represent an interesting means to obtain new kinds of historical evidence.[3] However, before presenting the principal results of our enquiry, it is necessary to explain how it has been conducted.

Method

Themes and sources

The principal problem in such research is in constituting a corpus of texts for analysis. Once chosen, such texts, inevitably limited in scope and number, provide the material from which a set of conclusions are drawn. The assumption is that two researchers working on the same evidence and using the same methods will arrive at the same conclusion.

To make such a comparison work the evidence chosen must be rigorously comparable. But this is unlikely for two reasons. The first, common to all historical research, is the haphazard availability and conservation of sources. But in this instance a second problem arises – very different trade union movements produce very different texts. The weakest of the three, the French labour movement hardly had a labour press to speak of. For that reason, we had to search for its voice in the Republican press, in *La Petite République*, for example. The German labour movement was much richer in publications of all kinds, including a wide variety of poetry. The strong links between trade unions and the Social Democratic party open the party's press to our analysis. But in the French case, with the exception of the *guesdiste* tendency, or in the British case, where the Labour party did not exist prior to 1900, such material is unavailable. We can remedy this gap in the British case by reference to the literature of friendly societies, associations without direct parallels in the other two countries.

It is thus impossible to construct a body of evidence which is strictly comparable. The differing structures of trade unions in the three countries produced different sources. Strictly speaking, a German text is only comparable to a French or British text if they are produced under similar conditions; if that is not the case, then distinctions arise from context and not from differences in social representations.

Taken to such lengths, a scrupulous methodology leads to the dead end of affirming that the comparison of differing social situations is impossible. But it is precisely because they are different that it is important to compare them. Better to defy the objection of logic than to be enslaved by it. For that reason we have tried pragmatically to constitute a relatively comparable corpus of materials. We admit readily to a compromise between a scientifically rigorous enquiry and one governed by the nature of the sources produced by very different trade union movements. The justification for the compromise is to be found in the objectives of the study – to comprehend workers' social representations. With Alain Touraine, we can distinguish, in the visions of workers, a principle of identity, a principle of opposition, and a principle of totality. Working-class consciousness coheres around these notions: a self-representation, that is, a representation of who are workers; a representation of their adversaries, employers or property-owners; and a representation of what is at stake in their conflicts.

These are the clusters of representations which we need to reconstruct: workers' sense of their own identity, of their opponents, and that of the conflict between the two. But which texts will disclose these representations? The most interesting seem to be those built into polemics, because the notions of 'us' and 'them' are implicit in confrontations. We therefore have sought three types of text: those centring on strikes or on working-class action; those concerning the law; and those dealing more generally with politics and society, in which we can find indications of the field of conflict on which workers and employers face each other.

To organise the body of texts on these three themes, we first need to recognise two sets of distinctions. The first arises from situations of communication, and requires us to consider speeches, articles, motions and tracts. Speeches and articles offer a contrast as between the spoken and the written, but they are both the products of a single voice: someone speaks, and we know who it is. Motions and tracts, in contrast, are distinguished by their collective voices: they are frequently anonymous texts, deliberately so in order to better speak for an organisation. But the motion arises out of the statutory deliberations of a group, whereas the tract concerns the action it pursues. This second distinction refers to different levels of the work of organisations: national or local, professional or not. Naturally, the combination of these distinctions is not always pertinent. On the local level, it is rare to find both minutes of discussions and motions; these texts are more abundant at a higher level of labour organisation. Conversely, at the higher levels, tracts are rare, since action is usually decentralised. But we were able to find calls for national action which mix the voice of the tract and the motion.

With these distinctions in mind, we searched for sources which could illuminate the three kinds of representations we have outlined above. But there the real problems emerged. Without discussing them in greater detail, it may be useful to point out the main difficulties at this point. First, it was evident that the German material was dominated by issues of organisation. Around 1895, the German trade union movement engaged in a broad discussion of its structures, whether centralised or federal, and of its functions, whether as units of struggle or as associations of aid and mutual support. Time and again they discussed their relationship with the party. The German material includes texts published in the socialist press, parallel to those found in the *guesdiste* press, which while not fully representative of the French workers' movement, is one of its main components.[4] The French material is thus more heterogeneous, and must include varied material, including those produced by Pelloutier.[5] It is both more interested in theoretical debates, on the general strike or political action for example, and more sensitive to local political and social situations. It discusses local strikes and debates arising from the organising commission of the London Congress of the Second International of 1896 which denied membership to those who abjured political activity, defined as action directed towards the ultimate conquest of political power by the vote. To this body of material we can add strike posters, though only in the British case can we add texts preparing strike activity and calling for solidarity before the outbreak of hostilities. The British material is more limited;[6] aside from conference reports, it includes local addresses sent for discussion by the whole trade union. The subjects treated are much more practical, many concerning the situation of the labour market.

One must not exaggerate, however, the differences among these three collections of sources. They all address similar subjects: for instance, the First of May. Moreover, the object of this analysis is to investigate the structure of their terminology, the language employed and the vocabulary used to describe the subjects raised, not their content. Behind the vocabulary of these discourses we try to discover the organisation of meaning which defines what can be said. Through the analysis of the contents of these documents, and their different thematic emphases, linguistic analysis enables us to uncover more fundamental structures of thought and meaning.

Method of analysis

We have tried to avoid adopting a method of analysis that is either too sophisticated or too elaborate; our objective is historical rather than linguistic.[7] Trade union or socialist discourse in France has been analysed in a substantial literature, reflecting different approaches and different methodologies. The laboratory of political lexicology at Saint-Cloud has developed techniques for scanning of texts and frequency analysis, enabling us to engage in elaborate statistical tests, factor analysis, or the study of singularities.[8] Although this laboratory has digitised a body of French texts, permitting the systematic study of particular terms, we have not engaged in such statistical work. The varied texts in our study are of such different lengths that distortions are inevitable in a strict application of these mathematical tools.

We therefore limited our study to the systematic comparison of specific terms in our texts which seem to be crucial to their semantic and lexical organisation – what is termed in French linguistics 'analyse de discours à entrée lexicale'. Take, for example, a term such as *ouvrier* or *Arbeiter*. We have constructed a table listing all sentences in which this term appears, and have identified clusters of terms which are associated positively or negatively with it. We are interested both in the frequency of usage (evident from the table) and the linguistic field in which the term is included.

Unfortunately, the German and British texts have not yet been digitised. This meant that the frequency of the appearance of particular words was registered laboriously through direct reading, which reduces the systematic character of the exercise. This distinction requires us to limit any claims arising from this simple exercise in the comparative linguistic analysis of the discourse of labour movements in the past.

Despite these problems, the exercise has produced some instructive results.

Workers' terms for self-reference

The first striking finding is the greater frequency of usage of self-referential terms than of terms designating workers' adversaries. References to workers outnumber those referring to employers or the bourgeoisie in general. Many of these texts are appeals, calling on workers to unionise or to demonstrate, for example on 1 May. That is why we find a large number of salutations and direct appeals at the head of a text or in its final sentences. Out of these forms, on both sides of the Rhine, emerged the vocabulary of camaraderie – *camarades* in France more frequently than *Genossen* in Germany, where the term of filiation was sometimes more precise, for example, *Parteigenossen*, *Berufsgenossen*. There are national specificities. In Germany the term *Kollegen* was frequently used, whereas we have identified only three appearances of the same term in French texts, and each usage is different. Twice in the same text where *collègues* designated members of the leading group of an organisation, and once in another text, where it is associated with *citoyen* – *citoyens* and *collègues*.

'Citizen' is not used in German texts, no doubt because German workers had yet to achieve the full rights of citizenship. The German equivalent of *citoyens* and *collègues* would be *Genossen* and *Kollegen*, terms which present the two faces of a community defined both politically and professionally. In France, in contrast, 'citizen' is frequently used, notably seven times by Pelloutier in a series of articles, in the form of *citoyens délégués*. The term seems to have preserved the egalitarian connotations of citizen's address established during the French Revolution. It remained active, even though not as active as the reference to *camarade*, which features 21 times as opposed to nine for *citoyen*, if we exclude Pelloutier's long textwhich doubles its frequency.[9]

In Britain, the two equivalent terms – *comrade* and *citizen* – are not used, at least in our texts. The way one addressed trade unionists was by saying *worthy brothers*, or occasionally (and more formally) *gentlemen*. When referring to a trade union official, French workers used *citoyen* or *camarade N*, whereas the English speak of *Brother N* or in the abbreviated form *bro. N*. The English term closest to *camarade* is *fellow*, often associated with other terms: for example, *fellow man, fellow-delegates* or *fellow signalmen*.

But the real originality of French usage is the reference to *travailleur*, either singular or plural, in salutations or closing remarks. This points to clear differences among the three languages in the terms conventionally used to designate those who socially were members of the trade union.

German uses one family of terms, derived from *Arbeit*, or *work*. The most frequent term used to designate a working-class group is *Arbeiter* (employed 60 times), but we also encounter terms derived from this noun, such as *Arbeiterschaft* (working-class collective) or, more frequently (26 uses), *Arbeiterbewegung* (labour movement). Our texts refer to *Arbeiter*, either *organized* or *class-conscious, without possessions, oppressed, without rights, dominated or exploited.*

The English use two roots for words designating work: *labour* and *work*. The first is used more generically, and refers to all workers. It is relatively frequently used, though it is not linked to more general terms in the way that *travail* leads to *travailleur* in French. In English a labourer is someone entirely different – an unskilled labourer. Conversely, *work* is not used directly, but words derived from *work* are abundant: *workers*, the most frequent, but always in the plural; the singular *worker* is less frequent than *working man*. The collective term reserved to designate the group of workers in the same trade is *workpeople*, as in *to pay his workpeople*, while *working class* refers to a social condition per se. These terms are used most frequently to designate the specific working-class group, though (no doubt referring to a shipyard or naval context) other terms are used, such as *men* or *hands*.

The French use two apparently synonymous terms: *ouvrier* and *travailleur*. In reality, the terms are different. The proper address among comrades or colleagues is *Travailleurs!*, and not *Ouvriers!* This latter term refers to particular workers: those employed at the arsenals, or workers *at Niort*, the *painting workers in the building trades*, unskilled workers in a particular enterprise. Of 38 usages of the term *ouvrier*, 22 referred to particular workers, and the others referred to particular situations: the workers *who had finished their day's work*, or a worker *returning home*. In contrast, *travailleur* refers to a group, defined by its solidarity and common condition. The term *travailleur* is much more frequently used: we noted 72 occurrences, including nine usages of direct address already cited. This term is clearly the most widely used by workers to designate their corporate identity.

In France the term *Classe ouvrière* is little used, certainly more rarely than in Germany or in Great Britain. But simple comparisons can be misleading, since the German language permits the use of complex words which do not exist in French or in English. In German (but not in French or in English) one may speak of the state of being in a class *Klassenstaat*; workers can be referred to as *klassenbewusst*, or being class-conscious; similar constructions cannot be found in French or English texts about class struggle.

The notion of class is certainly present, since we encounter here or there references to class enemies or adversaries, and the term itself is based on a notion of irreducible antagonism. And of what are *class-conscious* workers, present in France and Germany, though not in Great Britain, conscious of, if not of class stmggle?[10] Whatever the case, the expression 'class struggle' appears to be absent from the French material and even more so from the British.

The terms *proletarian* and *proletariat* are used relatively frequently on the Continent, but not in Britain. After *Arbeiter* in Germany and *travailleur* in France, the terms *proletarian* and *proletariat* are the most commonly used. The term *proletariat* is juxtaposed in almost every instance either to class adversaries (*patronat*) or to the state (control of which the proletariat must seize). The term has an international element, present in universalist references: *prolétariat du monde entier, universel* or *international*. In a way, the message of Marx's *Manifesto* of 1848 became a redundancy, a repetitive phrase: the proletariat is the body of proletarians of all countries in so far as they are unified.

In French, we also find words which designate labour through substantive adjectives: *exploited* appears seven times, as do other adjectives or past participles: *oppressed; suffering; miserable* (one appearance each). *Victims* and *producers* appear twice each. In German the most common adjectives are *oppressed* and *poor*. British trade unionists, in contrast, rarely use adjectives; there are exceptions – the *poor and distressed* designate those they defend.

The peculiarity of British texts is the use, in the singular or the plural, of the term *trade*.[11] The French equivalent, *métier*, is rare, and does not displace the term *ouvrier* in the same way as *les ouvriers du métier*. In English the term *trade* is much more frequent (53 in the singular, 29 in the plural) than *workers* (ten) and *labour* (28). It does not carry simultaneously connotations of profession (*engineering trade, building trade, printing trade*), and of trade (*our trade, the trade he belongs to*, or *the state of trade*). Building workers, for instance, *deplore bad trade and inclement weather*. 'We most earnestly hope the improvement in trade.' There are questions about '*the prospect of trade*'. The term combines not only with *union(s)* but also with *society(ies)* or organisations to designate labour associations.

The term *union* is associational too, since it gave birth to the generic term *unionism*, which surprisingly appears seven times in our evidence, where the word *syndicalisme* appears but once in the French material, although *syndicat* appears 34 times. Only in English is there a word for the non-organised – *non-unionist* – four occurrences, but none at all in French. Is it possible to conclude that the conviction that one must create a general labour movement is weaker in France than in the other two countries?

Whatever the answer to this question, it is evident that the terms designating the world of labour as a set of labour organisations is not the same in the three countries. The terms denoting the self-designation of the group in German surround *Arbeiter* and its compound words (*Arbeiterschaft* and so on); in French, the term is *travailleur*, and both use *Proletariat*; in Britain, the *proletariat* is absent, but we hear much of *trade* and *workers*. Again the differences with respect to organisations are clear: *syndicat* in France, *Arbeiterbewegung* in Germany and *trade union* in Britain, express three different social realities, the contours of which are beginning to emerge.

Designating the enemy

Here too we are in the shadow of specificities of each language. Neither English nor German has the precise equivalent of the French term *patron*, which is the most frequent designator of adversary in the French material (20 uses). The term refers to particular employers, those met in daily struggles: 12 uses are in two strike posters alone. Rarely, the term is used in the singular: the *patron* refers to his class, and we can find only five occurrences when the collective term *patronat* designates the group of employers. The term *patronal* is a bit more frequent (six occurrences, three of which are linked to *exploitation*). In short, when the French want to refer to employers as a class, they used the term *capital* and its derivatives.

Still, even the term *capital* is not very frequent (nine uses); *capitalisme* and the substantive *capitaliste*, even less so (four and two uses). The most frequent term used in this context is the adjective *capitaliste*, either as a class (five), order (two), or society (one). On this point, French and German are similar; in both languages *capital* and *capitaliste* are the terms most frequently used for labour's adversary. But in our French sample, we find the phrase *grand capital*. The British case is different from the two continental cases in having no recourse to this vocabulary. We find but one usage of the term capitalists and one of the conflict *between capital and labour*. The structured opposition of capital and labour in this discourse is not missing; it is just rare that this terminology is used.

To refer to particular employers, German uses *Unternehmer* (the entrepreneur), with its variants *Unternehmertum*, *Unternehmerwelt* and, sometimes, *Fabrikant* (usually specified, for instance as manufacturer of furniture). The English usage here is to *employers* and sometimes, to *industrialist*; the word *employeur* is rare in French as is *Arbeitgeber* in German. This latter term has none of the connotation of the French word *patron*, with its sense of authority and paternalism.

The particularity of the German texts is the centrality of terms derived from *Besitz* (property): *Besitzer*, the proprietor, the owner, and less frequently, the class of owners, or the propertied class, *die besitzende Klasse, die Besitzenden*. In French texts, *possédant* is unknown, both as a noun and as an adjective, and *possesseur* appears only twice; *propriétaire* is not used in this context. In the British texts, neither *owner* nor any other term related to property appears. Property connotes here the large domain of *landlords*. Once again we can see the evidence of a very different sensibility in Germany compared to the other two countries.

Another distinction arises when we consider expressions for domination. The German expression is to the dominant class or classes: *die Herrschenden*. In the French evidence, we find only one reference to *les classes dominantes* and six references to *dirigeant* used as an adjective or substantive. In contrast, *exploiteur* is very frequent (nine occurrences), as is *exploité* used as a substantive, to the point that we could refer to two classes – *les exploités* and *les exploiteurs*. There were terms used more rarely. In German, we find power holder, money holder, privileged, oppressor. We find too despot, torturer, or, ironically, bread-giver. In French, we find *riches* (two), *bourreau* (one), *oppresseur* (two). In contrast, *maître* implies adversary only once; the other uses of the term assign to the workers an objective – to become masters of the state or of their destinies.

In Britain, on the other hand, there is no vocabulary referring specifically to domination or to exploitation. Even the traditional word *master* appears in our texts only to connote an employers' association. Consider these distinctions: they oppose a universe where the class adversary is the possessor or the dominant class, to one in which the class adversary is the *patron* or *exploiteur*, and to a third, different from the other two, where the adversary is simply an *employer*.

But the enemy is not simply the employer. In French texts, he is also the *bourgeois* and the *bourgeoisie*. We leave the terrain of the relations of production to enter the terrain of politics – at least in the French case, since in the German materials, such terms are rare, and *bourgeois* is used only as an adjective. In the British case, the term disappears completely. In France, the use of these two terms is concentrated in the two texts of Pelloutier[12] – in which there are nine out of ten uses of *bourgeois* as a noun, two out of four of the term as an adjective, and six out of ten denoting the *bourgeoisie*. The connotations are generally political: they refer to ministers, or to the bourgeois state, or the need to get rid of the power of the bourgeoisie; they evoke the day of the battle between the bourgeois capitalists and the bourgeois socialists. Sometimes, pejorative connotations become explicit: one speaks of throwing away the overstuffed carcass of the dominant bourgeoisie. Pelloutier quotes a text of the workers' party which declares that it will not enter into elections to win a deputy's seat, and that he will abandon these seats to the *haemorrhoids* of bourgeois men; such seats are not for men like himself The bourgeoisie, is not just a class adversary due to his domination of the state; he is also and for the same reason, a repugnant, repulsive person. Moreover, one text states explicitly that 'what the worker aspires to is not to take the place of the bourgeoisie, or to create a "workers" state, but to render equality in the standards of living'.

This political argument is not general in France. Texts with a *guesdiste* leaning refer positively to municipal power or state power. One text aims to force governments to regulate hours or work and wages. We can see here the significance of the composition of the evidence. If we rely on texts reflecting rank and file discourse, such as posters or texts produced by trade union meetings, we are struck by the way politics is held in disrepute. The state is rarely present in our texts (one reference), and its organs, hardly more (two references to judges, five to justice and the police). The government is but lightly present (eight), but often used with negative connotations: *complice, renégat, réactionnaire, aux abois.* Governments are *sans scrupules et sans conscience*; it is *la bande gouvernementale qui nous opprime.* Senators are soft. References to public powers are almost always pejorative: *il n'y a rien à attendre, rien à espérer de ce qu'on appelle pompeusement 'les Pouvoirs Publics'*, or, to cite another text: *'il n'y a rien à attendre des pouvoirs publics, quelle qu'en soit la composition, le propre du pouvoir étant d'avoir des intérêts opposés à ceux des travailleurs'.*

This disgust with politics underlies a degree of indifference towards particular politicians. The term 'party' is to be found only in *guesdistes* texts and in the discussion of the rules of admission to the London Congress by Pelloutier. The only exception is the rejection of the conquest of power *au bénéfice d'un parti*. The adjective *politique* is used only in *guesdiste* texts. Elsewhere, one motion of Congress rejects all political discussion and seeks out a terrain *absolument en dehors de toute opinion politique*. The term *syndicat* is more frequent, but its use is generally in reference to the identification of the signatory or particular information, such as when one speaks on a motion to be adopted by a congress. Twice the usage is related to the question of trade union liberties, and juxtaposes political division to the trade union as a site of the unity of class: *uni à tes frères dans les syndicats et les fédérations, tu peux être invincible*. But these texts are in no sense a discussion by trade unions about their identity and work.

Here the contrast is clear with German texts, in which the troubles of organization are much more evident. This distinction arises not only from the body of evidence we have, but also from immediate German concerns. Still, the discussion of the functions of the trade union in German materials has no French equivalent. In Germany, there are discussions as to whether trade unions should limit their work to protest alone, or whether they ought to fulfil other social functions: for instance, the maintenance of unemployment insurance funds, even though the problem of retirement pay had already found a solution in Germany, not to be achieved for decades in France. There are discussions too about the relation between central and local trade union bodies. In effect, German trade unionists were more concerned with determining their own forms of organisation than were their French colleagues.

In addition, the representation of politics is very different. In the German material, references to public authorities are infrequent; they refer instead to the term *Behörde*, or authorities. There are also references to government, state, municipality and, sometimes, even ironic references to 'the representatives of the people', in inverted commas. Invariably, the authorities are on the side of the enemies of the labour movement.

It is here that we find another German specificity: the phrase 'labour movement' is very often qualified by one of two terms: 'socialist' or 'modern'. The French material never uses these qualifiers, referring instead to the 'revolutionary movement' or even to the 'socialist movement'; but when its authors speak of a movement, it always means a strike movement. There is no general term to encompass the trade union or the party or parties which, we might say, worked for the same aims.

The British evidence is entirely different. There is no reference to the state, but the government of Her Majesty is present. Here the question is the need to bring a question to '*the notice of Her Majesty's Government*'. The Parliamentary Committee of the TUC is mentioned on several occasions. There is a clear notion of the direct representation of workers in all governing bodies. These documents have a clearly deferential tone and they abjure all pejorative terms. Annual reports soberly note whether or not approaches to the government have succeeded, and if not, there is no tone of aggressiveness over the failure. One document expresses some scepticism towards legal solutions, or '*remedial legislation*'. Of course indignation is not appropriate to such reports; but such distinctions are precisely the ones we are looking for.

We must beware of possible bias in the evidence, but it still appears clear that the British evidence is overwhelmingly factual and juridical.

Steps taken are justified by reference to *trade union regulations*, the *code of rules*. The term also refers to the contractual rules governing labour in a locality, or *local rules*; for example, these refer to clauses in local rules barring non-union labour. The interests of the trade are treated as subjects to be discussed before a tribunal. The British evidence suggests that danger is to be found among employers and judges they control, rather than from the government. Here is the origin of their opposition to *judge-made law* and *the statute law of the nation*. Trade union struggles are aimed to secure *the rights and privileges of our trade* which the government can strengthen and the courts can only weaken.

In France and Germany, the vocabulary of the law is evident, though with very different meanings. In the French evidence, the term *droit*, either in the singular or the plural, appears frequently (44 uses), but it refers to very general rights without local settings. This discourse refers to the right to strike or the *right to existence through work*. The right is the moral foundation of protest. Whereas the British texts argue about the interests of the employees, the French texts appeal to legitimacy through asserting a right undermined by the employer. There are political forms of this appeal, for instance in the text which denounces the fact that workers are *outside of common rights*, and affirms: *Nous voulons entrer en possession des droits de l'homme proclamés par la révolution française*.

The German evidence, in contrast, never ceases to pose the problem of equality of rights, both civil and trade union. They speak of 'social equality', of equal rights for all (*gleiches Recht für Jedermann*), or equality of political rights (*politische Gleichberechtigung*). They denounce privilege, special rights (*Sonderrechte*), the mention of which is practically absent in the French material. These are fundamental features of the discourse of the German labour movement in this period, arising from well-known causes, described above.

The ethical dimension

In France, as in Germany, the ethical dimension to labour discourse is very important. Protest is not formulated in terms of interests, even collective ones, but of rights and values. Here is the salient difference with British discourse, where these issues are raised, but not in the context of protest. It appears when someone wants to underline in very general terms, the need to be generous. Thus the general secretary of the stone masons' union ends his speech thanking his members for re-electing him, by reminding them of the need to share tasks as well as benefits.[13] He adds these verses:

> He to no noble purpose lives
> Who much receives but nothing gives,
> Whom none can love, whom none can thank,
> Creation's blot, Creation's blank;
> But he who marks from day to day
> By generous acts his radiant way,
> Finds the same path the Master trod,
> The path to glory and to God.

His point is evidently to shame those non-trade unionists who refuse to join the ranks of the union.

The continental texts are written in an entirely different vein. The most rhetorical Geman texts aim to present the workers as the defenders of the cause of progress, as if they were advocates for the cause of the whole of humanity. This moralist's approach led the authors of French and German texts to underscore the human qualities of the militant. Certainly, the militant was different in this respect from the rest of the workers, at least in the French texts, which tend to denounce the egoism of the masses. But both the French and the German texts evoke the tenacity, the seriousness, the spirit of sacrifice, and the openness which characterise the militant. German texts denounced indifference and suggested that trade union militancy demanded more than political militancy. The French texts insist on the *energie* of the militant (seven references, plus two for *énergiquement*), his capacity for struggle (15 uses, plus two related terms), his firm and energetic will, his courage (three citations). One text even evokes the virility of the militant. Another shows, in contrast to the cowardice of the ruling class, that the worker would *donner héroïquement sa vie*. Militants must be *vaillants, patients, persévérants*. Above all, these texts appeal to *dignity* (four times, plus five references to *dignified*). The worker, bent over, reduced to the state of a brute, divested of his dignity, must *straighten up*, be *proud* – that is, *be a man*, that is, a man *worthy of the name*. The defence of his rights is, in effect, a moral question. In a splendid fashion, one text wrote: *in the entire civilized world, those who abandon their rights to avoid hardship only merit the title of cowards*.[14]

Differences persist, despite these similarities. The German material is marked by an emphasis on the ideal of legal equality which has as much a political as a trade union import. The employer is not subject to an irremediable condemnation. One text even argues that a rise in wages is also in the interest of employers. What is rejected absolutely in the German documents is inequality.

British texts are preoccupied above all with economic circumstances, affecting the balance of forces in the labour market and the defence or improvement in the rules of the trade; they appear to be associations respectful of their formal rules of functioning and which treat their claims as matters of business.

French texts are different yet again. The frequency of the term *travail* is not the least important (55 occurrences). There are also terms designating specific conditions of work, for example, *hours* or *day* (13 occurrences). But what is striking is the importance of work (*travail*) per se, or rather the term stands for the world of labour as a whole (26 occurrences). *Travail* in French has its equivalent in the term *labour* in English, but in reality the balance of usage is different: *travail* appears 28 times in the French texts; *labour* only seven times as the name of a collective, once as opposed to capital, in terms such as *labour representation* or *labour programme*.[15] In the field of semantics, in French, the term *the organisation of labour* combines also with emancipation, a term unknown in the British material. In France, it is *the army of labour marching towards its emancipation*. Elsewhere, we have the appeal *Vive l'émancipation complète, absolue du travail*. French workers' discourse is dominated by the terms *travail* and *travailleurs*.

A reader would miss the significance of these terms if he neglects the moral dimension of this discourse. Work here is not simply a constraint, a condition, a necessity: it is a positive value. Several texts illustrate this. They note that *Labour which is all, must occupy the first level of society*; or in the same text: *Society will be based on the power of labour which is the sole driving force of life and human activity*. Some evoked *the preponderance and the only true grandeur, of labour, creator and the unique source of wealth and of all well-being*.[16] In contrast, the class enemy, the employer in the factory or the bourgeois in politics, is an idler, a parasite. This is how they constructed the term *exploiter*, the importance of which we have already noted. One of our texts opposes the *producer* to the *employer* – that is, the employer produces nothing, since he does not work.

Under these conditions, the complete and absolute emancipation of labour is the emergence of labour as the universal class. The trade union discourse is performative; it has as its goal the transformation of workers in the full sense of the term.[17] In the construction of this discourse, Labour as a value (the capital letter is self-evident) is absolutely central in France, as one can see in the 1895 adoption of the name of the Confédération générale du Travail. No other term would do. *Travail* sounds like the affirmation of a conviction as well as a call to arms.

Conclusion

In the terms of this comparison, and in order to provide a kind of inventory of our findings, we must first emphasise the limits of our research. Even so, there are clear distinctions in the languages developed in these three labour movements. The distinctions among them are evident, as are parallels arising from the condition of wage labour and moral argument. British trade unionism appears to have been configured around the rules of the trade, leading to a preoccupation with unorganised workers and with the unions' strength in the struggle to improve the wages of labour. Their aim is to negotiate better on the labour market; theirs is an economic trade unionism. German trade unionism is obsessed with organisation, and envisions equality for the rights of labour in the whole of German society; it is a trade unionism of significance imbedded in a political and social movement. Finally, French syndicalism appears at one and the same time as both a movement of confrontation, and a movement of identity, resting on the notion of the exclusive and salient dignity of work and workers. This distinction is translated perfectly in the three general distinctions of type: *trade unions, Arbeiterbewegung* and *Confédération générale du Travail*.

Notes

I am greatly indebted to Dr Jay M. Winter for translating this essay and I thank him very much. In order to make it shorter, I did not include the annexe given in the French version. This annexe gives full details as to how each corpus has been constituted and from what sources. J-L Robert, F. Boll and A. Prost (eds), *L'invention Des Syndicalismes*, Paris, 1997, pp. 233–5.

1. Hayden White, *Metahistory. The Historical Imagination in Nineteenth-Century Europe*, Baltimore and London, The Johns Hopkins University Press, 1973.
2. Gareth Stedman Jones, *Language of class. Studies in English working class history 1832–1982*, Cambridge, Cambridge University Press, 1983, p. 20. This pioneering book, by taking into account seriously what the Chartists said, made obsolete and irrelevant previous social history of the working class. However, as Jacques Rancière, *La nuit des prolétaires, archives du rêve ouvrier* (Paris, Fayard, 1981) indicates Jones does not use linguistic methods which French linguists imported from Great Britain, mainly from Zellig S. Harris' *Discourse analysis* translated in French in 1969. I would make similar comments about Patrick Joyce, *Visions of the People. Industrial England and the Question of Class 1848–1914*, Cambridge, Cambridge University Press, 1991, especially chapter 8: 'The people's English', or about the collection of essays he edited, *The historical meanings of work*, Cambridge, Cambridge University Press, 1987.
3. I used this linguistic approach first to analyse the electoral addresses of French deputies, in *Vocabulaires des proclamations électorales de 1881, 1885 et 1889* (Paris, PUF, 1974), and later to discuss the patriotic and pacifist feelings of French veterans of the Great War in my book, *Les*

Anciens combattants et la société française, 1914–1939, tome 3, *Mentalités et idéologies*, Paris, Presses de la FNSP, 1977.

4. At this time, the French socialist movement was not unified. One of the socialist parties was led by Jules Guesde, who was a Marxist and then supported the idea of a close relationship between the party and the trade unions, and the need to achieve political power in order to realise the revolution. See Claude Willard, *Les Guesdistes* (Paris, Ed. sociales, 1965) and Claude Willard (ed.), *La France ouvrière. tome 1, des origines à 1920* (Paris, Ed. de l'Atelier, 1995). This faction was opposed by pure syndicalists who were hostile to the very notion of political action and thought that the state had to be destroyed, not conquered. Fernand Pelloutier, secretary of the Federation of Labour Exchanges, was the most prominent figure in this French revolutionary syndicalist movement, emphasising direct action. The revolution would arise from a struggle directly between workers and their capitalist exploiters, without reference to the state. Only in this way would the workers become truly free. See Jacques Julliard, *Fernand Pelloutier et le syndicalisme d'action directe* (Paris, Le Seuil, 1971).
5. I thank Stéphane Sirot for the French texts he kindly gave me.
6. Let me thank very warmly Chris Wrigley who was kind enough to provide the texts of British documents used in this exercise.
7. For another example of such methods applied to similar texts for a more recent period, see Alain Bergounioux, Michel P. Launay et al. *La Parole syndicale* (Paris, PUF, 1982); Anne-Marie Hetzel, Josette Lefèvre, René Mouriaux, Maurice Tournier, *Le syndicalisme à mots découverts. Dictionnaire des fréquences* (Paris, Ed. Syllepse, 1998) and the review *Mots*, edited by the Presses de Sciences Po.
8. This is a sophisticated method, permitting us to see whether a word is over- or under-utilized in each of the texts compared, according to the different length of each text and to the linguistic rules of frequency distributions (Stoup-Zipf law).
9. This evolution of vocabulary characterises French unions. By contrast the socialist party continued to use the term *citoyen* until the First World War, when it adopted the term *camarade*, according to Jean-Louis Robert's unpublished doctoral dissertation.
10. See the different formulations of Patrick Joyce and Gareth Stedman Jones on the nature of class sentiment and class consciousness. More basically, the lack or the scarcity of terms with class connotations in British texts are meaningful.
11. Keith McClelland, 'Time to work, time to live: some aspects of work and the re-formation of class in Britain, 1850–80', in Joyce, *The historical meanings of work, op. cit.*, gives similar examples of the use of *trade* earlier in the century, for instance p. 190 sq.
12. Four pages of his leaflet, *Qu'est-ce que la Grève générale* (Paris, 1895) and a series of articles in *Le Parti ouvrier* (29–30 August, 5–6, 12–13 and 19–20 September 1895).
13. Operative Stone Masons Friendly Society, *Fortnightly return sheet*, 9 May–23 May 1895 (W. M. Hancock).
14. Fédération corporative des mouleurs en métaux de France, *Compte-rendu officiel du deuxième congrès, tenu les 7, 8 et 9 septembre 1895[...]* Paris, Impr. J. Allemane, 1895, p. 20.

15. Tested with the chi square index, the difference between the two corpus is significant at the level of .05.
16. *IV° Congrès des Bourses du travail de France et des colonies. Compte-rendu des travaux du Congrès tenu à Nîmes les 9, 10, 11 et 12 juin 1895*, Nîmes, Bourse du Travail, 1896, p. 92.
17. Robert Benoit, 'Les figures du Parti. Formation et définition du groupe (1932–1946)', *Mots*, no. 10, 1985, pp. 109–32, analyses similar discourses from the communist party during the Popular front era. In such a sentence as: 'Nous devons faire de chacun de nos adhérents un militant', those who are supposedly the addressees of the discourse are grammatically the subject of the action, 'we have the duty' to make militants from members. This is a clearly self-performative statement: the party is telling the party that it must become fully the party ... .

CHAPTER EIGHT

The constraints of the law

Norbert Olszak and Chris Wrigley

The analysis of the role of legislation in the formation of the three principal models of trade unionism existing in Europe in the late nineteenth century immediately raise very important theoretical issues which raise some doubts about the possibility of carrying out such a comparative study of Germany, France and England.

One needs, first, to question what influences the legislation had in general on the countries' social structures. This is a vast question of judicial sociology which cannot be resolved here for this purpose, but it is very relevant when one tries to comprehend the significant differences in attitude to the law in the different countries. If France in the nineteenth century again gave a very important place to law clearly stated, in the spirit of the Revolution and the judicial monuments that it created, England gave primacy to common law and to consequent elaboration through judgments given by courts on particular cases (case law). In France jurisprudence is fully grown, whereas in England the lawgiver intervenes, especially in the social sphere, in order to correct common law or to correct aberrations in the way that the law has been applied. Germany equally appears to have a predilection for the law, because of its political and judicial unification and because, for our period, it saw the beginnings of modest social legislation which was soon to take place everywhere in Europe. These changes provide testimony to a common political willingness to seek to alter society. But one must not neglect the role of collective agreements, already fundamental in this period in England when France was still strictly upholding individual agreements. To sum up, if one wishes to be able to speak carefully of the 'constraints of law', in order to assess the different types of judicial systems, one must look beyond law in the strict meaning of the Acts to the general nature of edicts made by public authorities and by Parliament.

Next, it is necessary to know, for the three countries, the different ways in which they understood the judiciary's relationship with labour. France and England were both entirely marked, with some nuances, by a romanist culture which placed labour relations within the framework of legal obligations where the parties were considered as equal in their relationship. The German tradition – still strong at the end of the nineteenth century despite the weight of the new codification of laws – discarded intervention by contract and gave primacy to a statutory view of labour: relations were common relationships fixed by the integration of the actions of the workers within a community of workers and the stress was placed on a personal bond which could often be a bond of dependence.[1]

Yet, within all the cultures trade unionism was for some years forbidden. Everywhere, in different periods and for varying lengths of time, vocational groups were repressed and pursued for trying to establish their right to march in their early days or, later, for rejecting obstructive agreements offered by municipal or state officials, as in the Germany of Bismarck.[2] In France, the law *Le Chapelier* of 14–17 June 1791 and then the Penal Code of 1810 instituted severe penalties. In Britain there were the Combination Acts of 1799 and 1800 which defended individualism. In the German Lands, combinations were forbidden by various laws – in Saxony in 1791, in Prussia in 1794 and in Bavaria in 1809 – while the other states experienced the French regulations favoured by Napoleon.

It was a period where the constraints of the law were evidently at their maximum and most hurtful, with the penalties directly touching trade union activists. It was also to remain an heroic memory and a source of later distrust, which appeared to be cultivated longer in France. The heroic age of repression also remained a long-held memory especially concerning the tactics which were employed to evade some of the effects of these prohibitions. These measures often involved judicial tricks such as the creation of associations of mutual support to camouflage what were associations of resistance, or political action to obtain a tolerant regime or to secure pardons for condemned people.

This negative image of the law did not disappear quickly. It was often even reinforced after the repeal of laws against combinations. In England these laws were repealed in 1824, while France initially strengthened its legislation against associations in 1834 before legalising combinations in 1864. It was at about the same time that Germany, which had also witnessed a reinforcement of repression in various states between 1836 and 1857 in reaction to revolutionary agitation, rescinded many repressive measures in the new legal framework set up at unification. Freedom of combination was one of the rights guaranteed to industrial employees by the law passed in 1869 by the Confederation of North Germany. But after the period of repression, the working-class movement did not benefit quickly from genuine recognition. There was first a phase of toleration of trade union action: this amounted only to a simple, uncertain freedom, which if exercised had risks and perils, and was not a right which could give people the benefits of the protection of the authorities. When they existed, specific laws on trade unions contained numerous restrictions and limitations. It was not until the end of our period that one can note the first elements of a genuine recognition of the legality of trade unions. For all three countries it took the necessities of the First World War and the mood of *Union sacrée* before the trade union movements harvested the first fruits from being accepted and integrated by the state.

The period which saw the creation of the different types of European trade unionism corresponds, therefore, with the legal period of tolerance. The law was no longer displayed in a purely brutal manner. Henceforth, it was necessary for trade unionists to learn to use the legal rules in order to understand the scope of the new collective freedom and to be able to counter less favourable interpretations – notably those of employers. The true recognition of trade unionism required judicial activity which was beyond the political demands of an amending legislature. Certainly, when assessing the law, it is necessary to grasp that its impact went beyond trade union structures: our period was also marked by social pressure and the development of intervention by legislation and by government administration, and one can find in this situation competition between the state and the trade unions to establish a labour law.

Trade union and industrial relations laws

The ending of the ban on combinations did not lead immediately to the passing of legislation specifically dealing with trade unions, and they remained in an anomalous position in society. In France the law of 25 May 1864 removed the penal sanctions which had hit strikes. One is therefore able to speak of a liberty of combination, although nothing changed in regard to such matters as regulations which were very restrictive concerning meetings or associations, and, furthermore, protection of the freedom to work was reinforced against threats or violence. So workers who wished to meet to prepare a strike and to unite to negotiate or sign agreements were exposed to prosecution for penal offences and were faced with the severity of a generally conservative magistracy.

The situation was similar in England after the repeal of the Combination Acts in 1824 because the defence of the right to work provided all manner of opportunities to take legal actions which, in the absence of distinct trade union law, created great difficulties, both material and financial, for the trade unions. The ill-defined and unpredictable operation of laws on the trade unions also adversely affected the trade unions' ability to take collective action.

The legal status of the trade unions in Britain was established by the Trade Union Act, 1871. In France, the law Waldeck-Rousseau, 1884, established trade union law. Only Germany, of the three countries, did not introduce specific legislation recognising trade unions in this period, despite various attempts to do so.

The German trade unions were expected to fit in with the general laws dealing with associations. At first these were variable, their nature depending on the region of Germany. Unified legislation did not occur until 1908. However, throughout 1871 to 1914 there was tough administrative control, especially concerning political groupings and in areas where mistrust of workers was especially strong. In the case of Germany one needs to be aware of very great variations in the way that the trade unions were treated but, above all, one needs to remember the political character of the Kaiserreich and the widespread repression carried out in 1878 to 1890 under the Anti-Socialist Laws.[3] The fear that this repression might recur was always present. Many organisations refused to conform and carry out the obligations that the state imposed on associations.

In Britain the Trade Union Act of 1871 provided the unions with protection for many of their activities.[4] It safeguarded union members from legal action for being 'a restraint of trade', protected the unions from legal interference in their internal affairs, safeguarded their funds and permitted them to come within the scope of Friendly Society legislation. However, Gladstone and his government remained doubtful of the benefits of trade unionism, being believers in free market forces and as few restrictions as possible in the labour market. Hence, when the Trade Union Bill was drafted it also included clauses hostile to the trade unions. The Trades Union Congress (TUC), founded in 1868, successfully pressed the government to withdraw that part of the Bill which 'in its provisions presupposes criminal intentions or tendencies on the part of English workmen as a class'. However, Gladstone's government brought in another measure, the Criminal Law Amendment Act, 1871, which codified previous legislation which made collective action against employers very hazardous in law.

Thereafter, the British trade union movement campaigned to repeal the Master and Servant Act, 1867 (an amended version of medieval legislation concerning breach of contract) and the Criminal Law Amendment Act, 1871. The *Quarterly Review* reflected the view of many of the propertied classes when it expressed grave concern that the trade unions wanted 'nothing less than the repeal of the whole body of law by which a dangerous and encroaching despotism is at present held imperfectly in check'. After Disraeli and the Conservatives formed a government in 1874, Disraeli appointed a Royal Commission to investigate the operation of these two Acts. The Royal Commission recommended amending the Master and Servant Act but suggested that only minor changes should be made to the Criminal Law Amendment Act, 1871, and the law of conspiracy.

Under pressure from the TUC and its sympathisers, Disraeli's government did remedy the major legal grievances of the trade unions with the Employers and Workmen's Act, 1875, and the Conspiracy and Protection of Property Act, 1875. As well as dropping the terminology 'master' and 'servant', the first of these measures removed breaches of contract from criminal law, except in the public utilities of gas and water or where there was a serious danger to life or property. Initially, when introduced, the second measure dealt with the laws of conspiracy, freeing the unions from their operation where their actions were not in themselves criminal. Under further pressure from the trade unions and their parliamentary supporters, the government agreed to repeal the Criminal Law Amendment Act, 1871, and to add to the second Bill clauses which expressly legalised peaceful picketing.

Disraeli commented in a letter, 'We have settled the long and vexatious contest between capital and labour'; and in another expressed the hope that these laws of 1875 would 'gain and retain for the Tories the lasting affection of the working classes'.[5] Winston Churchill was still making much of this Conservative legislation in his major speeches in 1948–51 when trying to win working-class votes in order to return to power.

Gladstone's legislation of 1871, combined with Disraeli's of 1875, provided the British trade unions with considerable freedom in which to develop collective bargaining and be able to back their negotiations, if necessary, with strike action. The problem for the trade unions was that from 1893 there were several legal judgments which undermined what the trade unions had understood to be their rights. Between 1893 and 1896 it was ruled to be illegal to boycott the goods of a firm in dispute with the unions, to issue a blacklist of firms or to use pickets peacefully to persuade another employer not to provide materials to a firm engaged in a strike or lockout. These decisions, combined with a vigorous challenge to trade unions by major employers' organisations and growing disillusionment with both Liberal and Conservative Parties among some trade unionists, led the TUC in 1899 to pass a motion instructing its executive body, the Parliamentary Committee, 'to devise ways and means for securing the return of an increased number of Labour members to the next Parliament'. This led to the formation of the Labour Representation Committee (LRC) in 1900, which became the

Labour Party in 1906. Further adverse legal decisions brought increasing numbers of trade unions to affiliate to this new party.

The legal decisions of 1901 further threw in doubt the settlement of 1871–5. In the case of *Quinn* v. *Leatham* it was ruled illegal to strike or to threaten to strike in order to press an employer to discharge non-union labour. More worrying was the House of Lords' verdict in a case involving the Amalgamated Society of Railway Servants and the Taff Vale Company. The *Taff Vale* judgment undercut the trade unions' immunity from legal action to secure financial compensation for losses arising from strikes – an immunity which hitherto had been presumed to have been conferred by the trade union legislation of 1871.

Following the 1906 general election, in which the Liberals won a landslide victory and 28 LRC candidates plus further 25 Lib-Lab candidates were elected, Campbell-Bannerman's government brought in a Bill which would simply have provided limited protection for union funds. However, under Labour Party pressure, the prime minister agreed to widen the terms of what became the Trades Disputes Act, 1906, so that it gave unlimited legal immunity to the trade unions for damages incurred during the course of industrial disputes. This was to provide the basic framework of trade union activity in industrial relations in Britain until the series of hostile measures passed during the premiership of Margaret Thatcher (1979–90).

In Britain the trade unions could be involved in politics. Indeed, for most of our period, most trade unionists who had the vote probably voted Liberal (with regional variations, and these often adversely affected for the Liberals by anti-Catholicism), with a minority voting Conservative. With the trade unions funding the separate Labour Party, some active trade unionists who supported the other parties objected. A Liberal railwayman, Osborne, took his union to the courts. In the 1909 *Osborne* judgment the House of Lords ruled that it was unlawful for the unions to subsidise political candidates. With some difficulty, in the face of Liberal doubts and Conservative concern, the Labour Party secured the Trade Union Act, 1913, which allowed trade unions to fund political activity providing that a majority approved the establishment of a specific political fund and members who wished to could contract out of contributing to that fund.

So, in Britain in the last quarter of the nineteenth and the early years of the twentieth centuries, the trade unions had much freedom to operate, though at times this was limited by case law (notably between 1893 and 1901). Generally, legal regulation in Britain was fairly minimal, with the state intervening in the labour market to fix minimum employment conditions in particular areas (such as textile factories, coalmines and sweated labour).

In France, the first Article of the law Waldeck-Rousseau of 21 March 1884 formally repealed the 1791 law *Le Chapelier*. However, certain trade union activists, such as Jules Guesde, chose to deny that it did fully repeal that Act in order to denounce what they viewed as a modernisation and adaptation of the 1791 law to meet the new needs of the capitalists: 'Under the flag of sanctioning trade organisations for our working class, the new law is only intended to hinder our political organisations.'[6] This comment gives the tone of the criticisms which systematically attended the least of the working-class laws – criticisms which displayed suspicion that such laws inevitably represented various cunning manoeuvres by the bourgeoisie.

Certainly, the law of 1884 did contain a number of restrictions but this was quite normal at a time when it was giving a new and exceptional freedom only to labour, while the general right of combination had to wait a further 17 years. But then, each time when the law was developed and certain restrictions were repealed, the same criticisms were made and it was not until 1920 that changes deemed more acceptable were achieved. In fact the law reflected a republican idea of trade unions, the tenor of which was rejected by the working-class movement.

This concept rests on a strict principle of specialty.[7] According to Article 2 the 'trade unions and professional associations, those of more than twenty persons practising the same profession, similar trades or vocations linked through the creation of certain products, are able to set up freely, without government authorisation',[8] but, after Article 3, their object must exclusively be 'the study and the defence of their interests, economic, industrial, commercial and agricultural'. This thus excluded the principle of substantial class solidarity between workers and their sympathisers and firmly excluded civil servants. It also hindered all moves towards political action. Indeed, Article 5 gave the possibility of trade unions organising concerted action and uniting, but it was only a time for 'the study and defence of their interests, economic, industrial, commercial and agricultural'.

In this framework and for this object, the trade unions could enjoy all the attributes of a civil body – being recognised at law and using the sums coming in from subscriptions albeit under the restrictions which limited the acquisition of real estate to that strictly needed for their activities (this last point was a sign of the persistent distrust shown towards all company property and in no way manifested a special hostility towards the trade unions). The law also provided for libraries, professional training courses, mutual support and pension funds, labour exchanges, as well as for conferences of the trade and professional associations for 'all the judicial conflict and all the issues which linked their specialities'. But those attributes were denied to confederations of unions and were confined to simple organisation among union members.

This freedom to create trade unions was subordinated to one single formality: the deposition of the union's rules and a list of its officials with the municipal authority. Understandably, this demand helped crystallise worries and suspicions regarding police control, and many organisations, which existed before this law was initiated or which were created during this period, refused to conform with the law, not least in Paris. In 1893, during one of the crises which marked relations between the government and the Paris Bourse du Travail, it was stated that close to half the trade unions had not registered and this led to the prosecution of 50 activists.[9] Apart from this conflict, however, there does not seem to have been systematic control and if, increasingly, most trade unions abided by the rules, this was because it was in their interest for them to be recognised by the law – if, for example, they wished to use the law.

All things considered, the framework of legislation given to the trade unions was strongly influenced by the one which existed in England. It emphasised numerous and varied corporate activities, and a trade unionism of service. This type of trade unionism certainly did exist, but in the world of agriculture or among the shopkeepers and artisans; the workers' expectations were met only partly in the Bourses de Travail and partly in a revolutionary perspective. After the passing of the law of 1884, the working-class movement appears to have ignored the prescriptions of the text: their debates concentrated on revolutionary action – despite the ban on political action – and they were strongly preoccupied with the foundation of federations and of the CGT, although in the eyes of the law the unions were only a secondary matter.[10] The movement tried to impose its own vision of collective action, and this was all the more easily done since the legislation of 1884 in reality only gave a weak emphasis to the collective dimension in work relations.

The grip of the law on industrial relations was to develop progressively and with difficulty in a system where the individual nature of contracts had been planned to guarantee the balance of the market. Economists made fine demonstrations of how the changes in the industrial world now required that negotiations should take place between collective groups in order that a natural equilibrium was reached between capital and labour, although this did not lead immediately to significant changes in the rules and legal practice.[11]

In contrast, the trade union legislation took good care to affirm the primacy of individual liberty against collective constraints and especially against a proletarian vision of class solidarity.[12] Article 7 of the law Waldeck-Rousseau declared that 'all members of a professional trade union must withdraw at the moment of association, notwithstanding clauses to the contrary' and that 'all persons who withdraw from a trade union keep the law and can be members of societies for mutual support and for retirement pensions for their old age which utilise assets to which they have contributed by their subscriptions'.

This promotion of individualism can be found again in France, both in the attitude towards collective disputes and by the strikes that occurred in our period which were considered to be about individual freedom exerted collectively. Trade unions were not institutions for strikes, neither when strikes were initiated, nor as they developed and even less so in their conclusion. If the law of 28 December 1892 tried to provide a remedy for strikes by a conciliation and arbitration procedure, this only applied when the representatives were not connected with a trade union. In Germany the industrial professions' institutes (*Gewerbergerichte*) established by the law of 29 July 1890 and inspired by the councils of wise men (*Conseils de prud'hommes*) of the Second Empire, could intervene impartially in collective disputes, at the request of both parties, thus allowing a place for the trade unions but without necessarily requiring it.[13]

In Britain the state was wary of intervening in collective bargaining. Industrial relations were conducted on a voluntarist basis, in line with the dominant *laissez-faire*, free trade and free market principles then dominant in Britain. Trade unionists, with a few exceptions such as Tom Mann when addressing the 1891 Royal Commission on Labour, did not favour arbitration. On the whole, the stronger unions favoured unfettered collective bargaining. Some of the trade unions in the more weakly organised areas were well-disposed to joint committees with employers, which attempted to settle matters of contention peacefully. These dated back to the 1830s, but one of the most effective trade boards was that established by A. J. Mundella for the hosiery and glove trade in Nottingham.[14] The experience of working through such bodies, to try to secure benefits for their members through cooperation rather than confrontation with employers, reinforced the essentially moderate political and industrial views of many leading British trade unionists, including those who became ministers in Labour governments such as Arthur Henderson and Ben Turner.[15]

Individuals, and later the government, offered conciliation in major local or national disputes. Whether such offers of mediation were accepted was entirely a matter for the two sides to the disputes. The most famous of such nineteenth-century interventions was that of Lord Rosebery, the Foreign Secretary, in the great coal lockout of 1893.

During this period A. J. Mundella served for a second time as president of the Board of Trade (1892–94). In his efforts to encourage a balance between labour and capital within a prosperous capitalist economy rather than leave class warfare to take place, Mundella transformed the Labour Bureau (which he had set up in his first term at the Board of Trade in 1886) into a separate Labour Department with 30 local correspondents and funds to publish information on labour matters in the *Labour Gazette*. The officials of the Labour Department soon became involved in mediating in industrial disputes, as in the case of a lockout in the boot industry in 1895.[16]

Such activities by officials of the Labour Department of the Board of Trade were regularised by the 1896 Conciliation (Trades Disputes) Act, brought in by Lord Salisbury's Conservative and Unionist government and entirely in keeping with prevailing British voluntarist beliefs. The Labour Department of the Board of Trade could offer conciliation if one party to a dispute asked it to intervene and could arbitrate if both parties asked. If one party did not wish for such intervention, then they could reject it. In 1897 Lord Penrhyn, a notably tough employer, humiliatingly rebuffed the Conservative President of the Board of Trade, C. T. Ritchie, when he offered to arrange a conference to settle a dispute between him and his quarry workers. Later, when the Liberals were in office, successive presidents of the Board of Trade, David Lloyd George (1905–8) and Winston Churchill (1908–10), actively intervened in threatened or actual disputes.[17]

Such mediations by the Board of Trade did not affect large numbers of disputes. In the period 1897–1906 it was involved in under 4 per cent of disputes, and these affected only 5 per cent of the workforce involved in strikes and lockouts.[18] Yet, in time, the trade unions came to feel that in good times (such as much of 1910–21) they could hold out for government intervention in disputes and quite possibly gain better terms than if they had settled sooner with the employers. In 1912, to the dismay of the Liberal Prime Minister H. H. Asquith, the government was successfully pressurised into introducing legislation whereby a minimum wage could be fixed. At the time, Lloyd George observed, 'Asquith's declaration for a minimum wage sounded the death-knell of the Liberal Party in its old form'.[19]

In France, when the trade unions did occasionally sign collective agreements which fixed wage levels in order to prevent strikes or to end an industrial conflict, these were rarely successful. This was because the agreements could not be made to apply to recalcitrant employers as the courts upheld individualistic principles in regard to such agreements: only the signatories or, at a pinch, the members of a union which signed were committed. The unions had to wait until the law of 25 March 1919 to obtain partial recognition of collective agreements – a law which was deemed to be truly monstrous by classical doctrine.

It was during the same period, in 1918, that Germany firmly

established the legal validity of wage bargaining. Before then, the German legal system had allowed a small improvement, brought about because the German Civil Code of 1900 had introduced some new principles;[20] but nevertheless an employer and wage-earner could conclude an employment contract involving an inferior salary, this evidently removing much interest in collective bargaining!

Only in Britain was the practice of collective bargaining widespread. By 1910 one wage in five was fixed by collective bargaining, but such agreements could not be legally enforced; their strength lay in the goodwill of the parties involved, with them refraining from resorting to the courts. However, in many areas of the British economy, trade unionism was too weak to bring employers to the negotiating table. In some cases where both employers and workers were organised, there remained sufficient employers outside of the employers' associations to undermine such collective agreements that were concluded. Notable later cases of this were in the cotton and wool industries in the late 1920s and early 1930s. In the 1890s and at the turn of the century, employers in some major sectors – shipping, engineering and the railways – were notably hostile to trade union organisation. As has already been mentioned, some employers readily resorted to the law courts as one of several ways of defeating trade unionism. In the case of the Taff Vale Railway Company they resorted to the law to insist on trade union liability for financial loss through strikes, and secured the *Taff Vale* judgment of 1901.

It was at the turn of the century in France that Waldeck Rousseau, allied with the socialist Alexander Millerand, set out a series of plans to improve greatly trade union law. These proposals included strengthening the organisational ability of professional associations and trade unions, introducing penalties for employers who took hostile action against trade unions and the provision of formal procedures to try to resolve collective disputes, with trade unions a part of these and with seats allocated to them on the permanent representative institutions, the labour councils (*conseils du travail*).[21] But these ambitious plans, the inspiration for which had come from Australia and New Zealand, came up against a coalition of opponents. Those on the right were unlikely to appreciate legally strengthening trade unions, and the left was distrustful of the intentions of Millerand, whom they deemed to be a social traitor, even though the proposals had figured in earlier socialist plans. After the 1901 and 1902 CGT congresses there was no wish to institutionalise strikes and there was a fear of extending the scope of trade union law. In particular, there was no wish to be stifled by the pursuit of damages arising from strikes, as had happened with the *Taff Vale* case in Wales. The French socialists did advocate a vote on the principle of legal immunity for trade unions, but they did not have the same success as the British trade unions with the 1906 Act. However, in that case the unions had the benefit of the Labour Party acting on their behalf in Parliament while the CGT had instituted anarcho-syndicalist principles with the Charter of Amiens. It was, moreover, at the Amiens congress that Merrheim secured the rejection *en bloc* of all the proposed working-class legislation, on the grounds that Roman law smothered working-class action. The unions demanded a new law which would allow them to leave the vicious circle of the civil law, but it can be said that, by this, they understood such a law to be a post-revolutionary law.[22] However, this position was not representative of the whole movement and many activists were interested in securing social legislation.[23]

Social laws

The end of the nineteenth century saw an important extension of social laws in two respects. First, there was the development of an industrial law in which working-class legislation protected exploited and dependent labour. After the first measures of the mid-nineteenth century concerning children, a new law was formed and, in France, the *Code du Travail*, promulgated in 1910, was the first Code to complete the system of the five Codes put in place during the Consulate and Empire a century earlier. In Germany the successive versions of the Code of Professions (*Gewerbeordnung*) consolidated the various protective arrangements introduced between 1869 and 1891. In England there was a long run of legislation which protected women, children, and sometimes men, in factories, mines, agriculture and in home work. Second, the solution of the social question required, from the 1880s, the establishment of institutions intended to protect wage-earners from the principal risks that threatened their income. In both respects, trade unionism was concerned about the new structures, in terms of whether to support or oppose them.

If the creation of labour law seemed welcome, given some degrees of pragmatism in England and Germany, the political debates were more lively in France due to the fact that some people considered such labour law to be a 'poisoned chalice' intended to send the revolutionary ardour of the masses to sleep. If the measures placing working restrictions on women and children were more acceptable – particularly because they restricted annoying competition for men – making them applicable to all workers was more difficult to agree to because the skilled workers' dominant position in the labour market would then be weakened. But there was often a great contrast between the speeches at congress and actual practice: on the ground, workers and activists were more anxious to secure a favourable application of the legislation than to condemn it.[24]

Observance of the labour legislation was enforced by the creation of a specialised inspectorate. The English example of 1833 was to be followed in Germany in 1878 and in France in 1874 and 1892. But the inspectors were few in number and so were unable to appraise sufficiently all the workplaces to locate the distortions and evasions of the legislation. This led to the idea of introducing worker inspectors. In the German mines they elected 'men of trust', and the same was true in Britain, where trade union representatives could serve as checkweighmen. In France the trade unions aspired more towards their representatives being provided with an official status, like the safety representatives of working miners instituted in 1890 or the assistant inspectors discussed in 1907, but these examples completely failed to address the issue of trade union control of these elected representatives.

A new solution was suggested in 1899 by Alexander Millerand in a circular to labour inspectors. The Minister of Industry and Commerce recommended that they should increase their contacts with trade union secretaries and, in particular, with the Bourses du Travail (labour exchanges). This was an original attempt to rely on this institution, and was no less innovatory than the labour exchanges which had developed strongly in France, as well as being effective in Belgium, Switzerland, Italy and the Netherlands. It should be remembered that these involved buildings often constructed and funded by the municipalities to arbitrate trade unions and their corporate activities. The term *bourse* referred to an idea for organising the labour market introduced among the first plans of the mid-nineteenth century, and, other than in England until 1909, the concept of labour exchanges indicated an official employment service.

In France the Bourses du Travail were developed as an institution in the period after the trade union legislation of 1884 and the municipal reforms of the same year. Only two weeks after the passage of the law Waldeck-Rousseau, a law of 5 April transferred some state responsibilities to the communes, notably for the running of public services, and it also established the principle of electing the mayor and his assistants. These reforms favoured the emergence of municipal socialism in some communes controlled by the left, and the Bourses du Travail could be seen as one of the demonstrations of such socialist concern by the working-class movement. On the other hand, the creation and maintenance of the Bourses du Travail could also pass for an attempt to channel working-class strength into respectable activities (such as employment, vocational courses and libraries), but such attempts frequently failed, with this arousing tensions between the trade unionists and the municipalities hostile to schemes derived from revolutionaries.[25]

In any case, all such developments were carried out outside of general legal regulations, despite a plan which had been elaborated by the Council of State in 1894.[26] The government alone regulated the position of the Paris Bourse du Travail which did not enjoy the municipal autonomy of all other Bourses elsewhere. A decree of 1895, modified several times, ordered the administrative organisation of the Paris Bourse du Travail and defined its scope for helping the public, thereby gaining a strong control over this institution.

If anything, this eventual collaboration between trade unions and the labour inspectorate left open the question of breaches of the new labour law. The public prosecutor's department was not always favourable to penal prosecutions and it was not always possible to intervene in numerous cases which came within the scope of civil law, such as collective agreements or trade union rights. In certain cases, one can see that the French trade unions did use the law to defend the general interests of their occupations, but to do so they had to endure the worst kinds of procedural difficulties in order to get full acknowledgment of their presence before the courts, as the judicial system was universally hostile to collective action, especially in the case of the penal system. It was mainly the shopkeepers' associations and those of the wine-growers which took matters to be contested at law, notably in cases of fraud, and they were successful in obtaining, on 5 April 1913, the decree of principle, from the united chambers of the Court of Cassation, which preceded the legislative recognition in 1920 of trade unions' defence of vocational interests.

Despite doctrinaire requests for 'judicial socialism' advocating the systematic creation of a left-leaning interpretation of civil law, French trade union actions were limited enough in the area of the law and, in all cases, relatively conventional. There were the *conseils de prud'hommes* (councils of wise men) which made clear judgments on the predelictions of the working-class movement – those where they had taken 'direct action' among working people, without compromising with the bourgois professional lawyers.[27] The trade unions did not have a formal place in the 'prud'homal' system, but the election of its councillors played a major role in the renewal of the working-class movement in the 1870s and continued to represent an important activity afterwards, thus favouring their adoption of this tribunal. However, not all could make formal agreements through the *prud'hommes*, and, in some cases, Bourses du Travail developed judicial services to help workers appearing before tribunals, in particular in the cases of accidents at work where it needed great skills to secure compensation – at least until the appearance of legislation which provided social protection.

In England the range of ancient law which could be deployed against the trade unions, plus the frequent very unfavourable interpretations of the 1824, 1825, 1871 and 1875 legislation concerning trade unions, encouraged the trade union movement regularly to employ solicitors specialising in labour law and, mostly after the First World War, to develop their own research and specialist advice services. A famous early instance of such work was that undertaken by W. P. Roberts, a Bath solicitor, who worked for the Miners' Association in the 1840s.[28] The TUC, through its Parliamentary Committee, campaigned for legislation to benefit trade unionists generally or particular work groups, but it was not sufficiently well-funded to employ more than minimal administrative staff until after the First World War. Consequently, in the late nineteenth century it could offer unions advice, but not professional services.

Our period saw the achievement of national insurance. Reliance on personal savings or friendly society membership was inadequate as these did not meet workers' concerns, only adequately helped the better off, and in the case of small friendly societies with small reserves, could be financially risky. As for charity, which was tied to paternalism or patronage, it was incompatible with workers' feelings of dignity and independence. State provision bridged the gaps in private provision by organising insurance for sickness, old age and invalidity, as well as for unemployment and compensation for accidents at work. The important point which needed to be decided was whether such social welfare should be optional or obligatory. Should one make foresight obligatory or was it good enough to encourage it with a formula which was financially attractive? If the latter, then it was clearly compatible with liberal principles. Where it was obligatory, it was imposing on people in the names of social justice and efficiency, and was often limited to the poorer income groups, rather than for the working class as a whole.[29]

This solution was advocated by Chancellor Bismarck, who was convinced of the conservative value of social politics by the example of Napoleon III and followed his example when he attempted to check the rise of socialism in Germany. The laws of 31 May 1883, 6 July 1884 and 22 June 1889 successively put in place insurance against sickness, accidents and, finally, invalidity and old age. Membership was obligatory for workers earning less than 2000 marks per year, and their subscriptions were complemented by the payments of employers and the state. The funds, both national and local, were managed jointly. After several changes, the legislation was consolidated in the National Insurance Code of 1911, with an extension of its benefit to the employees.

In Britain before the turn of the century most provisions against adversity were personal – savings, membership of friendly societies, trade unions or private insurance schemes, family networks or even the goodwill of neighbours. Otherwise, there was charity. The last resort was the workhouse system, which by the turn of the century was under review. Between 1906 and 1911 the Liberal governments introduced a series of ad hoc piecemeal measures which helped differing groups of working people. The Old Age Pensions Act of 1908 still encouraged thrift and good character, but provided low levels of pensions for those of small income. It was notable that the funds came from taxes, so the measure appealed especially to the Labour Party as it redistributed income from taxpayers to the elderly poor. However, with the National Insurance Act of 1911, which dealt with unemployment and sickness, the funding came from insurance payments by the members of the scheme and was supplemented by payments from employers and the state. The coverage of the unemployment insurance was much more limited than the health provision. In turning to insurance for the 1911 measure the Liberal Chancellor of the Exchequer, David Lloyd George, avoided higher taxes and claims of outright socialistic legislation from the propertied. With his 'People's Budget' of 1909 he funded social welfare (and an increased navy) on Liberal lines, so avoiding the British right's desire, expressed by Joseph Chamberlain, to follow the Kaiserreich and fund social welfare by tariffs, at the expense of working-class budgets rather than by direct taxes.[30]

In France, outside of the railways and mines, where schemes to help those in need and for retirement were established in 1890 and 1894, the Third Republic seems to have preferred reforming mutuality by the law of 1 April 1896 and was not successful when putting in place an obligatory scheme for the retirement of workers and peasants on 5 April 1910. This law was defective in its financial provisions and in its organisation, which was uniquely statist. It was strongly opposed by the labour movement and was badly applied, despite being reformed in 1912. Much the same was true of the law of 9 April 1898, which was intended to guarantee compensation from employers to victims of accidents at work, but did not develop specific insurance.

At the end of the century, notwithstanding such developments there was one major social risk requiring attention: unemployment. The early obligatory schemes were rejected by referendum at Saint-Gall in 1897 and at Bale in 1900. On the whole, it was prefered to follow the town of Gand which, from 1901, subsidised the voluntary schemes of trade unions. Such schemes managed by the trade unions were judged to be very effective ways of using money contributed for hardship and for determining who should benefit from it. Only England made unemployment insurance obligatory by law (in 1911), although there it did not initially cover all occupations. Nonetheless, all the countries in our study were well aware of the importance of guaranteeing funds to ensure the well-being of everyone through social insurance, although the crises of employment were still considered to be essentially temporary.

All these plans left a place for the working-class movement. This was because the public institutions played only a marginal role. It was also because, as in Germany, they made an appeal for working-class representation in the bodies they created. But it is difficult to establish a correlation between judicial structures and the evolution of trade unionism. The example of France is a big enough topic. We have seen that the law of 1884 allowed the trade unions the opportunity to create friendly society provisions. Since the law of 15 July 1850 and a decree of 1852, friendly societies had been encouraged by the government but had also been subject to very strict administrative control, which went as far as to nominate the chairman in order to prevent any hidden forbidden activities and also to avoid doubtful financial practices. Under the Third Republic such close guardianship was progressively relaxed in practice, before being abandoned by the legal reform of 1898. However, these favourable conditions barely encouraged the trade unions to focus effort on social insurance or on unemployment insurance, with the exception of certain branches which were strongly corporatist such as *Le Livre*. It seems that the breach between trade unionism and mutuality was very close to being consummated after the intense political debates of the 1880s.

Conclusion

In the final analysis, with respect to trade union law, we already have a situation of 'a conflict of logics' where the 'true reality' of the workers is opposed by 'the old judicial notions which were without any point of support in the conscience or the interests of trade unionists'.[31] According to the thinking of the CGT, working-class law was based on the practical and took precedence over a law which did not sanction the *fait accompli*.[32] Beyond the divergences of the judicial systems, there was, then, a common belief in custom!

Notes

1. A. Supiot, 'Les voies du droit', *Critique du droit du travail*, Paris, PUF, 1994, pp. 15–22.

2. A. Jacobs, 'Collective Self-Regulation', in R. Hepple (ed.), *The Making of Labour Law in Europe. A Comparative Study of Nine Countries up to 1945*, London, Mansell, 1986, pp. 193–241.
3. On this point it is necessary to have local studies at one's disposal.
4. B. C. Roberts, *The Trade Union Congress 1868–1921*, London, Allen and Unwin, 1958; K. D. Brown, 'Trade Unions and the Law', in C. J. Wrigley (ed.), *A History of British Industrial Relations 1875–1914*, Sussex, Hassocks, 1982, pp. 116–34.
5. P. Smith, *Disraelian Conservatism and Social Reform*, London, Routledge and Kegan Paul, 1967, pp.215–18.
6. P. Schöttler, P. *Naissance des bourses du travail*, Paris, 1985, n. 53, p. 203.
7. F. Babinet, 'Dit et non-dit du texte: rapports sociaux et portée juridique de la loi du 21 mars 1884', in *Convergences. Etudes offertes à Marcel David*, Quimper, Calligrammes, pp. 19–41.
8. The reference to a threshold of 20 persons is explained by the existence of Article 291 of the Penal Code which required associations of more than 20 persons to be authorised by the government.
9. Schöttler, *Naissons des bourses du travail*, pp. 85–7.
10. This restrictive idea was more troublesome for some forms of Christian Socialism. Thus, the professional association of the employers of the North, which was under the mystical patronage of Our Lady of the Factories, was dissolved in 1892 because it was an association with a religious objective (Babinet, 'Dit et non-dit in texte', p.26). But it is true that the Republic found itself engaged in anti-clerical politics and that it refused to establish a general freedom of association precisely to avoid being placed in the arms of clericalism. It therefore would not permit the misuse of trade union freedom.
11. For the economic ideas see, for example, A. Batbie, 'La question des salaires et des grèves', *Revue des Deux Mondes*, 66, 1867, pp. 960–84.
12. M. Leroy, *La coutume ouvrière: syndicats, bourses du travail, fédérations professionnelles, coopératives, doctrines et institutions*, Vol. 2, Paris, 1913, p. 935.
13. A. Hueck and H. C. Nipperdey, *Lehrbuch des Arbeitsrechts*, Vol. 2, Mannheim, 1930, p. 371.
14. D. Knoop, *Industrial Conciliation and Arbitration*, London, King, 1905, pp. 45–79; I. G. Sharp, *Industrial Conciliation and Arbitration in Great Britain*, London, Allen and Unwin, 1950, pp. 1–269; J. H. Porter, 'Wage Bargaining under Conciliation Agreements 1860–1914', *Economic History Review*, 1970, pp. 460–75 and 'The Iron Trade', in Wrigley (ed.), *A History of British Industrial Relations*, pp. 253–65.
15. See, for example, C. J. Wrigley, *Arthur Henderson*, Cardiff, University of Wales Press, 1990, pp. 5–9 and 140–2; *Cosy Co-operation under Strain*, York, Borthwick Institute, 1987; and 'Trade Unionists, Employers and the Cause of Industrial Unity and Peace, 1916–21' in C. J. Wrigley and J. Shepherd (eds), *On the Move*, London, Hambledon Press, 1991, pp. 155–84.
16. W. H. Armytage, *A. J. Mundella, 1827–97. The Liberal Background to the Labour Movement*, London, Benn, 1951; R. Davidson, 'Llewellyn Smith, the Labour Department and Government Growth 1886–1909', in G. Sutherland (ed.), *Studies In Nineteenth Century Government*, London,

Allen and Unwin, 1972, pp. 227–62; and 'Government Administration', in Wrigley (ed.), *A History of British Industrial Relations*, pp. 159–83.
17. C. J. Wrigley, 'The Government and Industrial Relations', in Wrigley (ed.), *A History of British Industrial Relations*, pp. 135–58; R. Davidson, 'The Board of Trade and Industrial Relations 1896–1914', *Historical Journal*, 21, 1978, pp. 571–8; and 'Social Conflict and Social Administration: The Conciliation Act in British Industrial Relations', in T. C. Smout, *The Search for Wealth and Stability*, London, Allen and Unwin, 1979, pp. 175–97.
18. Davidson, 'Government Administration', p. 167.
19. Lord Riddell, *More Pages From My Diary, 1908–14*, London, 1934, p.42.
20. Hueck and Nipperdey, *Lehrbuch des Arbeitsrechts*, p. 34. G. Bender, 'Strukturen des Kollektiven Arbeitsrechts vor 1914. Ein Beitrag zu den historischen Grundlagen der rechtsförmigen Steuerung des industriellen Konflicts', in H. Steindl (ed.), *Wege zur Arbeitsrechtsgeschichte*, Frenchort, Ius Commune, 1984, pp. 271–3.
21. N. Olszak, 'Alexandre Millerand et l'organisation de la grève', in N. Aliprantis and F. Kessler (eds), *Le droit collectif du travail*, Frankfurt, 1994, pp. 135–49; and 'L'utilisation politique du droit des obligations dans la pensée de la Belle époque', *Revue de la Recherche Juridique – Droit Prospectif*, 1, 1995, pp. 31–45.
22. *Xveme Congrès National Corporatif. Compte-rendu des travaux*, Amiens, 1906, p. 129.
23. The Charter of Amiens recognised interests besides the daily trade union tasks slanted towards 'the increase in well-being of workers' by the improvements of their immediate conditions, such as the shortening of hours of work, the increase of wages, etc.', but one cannot say that these improvements had to be obtained by legislation.
24. P. Bance, *Les fondateurs de la C.G.T. à l'épreuve du droit*, La pensée sauvage, 1979, p. 315.
25. For the details see Schöttler, *Naissance des bourses du travail*.
26. Paul Pic regretted the absence of such regulations in his *Traité élémentaire de legislation industrielle*, (6th edn), Paris, 1930, pp. 292–3.
27. On these matters see N. Olszak, 'Les conseils de prud'hommes: un archetype judiciaire pour le mouvement ouvrier?', *Le mouvement social*, 41, 1987, pp. 101–19. It repeats some points made in his thesis, *Mouvement ouvrier et le système judiciaire, 1830–1950*, 3 vols, Strasbourg, 1987.
28. R. Challinor, *A Radical Lawyer In Victorian England: W. P. Roberts and the Struggle for Workers' Rights*, London, I.B. Tauris, 1990, pp. 71–169.
29. H. Hatzfeld, *Du pauperisme à la securité sociale, 1850–1940*, Paris, Armand Colin, 1971; P. Kohler, H. Zacher, and P. J. Hesse (eds) *Un siècle de securité sociale, 1881–1991*, University of Nantes, CRHES, 1982.
30. For the details of the British schemes see B. B. Gilbert, *The Evolution of National Insurance in Britain*, London, Michael Joseph, 1966. See also E. P. Hennock, *British Social Reform and German Precedents*, Oxford, Clarendon Press, 1987. For a shrewd assessment of social welfare and labour market policy see N. Whiteside, 'The Revolution that Failed: Public Administration and Labour Market Policy in Britain, 1880–1918' in E. V. Heyen (ed.), *Burokratisierung und Professionalisierung der Socialpolitik Europa, 1870–1918*, Baden-Baden, Nomos, 1993, pp. 57–81.

Chamberlain, however, had initiated the 1897 Workmen's Compensation Act.
31. M. Leroy, *Les techniques nouvelles du syndicalisme*, Paris, 1921, pp. 12–13.
32. 'Reconnaissance judiciaire du droit de signaler les faux-frères', *La Voix du Peuple*, 19 February 1905.

CHAPTER NINE

Employers and trade unions in the late nineteenth century in Britain, France and Germany

Marie-Geneviève Dezès, Kenneth Lunn, Arthur McIvor and Klaus Tenfelde

Overall view: similarities and differences

Especially in English language works, the historical literature on employers' labour policy seems to mirror a 'three-model typology'.[1] The picture of Britain is that of well-developed employers' organisations, although employers' policies in general seem to have been rather ineffectual and divided, which was partially due to the different market conditions they met in different branches. France seems to have been particularly fragmented and decentralised, showing very different stages of development at the same time, while Germany turned to a centralised and highly bureaucratic administration of employers' policies. The view on British employers, in particular, has been confirmed by various authors, concluding that their associations with regard to the labour movement 'typically lacked the internal coherence and capacity for sustained offensive action'.[2] As a matter of fact, on France Dezès shows that a high degree of variation according to region (centre and periphery) and branch of industry occurred whereby government policies intervened from the Napoleonic times, and created institutions designed to mediate labour conflicts especially on the regional level. A clear nationwide employers' organization, solely committed to all aspects of labour policies, did not evolve. Such aspects, it seems, would primarily include preventive and actual conflict management, and entrepreneurial opinion leadership concerning social policy and legislation.[3] In the German case, it must be said that during the first half of the nineteenth century, a certain French influence was felt although, since the foundation of the Reich, efforts at centralising the organisational capacity succeeded comparatively soon, and resulted in a system of leading organisations of the different branches, and a national organisation combining all entrepreneurial effort, after the turn of the centuries.

To a certain extent, A. McIvor has challenged the prevailing views, maintaining that, first of all, in a basic antipathy shared by European entrepreneurs towards the notion of collective organisation of their workers, British employers did not form an exception. Furthermore, internal variation of employers' strategies must be taken into consideration. In terms of organisational density, it is assumed that British employers around 1900 may well have had 'the most comprehensive network of employers' associations of any European country'. Through such organisations, British employers in several key sectors of the economy aptly took 'the initiative in regulating industrial relations', although their strength apparently laid 'primarily at the local and regional level'. Finally, it is indicated that British employers in particular may have taken a positive stance towards the trade unions in the decade prior to the First World War. Apparently, the advantages of stability and peace on the labour market, as well as at plant level, and the curtailment of competition reached by wage agreements, may have persuaded them to take a positive view.[4] Although in Germany, singular voices of that kind from social reform circles were heard, until 1914 the labour movement as a whole, and especially trade union influence, was fiercely challenged by employers' associations which, in pursuit of their policies, adopted a subtle and, at times, highly effective range of tools. There were only very few employers such as Robert Bosch or Ernst Abbe who were strong enough in terms of market control, personal standing and financial resources, to stay away from such policies.[5] In France it seems that compulsory participation in a network of institutions aimed at regulating labour conflicts preoccupied entrepreneurs as well as trade unions to a certain degree, although the latter diminished their strength by ideological fragmentation and lack of ability to effectually centralise.

Many authors seem to assume that, by this or the other national variation, most European nations and also the USA fit into the three-type model depicted above. In fact, the similarities of the organisational development of employers' interests throughout Europe are quite impressive. Apart from employers' strategies towards their workers at plant level, a scheme of organisational development seems to have occurred everywhere: in a first phase, lasting from the beginning of general entrepreneurial organisation until the occurrence of a labour movement of some local or regional strength, the interests of entrepreneurs as well as employers were organised within the framework of available types of organisation – that is, the local club system, chambers of commerce and regional or professional interest organisations which sometimes combined in this or the other way. This structure of rather accidental, but partially corporate interest organisations of entrepreneurs underwent structural differentiation according to need. Thus on the parliamentary level, entrepreneurs would develop different strategies to pursue their interests either by personal mandate, or by lobby organisation, or both. To meet their interests to develop or maintain infrastructures, to influence politics on local levels, to achieve favourable transportation prices and customs and so on, they would form different organisations. Specific employers' interests concerning workers during the early stages of development were usually covered by the old multifaceted types of entrepreneurial organisation. It was with the rise of trade unions that a need to cooperate evolved, aimed at strike prevention, at mutual help in case of strikes, at curtailment of the trade unions, and at favourable administrative efforts and legislation to these ends. Thereby, the influence on public opinion played an important role. Thus in the light of the results of the numerous parliamentary committees set up in Britain to investigate the conditions of work and the fate of the workers, British entrepreneurs could not but partially concede, and support social reform policies. The same was true in Germany in the case of Bismarck's social policies concerning sickness funds, old age pensions and national accident insurance in the 1880s.

The tendency towards forming specialised employers' associations usually became strong during massive strike movements.[6] From such conflicts, efforts at organisation evolved everywhere, and concerned both sides. Strikes, especially large strike movements which cover different regions and professions, tend to evolve especially in booming periods of the economy. It seems that, in the case of Britain, the economic boom which lasted from the middle of the century well into the 1870s led to a blossoming period of organisation in all parts of the economy. Strikes tended to end successfully, and wage agreements spread everywhere, being improved time and again during new conflict movements. During this time period, the German trade union movement was far from a massive market influence; it simply experienced its foundation period which was overshadowed by the early formation of social democracy, and also by the events of the Reich foundation period. Within the French economy, business cycles of those times did not lead to a comparable degree of growth, and the development seems to have been far more regionalised so that it is difficult to grasp general tendencies.

A turning point was reached during the European strike wave of 1889–90. It seems as if this first decisive period of highly active workers' mass movements brought employers' associations of all three countries under investigation to a new quality of effort. In Britain, it seems, the system of wage agreements was brought to completion, and conciliation as well as arbitration boards spread nationwide. In France, the period from the late 1880s to the turn of the centuries brought numerous employers *syndicats* into existence, although these apparently exerted only limited influences in strike movements, while in Germany in 1889 and 1890, and again from 1896 onwards, in all important branches employers' associations came into being. While the 'Central Association of German Industry' which had been founded in 1876, had until then dominated class conflict to a certain extent, especially in heavy industries, from the 1890s onwards, structural differentiation of entrepreneurial policies clearly led to a peculiar type of organisation designed to protect entrepreneurs' interests against the labour movement, and to limit its influence wherever possible, extending as far as parliamentary politics. It seems that, in terms of organisational structure, European developments have merged since the early 1890s. Yet quite different from the development in Britain, German employers – especially within the important branches of industries such as mining and smelting as well as machine-building – successfully avoided the introduction of wage agreements. The British culture of conciliation had come into being mainly in the blossoming period from 1850 to the late 1870s, and had created a set of institutions designed to manage labour disputes and to legalise working conditions by contract. In Germany, so far, the influence of government prevailed. Since the trade unions, except for the building industries, the printers and some minor professions, were unable to introduce wage agreements, the legalisation of work contracts proceeded rather by law than by agreement, leaving wages and working hours in particular to voluntary concessions on the part of the entrepreneurs, or to occasional achievements as a result of strikes. Thus in Germany, as well as in France, government influence remained strong.

Strategies of entrepreneurs towards their workers

Historically and systematically, the strategies of employers towards their workers are in the first place determined by their experiences at plant level. 'Historically' would mean that, except for a few cases especially in heavy industries, industrial undertakings did not grow up from nothing, but were rooted in family and market traditions usually within a local network of relations. The generation of 'pioneer entrepreneurs' emerged in Britain in the late eighteenth century and in Germany and France in the first half of the nineteenth century and thus received much of its social consciousness from family traditions. 'Systematically', it seems quite clear that the attitudes of entrepreneurs are determined to a large degree by labour market conditions, and the needs of the specific goods they produce. One would also have to take into account the features of specific branches, the propensity to organise on the part of entrepreneurs in regard of sales, the degree of interlocal cooperation in a given industry, and the sheer size of industrial activity.

So far, the case of mining is quite convincing.[7] Mining property was scattered in Britain, but rather centralised in France and Germany where strong government influence lasted well into the nineteentht century. It seems that, additionally, geological conditions and regional dispersion prevented the British mines from growing beyond a certain size, while the industry in Germany, once it was liberated from government influence around the middle of the century, grew fast and developed an urban landscape of its own. Within such new industries, severe labour shortage occurred, so that employers felt compelled to construct company housing on a large scale. The incentive to develop large-scale company welfare programmes within these industries must be clearly distinguished from that kind of paternalism which grew up from family and guild traditions in France and especially in Germany, although, in effect, the results were similar.[8]

Work conditions seem to have influenced such attitudes. At different stages of development, craft traditions could remain strong, while at certain workplaces, such as the textile industries, the structural composition of the workforce changed to include female workers. It seems that textile factories did develop paternalistic practices during the early phases of industrialisation, but failed to do so in the later decades, unless local conditions compelled them to do. Everywhere, labour shortage was a severe problem which had to be met by extraordinary measures so that company towns could develop in isolated areas. If managers and proprietors of the Ruhr heavy industries in the 1880s had been unable to recruit massive numbers of workers from the Prussian East, they would have been compelled to concede to union influence after 1890, as British employers bad been forced to in the 1850s and 1860s. Thus the availability of labour would determine union influence to a strong degree. In contrast, Silesian, Ruhr and Saar industrialists aptly developed a rough version of paternalism, the so-called 'master in the house' rule (*Herr-im-Hause-Standpunkt*) which enabled them to forcefully isolate their large plants from union influence, to successfully battle social democracy, and to exert important influences on social policies by paying unusually high wages, maintaining a strongly hierarchical structure of the workforce, and by provision of a refined company welfare system. For this, Krupp became especially famous. It seems that it was this attitude which, through the early foundation of a central association of German industries, flooded into many of the employers' associations which were founded after the 1890s, and nurtured the development of a range of subtle means to fight union influence such as blacklists, control of the local labour supply by employers' job centres, lockout strategies, and nurturing of yellow unions.

At least in Germany, social reform strategies, such as profit-sharing schemes or partnership statutes, remained weak and, for different reasons, the same seems to have been true in France, whereas in Britain, the system of wage agreements spread and institutionalised itself, so that trade union influence, especially at plant level, was secured at an early stage of development On the continent, employers succeeded almost everywhere in preventing even local trade union leaders establishing a physical presence in the factories. In Germany at least, employers rather successfully addressed government to support such attitudes and, especially in case of labour disputes, collaboration between plant officials and local authorities frequently went beyond what was possible in terms of law. It could be shown by numerous examples that such grassroot experiences from the plant level spilled over into the public. After all, the variety of such experiences may have been much too large to explain for a common direction of effort.

Trade unions and socialism

There was one thing that employers had in common everywhere – they all took an instinctively negative stance against the trade unions. Everywhere they had to realise that the sheer existence of trade unions would tend to decrease the power of decision-making and influence profits. Once trade union existence was confirmed beyond reasonable doubt, employers would turn to rather flexible policies even in Germany, where trade union existence was not recognised until 1916, but in fact became irrevocable after 1890. Yet, here, flexibility at best only resulted in making concessions without comment, while, openly, most employers would even deny the existence of Christian trade unions whose policies complied with the monarchial rule and market capitalism. Generally, the negative stance led to important concessions at plant level when faced with government social policies. For many, to concede to work protection legislation and social insurance schemes, or to invent and pursue the subtle means of paternalism, appeared to be a lesser evil.

The degree of affiliation, or connection of the trade unions to the different mainstreams of socialism, becomes important here. Without raising questions of exceptionalism, the fact that British trade unions throughout the nineteenth century dominated the labour movement, that a socialism which would have set its aims beyond capitalism did occur but remained weak, and that finally the Labour Party was formed on the grounds of trade unionism, must be deemed highly important, and is quite contrary to the German experience. There, in the middle of the nineteenth century, the middle classes (*Bürgertum*) gained strength in the light of a well-known spectre which materialised when the Social Democratic Party was founded in 1863, before trade unions could develop to sizable dimensions. On the contrary, it was socialism which seemed to have created trade unions which, in turn, were considered to be schools for socialism. Under the political conditions to be debated later in this chapter, trade unions and social democracy additionally merged, or were melded together so that, from the 1890s onwards, those people and powers in society who fought trade unions believed themselves to legitimately be fighting socialism. A British employer would not easily take such a stance.

Additionally, the different organisational modes generated by the trade unions in both countries must be considered. The early foundation of trade unions in Britain, and their major achievements during economic booms, had led to professional unions with a strong foothold at plant level, while in Germany the central association principle prevailed from the outset so that the tradition of localism which had played a certain role in a variety of professions was successfully defeated in the early 1890s. Hampered by the gravity of their own institutions, it took British trade unions quite a while to reach a new unionism, whereas their German counterparts, during the boom period which lasted from the middle-1890s until the outbreak of the First World War, apparently disposed of a more modern organisational tool. In terms of growth, they partially outnumbered their British comrades during those decades.

In general terms, there are two organisational modes which trade unions possibly may pursue: that is, a plant-level organisation which easily leads to closed shop principles and strengthens professional unionism, or a local organisation beyond single factories which emphasises the organisational hierarchy from the local to the regional and national level. Where the first prevails, the system would tend to reach plant-level agreements, while the latter would tend to centralise and put the bargaining procedure on a level beyond the local authorities. Thus the very trade union structure which accounted for the rapid growth of German trade unions may have hampered their bargaining capacity at plant level. Interestingly enough, this is a major issue of German trade union policy even nowadays.

In France, trade unions remained much more scattered until the end of the nineteenth century, and a clear principle of organisation did not evolve although at least a root organisation emerged. As in Germany, a rather strong inclination to the ideas of socialism could have served to unite employers' opposition, but factionalism and an overall weakness rather undermined such possible strength until the first decade of the twentieth century. To a strong degree, this weakness apparently derived from the influence of anarchism and anarcho-syndicalism which in turn strengthened local professional organisations. Additionally, the ideological fragmentation of trade unions between Catholic and socialist influences made things difficult – a fact which has to be accounted for in Germany as well. Thus the French case would appear to have a mixture of German and British trade union structures which resulted in considerable weakness, and allowed employers to abstain from powerful professional and national organisation. Hence the impression of rather accidental and scattered development of employers' unions until around 1900. Of course this did not prevent employers from using subtle and rough tools to fight trade unions: yellow unions (*syndicat maison*), compulsory professional records (*Arbeitsbücher* in Germany) and employer-organized employment offices (*Arbeitsnachweise* in Germany) were introduced as well. On the part of the unions, the frequently important role of the *mandat impératif* and of *action directe* could of course infringe or impede settlements on wages and work conditions.

The role of politics

Employers' attitudes towards trade unions, as well as the density and strength of their organisations, were much affected by the legal framework in which they operated. Perhaps even more important were the politics of the state, autocratic or liberal, and which classes or groups predominated in it.

In Britain, it is difficult to detect any infringement on the right to convene and to form associations on the part of entrepreneurs in the late eighteenth and throughout the nineteenth centuries. On the part of the workers, even the Combination Laws which lasted until 1824 rarely limited the existence of craft societies and artisan organisation. Thus the legal framework to form trade unions, and to use the strike as an ultimate weapon, was quite favourable, while employers' associations were not hindered at all. Roughly throughout the first two-thirds of the nineteenth century, the opposite is true for France and Germany, though such legal provisions increasingly came under debate. In legal terms, even employers were forbidden to form associations, but they enjoyed the advantage of the small number, and legally convened under different cover to spell out their strategies. Any kind of legalisation of trade unions was denied in France as well as in Germany, although factual recognition took place in both countries. A peak level of denial was reached in Germany from 1878 to 1890 when the Anti-Socialist Law prohibited socialist organisations whereby trade unions were included easily. Additionally, throughout the period under consideration, jurisdiction made it difficult for German trade unions to exist, while employers' associations never encountered such problems since they had come into existence.

There was only, therefore, a degree of balance between the legal rights and possibilities for action between unions and employers in Britain. In contrast, the constitutional provisions and the combination of political powers in Germany were very much weighted in favour of the employers. Time after time, the employers submitted legal proposals, such as on the breach of contract, to the Reichstag. Although most of these proposals failed, the right of combination remained under debate until 1912.

Things were different in France. When Alexandre Millerand became minister of trade in 1899, social reform policies were extended to industrial relations to introduce a new bargaining system (*parlamentarisme industriel*). The separation of the trade unions from reformist socialism (Charter of Amiens 1906) helped to separate such reformist policy, and cleared the way for the Parti Socialiste (SFIO). On the other hand, French syndicalism, and the kind of localism connected to it, survived and strengthened within the CGT. As a result, company and employers' strategies towards the trade union movement could vary to a considerable degree, resting on local conditions and traditions, but were increasingly regulated by law.

Organized capitalism and national distinctiveness

In the case of France, it was government that pressed ahead with legislation on industrial conciliation, especially after 1906.[9] At the end of the century, the *conseils de prud'hommes* had weakened, but Millerand established a new national network of conciliation boards, and tried to influence labour disputes by law. Although the bill failed to pass Parliament, the tendency seems typical for France because such regulation would have changed union bargaining into workshop bargaining. At the same time, labour disputes increased considerably. Only now, as a response, did employers' unions emerge to a considerable degree. Lockouts, which had been almost unknown in French labour disputes before 1900, now became possible. It seems that the employers' associations tended to form mutual aid systems rather than act as conciliators in trade disputes; it may well be that this was at least partially a result of government action to regulate the peace-winning procedure in labour conflicts.

Britain did not need all this. Whether British employers exerted strong political influence or not, at least they did not doubt that collaboration was necessary, and that the system of industrial relations had led to some sort of stability at plant level and within the branches of industry. Organised capitalism – if we limit the meaning of the term to the development of an efficient system of wages and work conditions settlement – had developed freely and without much government influence, although parliamentary debates and committees of investigation had influenced public opinion, and thus paved the way for the development of such institutions.

In Germany conciliation boards had been introduced in 1890 but, due to legal provisions, they never took the lead in major labour disputes. Settlement was reached by different means. Government action so far compared to France, but remained half-hearted. Especially in the important industries, wage agreements could not be reached by mutual bargaining procedures, but furthermore tended to look like concessions on the part of the employers. Almost all the employers' unions strongly refused formal bargaining procedures.

Thus it seems that the political framework decisively influenced the directions and convictions of employers' policies towards the trade unions. Semi-authoritarian government in Germany made it possible that employers could refrain from bargaining procedures while, in France, government at least attempted to care for an effective system of industrial relations. At the grass-roots, though, the tools of employers' policies remained similar throughout the countries under consideration. Yet it seems that such similarity was outweighed by the distinctiveness of the national frameworks of politics. On the other hand, strong tendencies towards the legalisation of bargaining procedures, and the institutional establishment of conciliation and arbitration, can be detected in all three countries. At least in Germany, and perhaps also in France, the two decades from 1914 to 1933–36 did provide little opportunity to further develop a conciliatory culture in industrial relations. This may explain why an academic culture of teaching and research in industrial relations has been well-established at Anglo-American universities, but gained a foothold in Germany only recently.

Notes

1. A. McIvor, *Organized Capital: Employers' Associations and Industrial Relations in Northern England*, Cambridge, 1996; S. Tolliday and J. Zeitlin (eds), *The Power of Manage? Employers and Industrial Relations in Comparative Perspective*, London, 1991.

2. J. Zeitlin, 'From Labour History to the History of Industrial Relations', *Economic History Review*, 40, 1987, p. 175.
3. M.-G. Dezès, 'La préhistoire des conventions collectives françaises' in *Les conventions collectives de branche déclin ou renouveau?*, Etude 65, Centre d'études et de recherche sur les Qualifications, November 1993, pp. 27–53.
4. A. McIvor, 'British Employers, their Organizations and Trade Unions, c. 1880–1914, unpublished paper, 1995.
5. G. Feldman and K. Tenfelde (eds), *Workers, Owners and Politics in Coal Mining. An International Comparison of Industrial Relations*, Munich, 1989; New York, 1990.
6. F. Boll, *Arbeitskämpfe und Gewerkshaften in Deutschland, England und Frankreich. Ihre Entwicklung vom 19. zum 20 Jahrhundert*, Bonn, 1992, pp. 154, 223 and 287.
7. See Dezès, 'La préhistoire des conventions', McIvor, *Organized Capital*, J. Michel's thesis, *Le mouvement ouvrier chez les mineurs d'Europe occidentale (Grande-Bretagne, Belgique, France, Allemagne). Étude comparative des années 1880 à 1914*, 6 vols, University of Lyon, 1987.
8. P. Fridenson, 'Herrschaft im Wirtschaftsunternehmen Deutschland und Frankreich, 1880–1914', in J. Kocha (ed.), *La bourgeoisie au XIXème siècle*, 2 vols, Munich, 1988. D. Geary, 'The Industrial Bourgeoisie and Labour Relations in Germany, 1871–1933', in D. Blackbourn and R. Evans (eds), *The German Bourgeoisie*, London, 1991, pp. 140–61.
9. M.-G. Dezès, 'La préhistoire des conventions', P. Fridenson, 'Le conflit social', in A. Burguière and J. Revel (eds), *Histoire de la France et des conflits*, Paris, 1990, pp. 355–458.

CHAPTER TEN

The multiple foundations of trade union organisation[1] in nineteenth-century Germany, France and Britain

Michel Dreyfus, Sandrine Kott, Michel Pigenet and Noel Whiteside

Introduction

In his study of world trade unionism, the French writer Paul Louis said in 1913: 'all over Europe, trade unions have adopted multiple bases for organisation'.[2] This expression, not customary to European trade unions, introduced implicitly a distinction between what contemporary British commentators called the 'trade' functions of unions and their provision of 'friendly benefits', which they provided to members outside periods of struggle. When unionists were not involved in disputes for higher wages or better working conditions, various social funds, unemployment funds and cultural associations took care of their everyday needs. This provision also served strategic purposes as it attracted – and retained – members. Louis emphasised nevertheless that 'certainly, this [multiple form of organisation] came up against more vehement opposition in Latin countries than in Germanic countries, where it is fully developed'. This established a distinction, dear to French unionists, between revolutionary and militant unionism, mostly found in southern Europe, and the type of reformist, administrative organisation dominating northern countries. This double opposition – contrasting revolutionary and reformist, fighting and functional – typifies a French vision of trade unionism. In Britain, and partly in Germany, the unions' protesting and administrative functions were closely linked with the movement's foundations. The existence of mutual benefit systems alongside industrial action was no contradiction; they were one of its foundations and the basis for its successful prosecution.

Using comparative analysis, we can re-examine the relevance of these common distinctions between reformist and revolutionary trade organisation in analysing the uneven roles reserved for mutual benefit systems in European trade unions. Surely other factors played some part in their development – most obviously, external constraints?

Genealogy

Great Britain and Germany: mutuality and the Poor Laws

In Great Britain, as in Germany, the essential character of organised mutuality found within the union movement sprang in part from the nature of the Poor Laws. In Britain, although we now believe that the 1834 Act was never implemented as harshly as intended, the threat of the workhouse and the social stigma associated with pauperism served as deterrents, pushing all sections of the working population into protecting themselves from the need for relief. Mutual insurance represented a good solution to this problem and even the poorest working-class households took out insurance policies with clubs or mutual aid societies, organised on the basis of locality, religious affiliation or trade. By 1900 friendly societies held over 4 million policies and formed the most common form of mutual protection. This movement was entirely voluntary. In Germany and particularly in Prussia, on the other hand, the greater impulse came from localities legally obliged to provide sustenance to the destitute. With industrialisation, the towns of western Prussia,[3] were faced with an influx of population from the rural areas in the East. In order to limit the financial burden of poor relief, they promoted providence, encouraging workers to subscribe regularly to mutual aid funds which, by and large, were trade-based. Under pressure from large towns on the Ruhr, the Prussian government passed laws in 1845 and 1849 which authorised local communes to pass statutes obliging first tradesmen, and later factory workers, to subscribe to mutual sickness societies. The old artisanal societies formed the foundations of this system but were transformed into compulsory funds under the financial control of the commune. This model was reproduced across northern Germany in the 1860s and subsequently – in a different form – in the South in the 1870s. By 1872 there were around 725 000 people insured within 4690 obligatory funds, to which we can add nearly 400 000 members of 2000 free societies, mostly organised on the basis of trade or profession.

Mutuality and trade unionism

In the three countries, mutual aid societies were conceived as a spontaneous substitute for the vanishing obligation of the rich to protect the poor. They were complemented by the development of cooperative movements which protected workers as consumers. The help provided by mutual aid organisations varied widely: funerals were highly important, as demonstrated by the continuing popularity of informal burial clubs in Britain. In France and Germany the importance of this sector declined, to the profit of sickness societies. This type of help was legally reinforced in all three countries (in 1852 in France, in 1875 in Britain and in 1876 in Germany). Such legislation imposed varying degrees of official control over forms of mutuality previously associated solely with developing workers' movements.

As with the German funds, a certain number of British friendly societies structured their organisations according to trade. The Friendly Society of Ironfounders, for example, created in 1832, offered a number of different benefits; it only recruited workers in the trade who observed conditions of employment (in terms of wages, working hours and so on) conforming to the society's rulebook. From any standpoint, this society was effectively a trade union, using mutual benefits to reinforce industrial demands. In Britain as in France (until 1852) and in Germany, society meetings were largely occasions for comrades and workers to meet to discuss future strategies and collective action.

During periods of reaction which, east of the Rhine, followed the collapse of the 1848 Revolution and also characterised the years of the Anti-Socialist Laws from 1878–90, mutual benefit societies became the secret organisational basis for the workers' movement,[4] while simultaneously helping to shape its structure. The first trade federation of free unions, the tobacco workers, also responded to the need to unite local funds which aimed to provide unemployment benefits. For the British 'new model' unions, bargaining and benefit functions were closely linked from the outset. Providing benefits to sick or unemployed members effectively protected them from being forced to accept work on non-union terms. High wages helped fund high union dues; successful unions thus indirectly obliged employers to pay for sick or injured workers, as well – in some cases – as those temporarily surplus to industrial requirements.

This model formed the explicit blueprint for the liberal German unions which, under the inspiration of Max Hirsch and Max Duncker, came together in a national confederation in 1868–69. Influenced by English trade unionism, they saw in trade unions instruments for industrial negotiation and for regulating the labour market. In this respect they remained opposed to the revolutionary movement around

Lassalle or Bebel. All the same, these last two also recognised the importance of social support. The funds played an essential role in union organisation because they attracted new members and provided the foundations for powerful trade federations. They formed a bridge between old, artisanal traditions from which they sprang and the newer organisational forms adopted by trade unions. This explains the nature of union help. During the 1870s traditional forms of union help, in particular tramping benefit (*viaticum*), were still largely dominant but, following the British example, contributions became more specific and benefits more diverse.[5]

France: the break of 1852

In both Britain and Germany governments favoured this more managerial orientation, from opposite political perspectives. In Britain, the Royal Commission on Labour saw in it signs to a 'highly remarkable degree, the power of organisation, self government and self help'.[6] In Germany, although official views varied, the social conservatives, who liked to see trade unions as descendants of the guilds, favoured the provision of benefits because if 'we prevent workmen's organisations undertaking this new activity, we will push them to the left onto the territory of social agitation and into the arms of social democracy'.[7]

By contrast, the French law passed in 1852 distinguished neatly and clearly between the two elements of confrontation and mutuality. The *Le Chapelier* law of 1791, this 'terrible act,'[8] outlawed all forms of worker organisation until 1884. In the interim, the mutual aid societies, as in Germany, constituted the matrix of union organisation. Following legislation in 1852, mutuality was no longer organised on a trade basis, but on a geographical one, controlled by the local establishment. In this way, mutuality became cut off from the workers' movement. By 1870, these 'approved' societies covered more than three-fifths of mutual aid, comprising 670000 members, observed by 110000 honorary members. These societies kept completely apart from the struggles of the communes, which led to the total dissociation between the two branches of the social movement. From that point, the two histories coincided only chronologically. The first National Congress of Mutuality was held in 1883 at Lyon, one year before the Waldeck-Rousseau law legalised trades unions. The Fédération Nationale de la Mutualité Française (FNMF) was constituted in 1902, the same year as the 'second birth' of the CGT at the congress of Montpellier. Throughout, the two movements remained completely separate.[9]

Union dues and union benefits in practice

Contrasts and similarities

At first glance, the comparison of contributions and union benefits in these three countries conforms to the classical picture of opposition between two types of unionism: confrontational in France and managerial/administrative in Britain and Germany.

The statistics do not contradict this impression, notably in the British case where 70 per cent of union expenditure was taken up by benefit payments in the years 1905–07, years of high unemployment, while less than 8 per cent funded strike action.[10] Further, over 50 per cent of the 4.1 million trade union members at the start of the First World War could claim benefits from their unions.[11] While, originally, only the older artisanal trades had provided benefits, conditions had changed by the late nineteenth century. The largest and most comprehensive schemes were then to be found in national unions of skilled industrial workers in engineering, shipbuilding, metalworking, construction and printing. Excluding the miners and textile workers (the latter also gave help to sick members), these unions dominated the TUC until the renaissance of 'new unionism' in 1889, dedicated to strike action, temporarily reconstructed the general balance of power. The provision of unemployment benefit, a risk not covered by the friendly societies, illustrates this evolution. In 1891 nearly 682 000 members belonged to unions offering help to the unemployed – a number reaching nearly 2.36 million by 1908.[12]

Less well-developed, the German union movement, which was restructured following the repeal of the Anti-Socialist Laws in 1890, totalled around 2.9 million members on the eve of the war. This spectacular growth in power was based on organisations which had developed a very broad range of union services. Although strike benefit took pride of place in union expenditure, the total spent by the free trade unions with socialist sympathies reached 48 million marks in 1913, or 18.75 marks per union member. This total reached 2.5 million marks (7.29 marks per member) and 1.5 million marks (14.36 marks per member) in the Christian and liberal unions respectively.

In terms of the numbers covered and the sums of money dispensed, the rare benefits bequeathed by French organisations indicates a completely different sociopolitical context. Fewer than 9 per cent – 8.4 per cent – of the 2 178 trade unions surveyed in 1894 had precise policies for helping unemployed members.[13] Further, the funds accumulated did not always permit the observation of statutory rules. In that year, 87 unions with 16 250 members – around 4 per cent of French trade unionists – actually paid out benefits. Eight years later, the expansion of the movement was not accompanied by any real expansion in funds or range of help. Only 30 297 workers were covered by a trade union unemployment scheme.[14] When inspected, the financial receipts of 285 out of 310 societies were found to cover only 80 per cent of expenditure.

On the basis of statutory obligations – which are certainly exaggerated and give a false impression – a statistical survey made on 1 January 1911 revealed the dominance of cheaper services. Of 5325 unions, 26.8 per cent claimed to have a library and 19.7 per cent had a placement bureau.[15] Following this, specialised societies offered (in descending order of importance): sickness benefits (15.3 per cent); unemployment protection (11.1 per cent); and travel benefit (9.3 per cent). More complex services were offered on an even smaller scale: professional courses (6.6 per cent); union bulletin (2.5 per cent); cooperative and pension funds (1.5 per cent). The matter might be better understood if a more detailed analysis did not stretch out these national contrasts and moderate the picture through oversimplification.

In all three countries, effectively the same group of traditional trades, incorporating real skills and knowledge – cabinet makers, carpenters, typographers, mechanical engineers and so on – were able to construct solid organisations, endowed with important benefit funds of diverse forms.

Such broad similarities aside, many variations can be observed. For example, the organisational capacities of the English engineers (ASE) varied over space and time. In this case, sustaining national rates of pay and working conditions was unrealistic in a sector as technologically heterogeneous as engineering. In periods of slack trade, one branch might accept lower wage rates to protect members' employment. When times improved, demands for a shorter working day or a higher wage rate resurfaced. During the years 1871–72, the ASE's national executive supervised rolling strike action, district by district, supported by a mix of unemployment benefit and strike pay, in a successful struggle to win the nine-hour day. Twenty-five years later, the same strategy failed to win an eight-hour day because the newly formed Engineeering Employers' Federation declared a national lockout – an episode which revealed the vulnerability of union benefit funds to mass conflict of this type.

In the printing trade, the powerful London Society of Compositors (LSC) could bypass negotiations and fix wage rates unilaterally, leaving their enforcement to local branches. This union operated rigorous systems of work-sharing among casual hands and also sustained high levels of unemployment benefits, emigration grants and sickness benefits. A similar degree of collective protection existed on the other side of the Channel. From 1881 the constitutional congress of the Fédération française des Typographes – soon the Fédération du Livre – introduced, over and above travel grants, payments to strikers who, for the duration of ratified conflict, became the 'salaried' employees of the organisation.[16] At the turn of the century, the Federation introduced unemployment and sickness benefits, then a contractual funeral grant.[17] On a more modest scale, French inquiries noted a relative frequency of unemployment funds among mechanical engineers, older wood, leather and fur trades, among hat-makers and makers of precision instruments.[18] Organisations of workers in the food trades preferred, by contrast, to give precedence to the placement of unemployed members, while the provision of professional training courses were to be found in a few specialist sectors among clerks, white-collar workers, draughtsmen and accountants.

On the margins of unionism: the cooperatives

Although they maintained ambivalent relations with the union movement, consumers' cooperatives merit special mention. In Great Britain, where the movement was born, their operation, founded on the principles of consumer democracy, excluded any notion of workers' control. The employees were kept at a distance from management. The Co-operative Wholesale Society (CWS), which had over 2 million members by 1901, recruited – like the friendly societies – among skilled workers and artisanal groups.[19] The CWS, through the activities of its bank, became a repository for union funds and participated in the financing of strikes. During the 1912 miners' strike, for example, it loaned the Miners' Federation around £750 000.[20]

Even though similar reports can be found in France, the boom in union growth occurred after the movement had ceased to view cooperation as a form of worker emancipation. Although consumer cooperatives multiplied during the 1880s, the organised workers' movement saw them as institutions peripheral to their interests, until the guesdistes changed their minds, following the success of the Belgian cooperatives. Even so, the relationship between cooperatives and unions was neither exclusive nor systematic. The *L'Encyclopédie* of Compere-Morel underestimated the numbers of cooperative stores created by the Bourses du Travail, but strictly union-inspired ventures remained exceptional.[21]

Union–cooperative links were even more distant in Germany, where the central Federation of Consumers' Associations, founded in 1903 and close to the Sozialdemokratische Partei Deutschlands (SPD), kept a strict neutrality, aiming to compete with the Cooperative of Purchasers in accordance with the inspiration of liberal market principles.

Union services: between strategy and ideology

The impossible French system

The very limited range of French achievement in this area was not the consequence of any principled opposition. Until very late in the nineteenth century, neither external observers nor those involved could easily distinguish between a union branch and a mutual aid society. Some sought to build on this confusion inherited from the past. Jean Barbaret, founder of the Union Syndicale Ouvrière in 1872 and one of the architects of the legislation of 1884, admitted in 1901: 'I saw the possibility of making these two institutions, the professional trade union on one side and the mutual aid society on the other, two parallel actions which could be fused together' to the great advancement 'of peace and social security [sic]'.[22]

The gradualist approach promoted by Barbaret's followers was only faintly supported at the time when union organisations were being created. Nonetheless, this did not mean a categorical rejection of this means to 'raise the moral and economic standard'[23] of workers. Structural impediments also proved problematic. Although founded with the purpose of facilitating the collection and distribution of strike benefits and with their activities confined by low levels of subscription, French federations had grave difficulties in collecting promised allocations from their union members. As a result, many cut back their activities and stopped warning in advance of higher future contributions.[24] It would, however, be wrong to argue from the attitudes displayed by the Gambetta-inspired organisations of the 1870s, from the initiatives of the Christian trade unions or from the leaders of the Fédération du Livre, that a narrow correlation existed between the political orientation of the union and the amount of help it distributed. In other words, we must be careful not to understand mutual benefits in terms of the classical opposition between reformist and revolutionary unionism.

In France, the unions were never the principal advocates of reform among workers. Reformism was associated with the mutual aid societies and the cooperatives. Numerous trade unionists, both revolutionary and reformist, came together in criticising the servile attitudes and narrow perspective of both these movements. The revolutionaries were more vehement in their denunciations of widespread 'illusions', which Sorel termed 'the leprosy of social peace'.[25] But the reformists were equally disturbed when they saw activists weighed down with peripheral administrative tasks.[26] Advocates of direct action feared that members would be transformed into 'subscribing machines, no longer attending meetings'.[27] They feared the growth of organisational chauvinism, the development of discrimination through contributory record, contrary to the principles of solidarity.[28]

The revolutionaries did not condemn all this irrevocably. Fernand Pelloutier pushed the militants in the Bourses du Travail, these 'schools of social economy', to expand these 'noble deeds'.[29] In his view, these were a means of instruction, anchoring in the present the means to promote workers' self-emancipation and preparing white-collar workers for their future duties. Hostile to permanent funds and to capitalist forms of mutuality, the leaders of the Fédération de la Metallurgie decided in 1903 to devote themselves to 'work for social purposes'.[30] Collaborating with Monatte and Merrheim, the moving spirits behind *la Vie Ouvrière* became reconciled with Pelloutier's ideas before the end of the decade.

This renewal of interest, interrupted by the war, arrived all too late. The unions did not enjoy the exclusive provision of mutual benefits, which were buttressed by the law; further, other associations provided them extensively as their sole objective. The mutual aid societies never ceased to represent the most reasonable solution to 'social problems',[31] whether they embraced imperial notions of mutuality, the republican equivalent or were based on employer paternalism. All were preferable to a trade unionism based on struggle and agitation. The law of 21 March 1884, encouraging unions to develop mutual benefit systems, met with little success.

The law of 1 April 1898 recognised and confirmed the impregnable lead established by societies external to the union movement. On the eve of the war, these had 5.3 million members, a total five times the membership of all unions of wage-earners.[32]

The trade unionists appear to have resigned themselves to this reflection of natural forces, to the comfort of the more reticent revolutionaries. Even so, they continued to dispute control over paternalist societies with employers, in some areas.

Workers' protection and union discipline: the British model

In England, where this type of workers' mutuality was much older, union benefits were located more explicitly within organisational strategies. Unlike the industrial unions like the miners' or the general labour unions found on the docks, organisations of skilled workers were better able to defend their members through the astute use of indirect pressure rather than open struggle. Unionists incapable (through sickness, age or slack trade) of finding work on union terms, or working for an employer in breach of agreed work practices, were expected to become a charge on the union funds. As a result, the difference between unemployment and strike action became blurred as mutual benefits were used to enforce collective agreements and union rules. Members in breach of rules could be fined and, as unpaid fines carried the same penalties as membership arrears, all benefit rights were suspended until they were paid. As it was not unusual for both the amount of benefit and the period of cover to expand with length of membership, this sanction operated with some force: particularly on older unionists, who were more vulnerable to sickness and unemployment. By the 1890s a powerful union like the Boilermakers claimed to punish members guilty of drunkenness, poor timekeeping, substandard workmanship or disobedience of union rules. Branch meetings determined the right of claimants to union support, discussed local work practices and fixed sanctions imposed on offenders. In a broad variety of trade unions, branches ran their own contingency funds, which complemented 'legal' benefit systems in helping local trade unionists in distress. Schemes of benefits thus contributed to sustaining the numbers, fidelity and discipline of members, affirming the authority of the union operating them.

In this manner, union benefits served to strengthen skilled workers' organisations. For this reason, some employers – notably in the railways, the gas industry and coalmines – started to operate their own sickness funds; membership was sometimes made a condition of employment.

Practical and universal: the German system

At the turn of the century, the provision of sickness benefits took an upturn. By 1914 they were provided by 45 federations which organised 97 per cent of free union members (only 8 had been involved in 1897), which paid out more than 13 million marks, or 5.43 marks per union member. After strike benefit, they occupied first position in free union expenditure (over a quarter of the total). Further, they had changed their nature. Union sickness funds had lost the exclusive character they had possessed until the 1890s. In particular, they opened up more to women; in the case of the tobacco workers' federation, they provided maternity benefits. Undoubtedly, the sickness insurance law and legislation on work, making maternity leave obligatory, played an important part here. In more general terms, this evolution was symptomatic of what one might call the 'modernisation' of union benefits. Tramp benefit, which had represented one of the most important provisions in the period of trade union construction, only absorbed 3 per cent of union expenditure by 1913, at a time when payments to families to aid house removal were becoming more commonplace.

All this demonstrates a reorientation in the politics of union benefits.

Payments were increasingly made to sedentary workers, tied to their place of work by their families. In this, we can observe a change in the purpose of organisation: unions ceased to be instruments in the hands of a minority of agitators but came to recruit a growing part of the labour force, counterbalancing the influence of industrial employers. The growth of unemployment benefits underlines this transformation. For their advocates, this allowance gave the unions the means to participate in the regulation of the labour market alongside employers and in parallel with the appearance of labour bureaux which represented both sides of industry. On the other hand, before 1900, some members of free trade unions fought against the introduction of unemployment benefits which were perceived as an acceptance by the workers of the laws of a capitalist market economy. By the outbreak of war, the movement for unemployment benefits had triumphed. Such benefits now covered the majority of unionised workers: 40 federations of free trade unions (80 per cent of members) had introduced them. By 1913 these benefits absorbed nearly a quarter of total union expenditure.

Relations with the state: evidence of national constraints

It seems that both the size and nature of union benefit schemes were determined less by ideological preference than by judicial constraint and national politics. This conclusion is reinforced by the point made above concerning the operation of the Poor Laws in Britain and Germany. In more negative mode, the same is true for France, where the 1852 law favoured the evolution of mutual insurance based on geographical localities and controlled by the local establishment, while workers' organisations remained illegal.

State initiatives: the emergence of social policies

Confronted by a powerful movement, the German authorities sought to sustain institutions capable of underwriting social stability, while seeking to regulate their activities. The sickness insurance schemes set up in 1883 allowed free trade union systems to continue alongside other fund-holders; the most important were those which, at local level, took over obligatory schemes run by local authorities or individual enterprises. In opposition to these, free union funds were financed – and run – by workers themselves. These funds were free to select their members and were attractive because they did not hand out benefits in kind. In 1889 free funds insured nearly 13 per cent of the total numbers covered by the statutory sickness benefits. Among them were 12 organisations with more than 10000 members. The largest, the metalworkers and the masons, were closely linked to the social-democratic movement. They still observed regulations inherited from the old union schemes, in particular the double exclusivity of trade and sex, as well as a partial provision of medical treatments.

The explosion of worker militancy in 1889–93 threatened neither the established social order nor the English political system. It did, however, encourage British authorities to pursue the reform of union management, to require the separation of strike funds from sickness funds in order to offer legal protection to the latter alone. Following the infamous *Taff Vale* judgment in 1901, trade unions found themselves liable for breach of contract – which threatened to undermine their full range of benefits. The position was reversed by law in 1906, which restored the immunity of union funds from legal prosecution. The idea of establishing a distinction persisted, however, and was introduced under the 1911 National Insurance Act, which obliged participating trade unions to adopt the management of their benefits in a manner approved by the state.[33]

First suspicions and the diversity of subsequent progress

The National Insurance Act reflected the purpose of the social reformers, which aimed to secure economic efficiency and uniformity in the management of the labour force.

This new law created an insurance scheme in two parts – health and unemployment. Both were open to union administration. Those participating in the first – compulsory for all workers – registered as 'approved societies' under the Act. Two-thirds of funds for health benefits were provided by employers and the state, and unions wishing to administer benefits to their members were obliged to conform to the central regulation of their administrative practices, or risk losing members. In reality, after many repercussions and conjunctural crises for their funds, the unions accepted official intervention in this area. In the course of the deep depression of 1906–08, most union leaders had examined the possibility of state subsidies to their benefit funds, on the assumption that they would continue to control their management. A visit by German union delegates to the TUC congress in 1908 reassured British union leaders; state help would not enfeeble their organisation, but reinforce it. The initial hostility of British militants was not unusual. Their continental equivalents all displayed more or less equal mistrust of official initiatives, widely perceived as a threat to both union funds and union autonomy.

In France this danger was not great because union benefits were so modest. Even so, a number of unionists adopted an ideological opposition to the proposal for pensions for peasants and workers, whose 'integrating effects' they denounced. In 1898, Pelloutier asked: 'How can workers who accept the class struggle demand retirement pensions from a capitalist society?'[34] While rallying to the principle of pensions, the majority of federal leaders criticised the conditions – workers' contributions and conditions of age – embodied in the law passed in 1910. Termed aggravated 'swindling' and 'pensions for the dead', this rough draft of obligatory social protection limited to the lowest paid, incited the fury of the militants.

Socialist or liberal, the German trade unions had shown no great enthusiasm before the introduction of the Reich's first social legislation. By and large, most encouraged their followers to join the free union societies. German trade unionists always opted for maintaining a political presence.

With the removal of the Anti-Socialist Laws, the free funds which, from the 1880s had gone slowly into decline, ceased in effect to be central to the survival of the workers' movement. By the mid-1890s, the free trade unions, followed by the liberal and Christian organisations, were showing a growing interest in the councils governing local funds; these, in accordance with the principle of self-administration – the *Selbsterwaltung* – were two-thirds composed of subscribers' representatives. The election of these representatives became a focus for union action; by 1900 about 30 per cent of subscribers were involved, as opposed to 1 per cent in the years immediately following the passage of the law. The main local funds, at Dresden (84 000 members) or at Leipzig (100 000 members), came under the control of the free unions by 1895. Eight years later, J. Frassdorf, social-democratic deputy in the Saxony *Landtag*, took over the federation's direction of local sickness funds. Among other things, this constituted a reservoir of employment for union officials.[35] By the start of the First World War, three-quarters of the administrators had been elected on a union ticket.

In this situation, the workers' leaders began to develop a politics of hygiene which underpinned their social programme. The federation of local funds fostered inquiries into living conditions, a point of departure for a preventive programme for the 'three social diseases': tuberculosis, alcoholism and syphilis.

Redefinitions and reorientation: subsequent developments

This direction of policy helped to install the workers' movement into bourgeois society, even though it represented a recognition of workers' demands. This was particularly true of the 'workers' secretariats',[36] the antecedents of future union officialdom and supporters of the reformist tradition within the politics of social democracy.[37]

In Britain, Part 2 of the National Insurance Act provided benefits for the unemployed in a restricted number of trades, on the essential condition that their unemployment was 'involuntary'. As with health benefits, two-thirds of the contributory income came from employers and the state. The centralised management of claims placed the unions involved in a delicate position. Before workers' organisations could claim reimbursement of state benefits paid out to their members, they had to submit audited accounts for Treasury inspection. Initially at least, many such payments were deemed illegal and union funds suffered heavy losses. This was largely because the problems of sickness and unemployment were officially redefined and rendered uniform. Inability to work for reasons of sickness no longer simply referred to a particular trade, but described an incapacity for any type of work at all. To be unemployed no longer signified an inability to find work conforming to union terms and conditions. Under the new legislation, a worker unemployed following dismissal for differences with his employer lost all right to state support.

These differences created by the Act rebounded on the internal life of the unions. Under the threat of financial losses resulting from local maladministration, reform of union management increased the authority of the national executive and reduced the autonomy of the union branch. The obligation to submit separate accounts for each type of benefit paid, furthermore, led unions to distinguish more exactly their trade activities from the provision of 'friendly' benefits to their members.

Unemployment benefits and municipal subsidies

In the absence of comparable legislation, there was no similar transformation on the continent, where their provision of unemployment benefits led, here and there, to unions fostering closer contractual relations with local authorities in imitation of the system inaugurated at Ghent. By contrast, no local support for trade union benefits was ever introduced in Britain.

In France the municipalities first at Roubaix, and later at Dijon, Limoges, Paris and Lyon, all subsidised workers' organisations recognised by the law of 1898 as administering unemployment benefits.[38] Official councils and the state itself followed these examples. In 1910 aid was given to 106 funds which supported 8500 unemployed workers. The attraction of public funding converged with liberal opinion to preserve the voluntary character of these insurance schemes. Marginal help, not major upheaval, this small advance did not stimulate any reevaluation of trade union activity.

Taking account of the nature of the risk and the absence of social support, unemployment benefits occupied a central place in German trade union propaganda. The burden of union benefits in periods of crisis led the free trade unions, from 1902, to demand a contribution from the state and, here as well, to collaborate with municipal authorities. By 1913, nine towns offered unemployed unionists additional benefit to that provided by their own organisation, thereby confirming their partnership.

Conclusion

Overall, the analysis reinforces nuances of the convenient framework of a duality in European unionism. Certainly, when compared to the widespread and varied systems found in Britain and Germany, the social assistance provided by French trade unions appears marginal. Nonetheless, French schemes were not totally ineffectual. In every country, the established trades with a long tradition of collective organisation were distinguished by their select and diversified benefit funds. In France, both the federations and the Bourses du Travail could have provided the support required to aid the expansion of union-based systems of social support. The impetus was not missing. This type of comparison validates an exclusively ideological approach. In Germany and Britain the partisans of a conflictual form of unionism nonetheless persisted in viewing the provision of union help as part of the struggle, as a means of exerting pressure on employers and as an affirmation of worker solidarity. In France, by contrast, the implications of the principles of federation, which threatened the autonomy of local unions, became an obstacle to the growth of a centralised system of union services.

Behind the identity of national models, comparison underlines the influence of external political and legislative constraints. On the one hand, English workers saw voluntary mutual schemes as a means of escaping the dreaded workhouse. On the other, the German communes sought relief from the burden imposed by aiding the poor. In France the 1852 law attempted to remedy the 'backwardness' of municipal assistance, leading to a controlled mutuality, voluntarily maintained at a distance from the workers' movement which was repressed and pushed back to the margins of legitimacy. Faced with powerful organisations, the British and German states did not seek to constrain the growth of union benefit schemes. Up to a point, they seem even to have chosen to encourage them because they fostered social stability.

Initially sensitive to the threat posed by state social policy to their autonomy, the unions in these three countries subsequently developed in different directions. In Germany, and subsequently in Britain, they did not refuse to participate in the systems created by the law. Paradoxically, it was in the authoritarian German Reich that the principle of auto-administration was pushed the furthest. If this association favoured the integration of trade unionism into German society to the point of deadening its earlier revolutionary ambitions, it also undoubtedly contributed to its enrichment and expansion.

In Britain, by contrast, the participation of trade unions in the administration of state insurance initiated a fundamental reform of the system which, before, had linked the administration of union benefits to union control of the labour market. This was the price paid for preserving union power and union membership. However, this transformation arrived very late. In contrast to both continental countries, union benefit systems in nineteenth-century Britain developed in the absence of legal constraint or political intervention in their nature or operation.

Willy-nilly, the French union movement opted, for its own part, in favour of confrontational politics at the price of renouncing, in practice more than in principle, functions previously fundamental to their original project. The poverty of the proposed services could only reduce their attraction for workers. This carried the risk that unions would remain a minority force among a working class whose political inclinations led it to turn to the Republic and to make the best use of that supreme form of indirect action – the vote.

Notes

1. Translators' note: '*Les bases multiples du syndicalisme*' does not translate directly or easily into English; the concept is not found in Anglo-Saxon trade union studies.
2. P. Louis, 'L'état present du syndicalisme mondial', *Mémoires et Documents du Musée Social*, 1913, pp. 165–84.
3. Cf. U. Frevert, *Krankheit als politisches Problem, 1770–1880. Soziale Unterschichten in Preussen zwischen medzinischer Polizei und staatlicher Sozialversicherung*, Gottingen, 1984; see also S. Kott, *L'Etat social allemand, représentations et pratiques*, Paris, Belin, 1995, pp. 25–46 which contains a full bibliography.
4. G. Bruggerhof, *Das Unterstutzungswesen bei den deutschen 'freien' Gewerkschaften*, Jena, 1912; K. Schonhoven, 'Selbsthilfe als Form der Solidarität. Das gewerkschaftliche Unterstutzungswesen im deutschen Kaiserreich bis 1914', *Archiv für Sozialgeschichte*, 1980, pp. 147–93; and

statistical supplements of the *Correspondenzblatt der Generalkommission der Gewerkschaften Deutschlands*.
5. *Viaticum* is simply the Latin expression (used, I suspect, in Germany) that describes the early alternative to unemployment benefit. Members were required to travel in search of work if unemployed and would receive shelter and support (possibly even a job) from other branches of their union/association/society. Those who refused to travel forfeited this assistance. By the late nineteenth century, thanks to cyclical unemployment (which meant that depression tended to have a more widespread effect on trades – even nationwide) this tradition was dying out and 'stationary' unemployment benefit was replacing it.
6. Royal Commission on Labour, *Fifth and Final Report*, C. 7421/1894, p.24.
7. Cited in H. Rothwells, *Theodor Lohmann und die Kampf. Jahre der staatlichen Sozialpolitik, 1871–1905*, Berlin, 1927. Theodor Lohmann was the originator of the sickness insurance laws of 1883.
8. J. Jaures, *Histoire sociale de la Révolution française*, Vol. 1, Paris, Ed. Sociales, 1969, p. 903. Cited by B. Gibaud, *Révolution et droit d'association au conflit de deux libertés*, Paris, Mutualité française, 1989, p. 83.
9. M. Dreyfus, *Histoire de la CGT*, Brussels, Ed. Complexe, 1995, esp. p. 42.
10. 'Introduction', *Report on Trade Unions, 1905–1907*, Cd. 4651/1909, p. xiii.
11. E. H. Hunt, *British Labour History, 1815–1914*, London, Weidenfeld and Nicholson, 1981, p. 297. See also N. Whiteside, 'La protection des métiers', *Cahiers d'histoire de l'I.R.M.*, (51), 1993, pp. 29–51.
12. *Report on Agencies and Methods for Dealing with the Unemployed*, Cd. 7182/1893-4, p. 18; LAB 2/184/LE 22733/24/1911, Public Record Office; J. Harris, *Unemployment and Politics*, Oxford, Oxford University Press, 1972, p. 298. The figure for 1908 includes members covered for removal expenses, travel or unemployment benefit.
13. Office du Travail, *Documents sur la question du chômage*, Imprimerie Nationale, 1896.
14. Conseil supérieur du travail, Report by Mr Fagnot, *Les caisses de chômage*, Imprimerie Nationale, 1903. One-third of unionists so covered were affiliated to the Fédération du Livre (printers' union).
15. M. Pigenet, 'Prestations et services dans le mouvement syndical français, 1860–1914', *Cahiers d'histoire de l'I.R.M.*, (51), 1993, pp. 7–28.
16. P. Chauvet, *Les ouvriers du Livre et leur journal*, Ed. Ouvrières, 1971; and M. Rebérioux, *Les ouvriers du Livre et leur Fédération*, Temps Actuels, 1981. La Fédération lithographique adopted a similar system.
17. The greatest part of members' subscriptions went to the Federation, an exceptional practice among French trade unions.
18. In France, these inquiries were instigated by the Office du Travail, *Documents sur la question du chômage*, or the Conseil supérieur du Travail, M. Fagnot, *Les caisses du chômage*.
19. S. Webb and B. Webb, *The Consumers' Co-operative Movement*, London, Longmans, 1939, p. 17.
20. G. D. H. Cole, *A Century of Co-operation*, London, Allen and Unwin, 1945, p. 259.
21. P. Brizon and E. Poisson, *Encyclopédie socialiste, syndicale et cooperative de l'internationale ouvrière. La coopération*, Quillet, 1913. Cf

E. Furlough, *Consumer Cooperation in France. The Politics of Consumption*, Ithaca and London, Cornell University Press, 1991, p. 312.
22. *VIIe congrès national de la mutualité*, Limoges, 1901, p. 100. Barberet was one of the founding fathers of professional trade unionism. He was close to Gambetta and the Republican Partisans for Social Peace.
23. An expression frequently used in union constitutions in the 1890s.
24. This happened in the case of the Fédérations des Chapeliers (1892), des Cuirs et Peaux (1893) and des Mouleurs (1897).
25. G. Sorel, 'L'avenir socialiste des syndicats', in *Matériaux d'une théorie du prolétariat*, Rivière, 1919.
26. *La Tribune Ouvriére*, 23 November 1907.
27. Intervention by Lapierre, *Compte-rendu* du XVIIe congrès national corporatif, Toulouse, 3–10 October 1910, Imp. ouvrière, 1911.
28. Some reformers agreed with this argument. Isidore Finance deprecated the way in which union work cut officials off from the mass of workers. Cf. L. De Seilhac, *Syndicats ouvriers. Fédérations et Bourses du Travail*, Paris, A. Colin, 1902, pp. 90–91.
29. F. Pelloutier, *Méthode pour la création et le fonctionnement des Bourses du travail*, 1895, Memoire reproduced in J. Julliard, *F. Pelloutier et les origines du syndicalisme d'action directe*, Seuil, 1971, p. 482.
30. M. Leroy, *La coutume ouvrière*, vol. 2, Giard et Briere, 1913, pp. 765–6.
31. M. Radelet, *Mutualité et syndicalisme*, Paris, PUF, 1991.
32. M. Dreyfus, *La Mutualité* in Y. Saint Jours (ed.), *Traité de Sécurité sociale*, Vol. 5, LGDJ, 1990. In discussing mutual benefit schemes, we must remember the possibility of multiple membership. We should also note that the professional mutual aid societies, above all, helped hold back union growth. On 31 December 1896, these societies had 354 778 members, only 72 406 less than the unions (427 184).
33. N. Whiteside, 'Définir le chômage' in M. Mansfield et al., *Aux sources du chômage*, Paris, Editions Belin, 1994.
34. Cited in B. Dumons and G. Pollet, *L'Etat et les retraites. Genèse d'une politique*, Belin, 1994, p. 158.
35. K. H. Pohl, *Die Münchener Arbeiterbewegung, sozialdemokratische Partei freie Gewerkschaften. Staat und Gesellschaft in München, 1890–1914*, Munich, Saur Verlag, 1992, pp. 336–7.
36. Their job was to render accounts required by the social legislation. The first was formed by the Christian unions in 1890, followed by the free unions in 1894, then by the liberal unions. On the eve of war, 232 free union and 134 Catholic secretariats were in existence.
37. *Die Rechtsberatung der minderbemittelten Volksreise im Jahre 1913. Sonderbeilage zum Rechts-Arbeits-Blatt*, 7, Berlin, 1914 and M. Martiny, 'Die politische Bedeutung der gewerkschaftlichen Arbeitersekretariate vor dem ersten Weltkrieg', in H. Vetter (ed.), *Vom Sozialistengesetz zur Mitbestimmung*, Koln, 1975, p. 153 et seq.
38. R. Rougé, *Les syndicats professionels et l'assurance contre le chômage*, Paris, Thèse de droit, 1912.

CHAPTER ELEVEN

The structure and organisation of British, French and German trade unions before the First World War

Peter Berkowitz, Rebecca Gumbrell, Richard Hyman, Michel Pigenet and Michael Schneider

In 1903 Georges Sorel asked the question 'What is a union?' in an article in *Pages Libres*.[1] It examined the French case, but referred to other national examples and distinguished three families according to forms of mobilisation and action, and their relationship with employers, parties, the state and the labour movement. Yet at the same time he observed that the movement was 'multiform and contradictory' and concluded the absence of any single model of unionism. It is hard to disagree with his conclusion. Indeed, as the rest of the contributions to this collection demonstrate, geography, occupation and politics conspire to undermine any clear notion of what can be meant by a national model. This picture of organisational diversity should, however, be qualified by two observations. First, divergences from national models of organisation can often be explained in terms of sectoral specificities. The importance of occupational communities in mining and printing has led many to argue that they have transnational organisational features.[2] In contrast, other sectors such as engineering seem to lend themselves to national models more easily. Second, much of the research that has informed comparative studies of union organisation has been institutional rather than sociological, emphasising written rules and procedures rather than the reality of organisational process. This chapter does not seek to provide a comprehensive picture of the shifting forms of organisation in the period 1890–1910. Rather, it seeks to identify two central features – the structures of membership and the organisation of the relationship between the centre and local groups – and argues that among competing organisational tendencies there are underlying organisational dynamics that allow us to speak of dominant models. This focus is at the expense of other important questions such as political cleavages, finances and the relationship between leaders and the rank and file. But this simplification allows us to make a more fundamental argument: that among all the factors that explain organisational variation there is a permanent tension between the spontaneous attempts of unionists to organise themselves and the attempt by external groups to impose their own projects.

I

There is a principle to craft unionism that goes beyond occupational boundaries. It is the attempt to influence the labour market by controlling access to it. In Turner's classic formulation, closed unionism delineates those unions which had the ability to restrict entry into the trade or occupation. As a result, they maintained an exclusive approach to their membership pattern and had little interest in recruiting outside their area of control. Open unions lacked the ability to control entry into the trade or occupation and therefore relied on the numerical strength of their membership to provide bargaining power.[3] This distinction between open and closed unionism allows greater clarity than the traditional language of craft and industrial unionism since it reflects organisational practice. For example, many 'industrial' unions in the three countries were able to maintain a closed structure of membership. In the period 1870–1914, the key distinction between Britain, on the one hand, and France and Germany on the other was that in Britain a significant number of unions were able successfully to pursue strategies of closed unionism before the massive influx of semi-skilled and unskilled workers into the union movement.

France

The composition of the unions that formed in the early 1880s was almost exclusively craft workers, although workers in mining, textiles and railways were also beginning to organise.[4] Two factors undermined the viability of closed unionism for these unions. The first was the inability of French workers to control access to labour markets in a way similar to their British counterparts: French employers were often far less interested in finding an economically viable solution to work problems than in maintaining their own workplace authority. Second, the objectives of craft-based unionism had already been radicalised by 60 years of artisan class theory that understood regulating access to the labour market in terms of worker control[5] rather than unilateral regulation. From its origins after the 1830s through to the 1870s, the main objective of the French labour movement was a federalist trade socialism in which the means of production would be owned collectively within the framework of skilled trades.⁶ Neither employers nor employees pursued objectives that were likely to encourage stable closed unionism.

There were, of course, exceptions such as the printers and the mechanics. But they were fighting a losing battle. By 1902 – the year that the CGT fused with the Bourses du Travail – Coupat, leader of the mechanics, had begun a long rearguard action against the encroachment of the metalworkers. Craft organisation corresponded to the needs of workers: first, it was the dominant tendency in the USA, Great Britain and Germany; second, in Germany trade union density was higher in craft unions; and, third, solidarity and contributions were stronger. 'Man is selfish. Where he has to defend his direct interests, he will group together straight away, but if he is presented with a distant goal, he hesitates.'⁷ Reisz of the metalworkers, argued, in contrast, that competition between unions was confusing workers and leading to demobilisation.⁸ Industrial unionism corresponded best to class spirit and the autonomous organisation of industry⁹ and was needed to avoid division in the general strike.¹⁰

For many supporters of industrial unionism the clearest evidence for the superiority of open unionism was the transformation of the work process. Its strongest advocates came from unionists in the metalworking industries, such as Merrheim and Latapie, and those in traditional crafts under assault from mechanisation such as Griffuelhes in leatherworking. For Latapie the evolution of modern industry made closed unionism irrelevant to union organisation. In the USA crafts in the metalworking industry had disappeared as apprenticed craft workers were replaced by semi-skilled workers trained in eight days.¹¹ Griffuelhes argued that machines were fragmenting the work process into discrete specialised activities and to attempt to continue to organise workers according to what they do would lead to an ever-increasing number of specialised unions. Industrial unionism would reduce the resulting fragmentation of organisation and class-consciousness.¹² Merrheim's commitment to industrial unionism was based on his analysis of modern mechanisation and the concentration of employers in organisations such as the Comité des Forges. Open unionism was inevitable and it was only through strong industrial unions that workers could be defended from the increased exploitation inherent in this new stage of capitalism.

The process of concentration accelerated after 1906 when the Amiens congress, at the peak of the influence of revolutionary syndicalism, voted at the request of the federation of building-workers to admit only federations of industry, although tolerating craft federations that were already members. A national building congress in 1907 saw the fusion of masons, stoneworkers, painters, carpenters and joiners. The CGT congress of 1908 supported the metalworkers against the mechanics (voting 889 against 178 in favour of the motion[13]) while miners, quarryworkers and slateworkers merged into one union (the Sous-sol) in 1911. Other mergers were initiated at the Congress du Havre in 1912 involving clothing, leatherworking and agricultural workers.

This represented a victory of the principle of industrial unionism over craft unionism, and to a lesser extent of open over closed unionism, but it also represented a compromise. Individual unions were not obliged to obey the principle of open unionism. This gave the CGT great flexibility. The standard pattern was adherence to an industrial federation by craft unions which remained the primary focus for collective action at a local level composed mainly of skilled workers.[14] For example, in 1912, among the federations represented at the Havre Congress it is possible to identify 35 different crafts in the federation of building workers and 14 among the textile workers. Thus some federations were open, such as the metalworkers; others were closed, such as the printworkers; while others, such as the building workers, would behave as closed unions at the local level while agitating for the industry as a whole.

Germany

It has been argued that had German unions been able to develop uninterrupted they would have evolved in a far more English way.[15] This is certainly true in organisational and political terms. However, it is equally important to note that German journeymen often did not have the craft controls and privileges necessary to defend their position on the shopfloor and that in many trades there was no tradition of workplace autonomy.[16] In some trades, such as printing, this was clearly not the case but in many sectors of metalwork and woodworking unions were to be built on craft identities that had no experience of the solidarity created by autonomy within the workplace.

The *Sozialistengesetz* of 1878 to 1890 both radicalised and politicised the union movement and further weakened the position of skilled workers *vis-à-vis* employers. National unification, international competition and a transformation of the legal environment in which companies operated encouraged employers to concentrate and improve their organisation.[17] The wave of strikes at the end of the 1880s and re-emergence of union organisation preceded the non-renewal of the *Sozialistengesetz*. Apart from the miners, this mobilisation took place largely among traditional skilled trades. With the lifting of the exclusion law the mobilisation widened to other politically more radical groups such as the metalworkers who became the spokesmen of industrial unionism. The tobacco workers and the association of manufacturing workers (the predecessors of the textile workers) both had open membership patterns but, unlike the metalworkers or the woodworkers, they were not to become important actors in the debate over structure.

At the Social Democrat *Parteitag* of October 1890 a discussion of union structure and organisation led to the founding of the General-kommission under Karl Legien's leadership in order to work on the organisational question. At Halberstadt a year later, four main groupings emerged. The first were the supporters of the Generalkommission who wished to see a weak form of branch model with weak contractual links between occupational unions. According to Legien, experience had shown that branch-level organisation was most effective for agitation and strike support, since craft solidarities and 'caste-consciousness' (*Kastengeist*) are inward-looking. However, industry was not yet sufficiently evolved to facilitate the formation of industrial unions. Practical problems would arise from bringing craft unions together due to failing contributions as less organised workers were brought into the unions. Even the richest union, the printers, had problems with contributions. Hence, three factors militated against industrial unionism: underdeveloped industry, variations in contributions and benefits between groups and *Kastengeist*.[18]

The second group, led by the metalworkers favoured industrial unionism. Segitz argued that duplication of administration was wasteful and divisive, that exclusive class solidarity was not so strong and that finances were not such a problem, citing his own union as an example. Von Elm, representing a third group of craft unions, argued that the basis for industrial unionism was not yet in place and cited the example of the success of craft unionism in Great Britain. A final group of localists supported the right of all types of organisation to exist free of central control.[19]

Legien's resolution was supported and in practice did not resolve the question of union structure. The *Kartellvertrag* that was supposed to bind occupational unions together turned out to be of little use.[20] The tradition of occupational solidarity was maintained in the trade union movement in spite of the transformation and levelling of the nature of occupations through mechanisation and division of labour.[21] Although Legien argued in 1897 that the form of organisation depended on economic development, closed occupational unions were able to adapt to these processes.[22] Many widened the concept of occupation to cover semi-skilled or similar occupational groups, because the mechanisation of the production process weakened distinctive features, and made it possible to replace apprentice trained workers.

In the years after 1890 most craft unions refused to merge with related trades, because their membership, which came mainly from the craft/skilled workforce of small and medium-sized businesses trusted them to vote for *Handwerk*-oriented organisational forms.[23] Closed unionism was dominant before 1914 in terms of shaping the goals and aspirations of the union movement, although the movement's leadership was committed to industrial unionism in the long term. While industrial unions comprised approximately 70 per cent of union membership in 1914, membership fluctuation was far greater than in the craft unions. Of the seven largest open unions only the metal- and woodworkers were significant actors within the union movement. The transport, textile and factory workers were still relatively weak organisations. The miners were internally divided and the building union still retained much of its craft heritage. However, in contrast to Great Britain, closed unionism was able to coexist with open unionism within industrial structures. The occupational segmentation of the workforce did not therefore become a significant factor in the interaction with employers.

Britain

The growth of the early 1870s led to the establishment of new, less exclusive unions – gas-stokers, dockers, agricultural workers – outside traditional craft sectors. To this must be added miners, ironworkers, and railway workers. The first two, to which can be added spinners, have been called promotion unions (where unions tried to control a promotion process that no longer depended on apprentices) and, with the craft societies, were able to ride out the very unfavourable conditions of the late 1870s and early 1880s. They are clearly hybrid models with respect to the distinction between open and closed unionism – recruiting openly but attempting to maintain control over skill distinctions within the labour market. It is important to note that their ability to do so depended on their strength outside the workplace and the willingness of employers to deal with them. Promotion unions were, in many respects, closed unions without a craft tradition.

What has been called the New Unionism was indicative of a new type of union structure. The unions of the 1870s were a mixture of crafts and promotion unions. By the late 1880s general unions were becoming far more prominent. They were a product of high employment and the problem of absorbing casual workers into existing union structures. However, although this proved a useful way of organising mobilised workers it proved much harder to establish it as a method of keeping them organised. As New Unionism declined it became clear that its principal beneficiaries had been the old craft and promotion unions which had been able to consolidate their membership. Certain new unions did survive the economic downturn, the employers' counterattack, poor leadership and destructive strikes. But they tended to be in expanding industries such as transport or in municipally-owned industries such as gas, water or electricity where management had an interest in stability. Moreover, it was skilled workers in these industries who once again were to form a core of membership: 'organisational innovations were remarkably few, apart from the grouping of more or less skilled local trades incongruously within the same "general" union in place of the unskilled whom the leaders had set out to capture'.[24] Hobsbawm characterises the general unionism of the period as 'the offspring of marriage between the class unionism of the socialists and the more modest plans of the unskilled themselves'.[25] If, as the Webbs would argue, socialism provided a prerequisite for durable general unionism, it was probably less as a basis for organisation than as a rationale for solidarity between those who had resources – skilled workers – and those who had not. For these general unions of the 1890s formed the basis for the general unions of the pre-war and post-war periods.

In Great Britain those that could avoid dilution did so, leaving other groups of skilled workers isolated within the labour market to group together and adopt a more open attitude to less skilled workers. This pattern of craft and general unionism was to prove resistant to all attempts at change. The only significant attempt at reform was linked to syndicalism in the pre-war period. Influenced by French and American syndicalism, Tom Mann founded the Industrial Syndicalist Education League. However, its influence proved to be short-lived and had a greater impact at a political than organisational level. At each phase of the development of the trade union movement closed unionism was able to dominate open unionism. Furthermore, the union movement remained too weak and divided to impose any principles from a centre that had little legitimacy in the pre-war period. As Clegg has noted, at no point between 1892 and 1910 could the new unions have resisted efforts on the part of craft unions to integrate them into an industrial structure; the craft unions merely had no desire to do so.[26]

II

In both France and Britain workers were able, in Julliard's words, to turn craft autonomy into union autonomy before the influx of semi-skilled and unskilled into the union movement.[27] In Germany the strength of integrated organisation had overwhelmed attempts at autonomy by 1900. There would be no significant conflict over the principles of organisation: the need to create strategic leadership by delegating authority and by centralising resources was a lesson that was learnt in the context of industrial relations but equally in that of organised interest group politics of the Kaiserreich. The pillarisation of German society, the rapidity of industrialisation and urbanisation, the process of nation-building, the endurance of guild structures and the absence of a liberal economic interlude contributed to the homogenisation of labour and capital and inhibited groups from creating alliances that cut across the class barrier. In Great Britain and France it was easier to build on local solidarities and exploit the competition between employers.

Germany

At Erfurt in 1872, the idea of an integrated movement gained support from Bebel who saw the possibility of unions overcoming class fragmentation – unions could foster class-consciousness and socialism. A central federal body would be set up and convene an annual congress. This congress would determine the availability of strike support, agitate for union mobilisation and organise unions in weak sectors. Centralisation gained in standing[28] among party members but trade unionists remained suspicious. The founding of the SPD in 1875 at Gotha reinforced the commitment of the party leadership to centralisation, resulting in tension with the aspirations of craft-oriented local unions.

Within a few weeks of the end of 1878, 17 centralised unions and 62 local unions had been dissolved by the police.[29] Despite efforts at the end of the 1880s to establish mutual assistance funds the ability of unions to establish relatively autonomous and local craft unionism was limited before 1890. But they became important structures of political agitation, education and organisation during this period. This greatly strengthened the ties between party and unions and reinforced the influence of the party preference for centralisation: 'among unions, patient organisation, coordination from above, and cautious planning would be the hallmarks of Social Democrat leadership'.[30]

Three consequences of the *Sozialistengesetz* were of particular importance for the organisation of the union movement. First, the 12-year period of repression brought a strengthening of core groups and particularly of the solidarity of the individuals who would lead and administer the party and the unions. Second, it brought great suffering to union leaders and their families, reinforcing their sense of common purpose. Finally, and perhaps most importantly, it delayed the foundation of confederal organisation and allowed employers to improve their organisation: 'the traditional inequality between employers' associations and unions in Germany with its unfortunate consequences has some of its roots here'.[31]

With the re-emergence of national trade unions at the end of the 1880s the autonomous tendencies of local groups was increasingly restricted. At the SPD congress in 1891 it was decided to encourage centralisation and the formation of a *Generalkommission* in order to deal with union organisation. Centralisation was, in many respects, a compromise between the unions favouring industrial unionism and those favouring craft unionism.[32] The *Generalkommission* under Legien was able to influence the debate on union structure in 1891 in a plan which saw the *Kommission* connecting individual union centres. Objections to this centralisation came in particular from Berlin where there were intensely political local unions in building, specialised crafts and metalwork.

The fundamental objection to centralisation was that this would involve the depoliticisation of union activities.[33] This would be a recurrent feature of calls for decentralisation within the German labour movement, assimilating the bureaucratisation of the union movement to reformism, in the syndicalism of the FVdG founded in 1897 and the workers' councils of Berlin metalworkers in the post-war period. In the pre-war period the elements of German localism were the craft union, the general meeting and shop steward system. This was a clear contradiction of the aims of the *Generalkommission* which was committed to delegated authority and the elimination of local autonomy. Legien rejected all versions of the localist idea and argued for the necessity of centralisation in a capitalist economy and the role of unions as the training grounds for solidarity.[34] While artisans produced for the local market, local organisations had been in a position to influence working conditions. But mass production using craft skills brought workers from different towns into competition with each other and needed to be regulated. Companies now pursued strategies in a world market and local unions could no longer control the supply of labour. Methods of production and the nationalisation of labour and commodity markets created the need for a strong organisation. In order to be effective such an organisation would need to be centralised.

By 1907 the localist movement had been neutralised and the lessons of the organisational setbacks of 1891 to 1894 had been applied to a massive influx of union members after 1895. This crisis had seen increased employer resistance, bad economic conditions and new forms of repression. Rather than questioning the model elaborated at Halberstadt, the unions concluded that there was a greater need for organisational strength, better organisation and the nationalisation of activities.[35] Above all there was a need for a greater rationalisation of strike activity. Attention was turned to integrating a mobile and fluctuating membership into organisational structures through associations and welfare plans.[36] This was greatly facilitated by the structure of state provision for welfare that institutionalised the involvement of union members in local provision. The unions were thus able to develop a very strongly integrated organisation outside the workplace.

France

The sources of the strength of the principles of organisational autonomy and decentralisation lie in pre-Republican France. Perrot sees the idea of federation as a legacy of the French Revolution in which diverse groups could organise at a national level without renouncing their individual autonomy.[37] In the period preceding the Commune the labour movement's attempts at organisation were dominated by federal trade socialism. Slow industrialisation and economic liberalism encouraged workers to build organisation around local occupational identities. A mutualist cooperative vision of worker organisation was reinforced by the distrust of the bureaucratic state of the years of the Empire.[38]

The failure of the Commune both radicalised the federalists and strengthened those groups in favour of centralisation. For a time the socialist *guesdistes* were able to dominate the union movement. Guesde had founded the POF at the 1879 National Workers Congress. The first nationwide federation of unions, the FNS, which had been founded in 1886 as a federal body was almost immediately taken over by the guesdistes. Where they were strong, particularly in the north, they were successful in building centralised unions; however, their main impact on the national labour movement was to encourage unions to favour decentralised structures.

Parallel to this centralised organisation, Pelloutier had begun to organise *Bourses du Travail*, government-supported local interoccupational bodies. The first Bourse was created in 1886 in Paris; by 1892 there were 14 Bourses and by 1901 there were 78. The creation of the Bourses had been intended to establish a close link between labour organisations and the state, but in fact its effect was to reinforce worker and union autonomy by providing a structure in which unionists influenced by anarchism and individualism could operate independently of the *guesdistes*.[39] For Pelloutier, the emancipation of the working class had to be self-emancipation: they could depend neither on parties nor the state. By 1892 a national federation was formed to assert the independence of the Bourses both with respect to parties but equally to unions considered to be under the control of socialists. Based on a unitary conception of class, the Bourses reflected practical preoccupations. They provided unions with premises, sought to fulfil the role of a local labour exchange and created a focus for local collective action that was beyond the capacity of the national federations.

The POF was too weak to dominate the union movement as the SPD had done. Unions increasingly rejected involvement with the POF and in 1895 a new central organisation, the CGT, was formed at Limoges. It united non-*guesdiste* trade and industrial federations and accepted membership from local unions, Bourses, national craft and industrial unions and federations. However, without the support of the federation of Bourses it was little more than an umbrella organisation. Even with the affiliation of the former in 1902, the CGT did not represent the majority of trade unionists.[40] This, however, raised the question of the relationship between the constituent parts of the confederation. From the merger the CGT acquired a system of dual territorial and functional representation based on local unions. Each would be affiliated to a regional body and a national craft or industry federation. Each union had one vote in congress and this was to strengthen the position of the localists and syndicalists.

The federations were divided into three types: strongly centralised unions such as the printers; national unions such as the railways; and decentralised unions such as the metalworkers. In the period before 1908, those in favour of decentralisation held the upper hand. This manifested itself in two ways: first, in the organisational weakness of the federations and their inability to collect dues; second, in a reluctance to delegate authority to a higher body. This was apparent at all levels in the relationship between unions and federation and between federation and confederation. Strikes, unemployment and mutual aid remained the province of the local union and the local interoccupational structures. The administrative mechanism of the unions and federations tended to have two main bodies: a general assembly and an administrative council. The majority of unions refused to delegate the power of decision to the council and remained attached to direct democracy.[41] Most ballots required only a relative majority in the second round and secret ballots were rare.[42] Moreover, the posts of administrator were revocable in order to avoid creating a hierarchy and there was a clause of autonomy in favour of the unions inserted in the statutes of the federations.[43] The role of the federations and the CGT was to represent only those collective interests that individual unions were unable to represent.

The weakness of French unions to collect dues is well-known.[44] It was felt that the fighting spirit of the unions would be weakened by the need to protect and generate funds. It was not seen to be effective in attracting members, it generated selfishness in those who paid with respect to those who didn't and made it difficult for unions to unite the whole workforce in the union movement.[45] In Pouget's words: 'the worth of a union depends less on its cashbox than on the multiplication of the coherent energy of its members'.[46] However, the need to constitute reserves was always a minority strategy favoured by the printers. As many commentators have remarked, this attitude to union finance was influenced perhaps more by necessity than virtue[47] and such a commitment was fundamentally incompatible with the attachment of a large number of members to autonomy.

In the years before the First World War the decline of revolutionary syndicalism and changes in the work process strengthened the hand of the reformists and convinced many syndicalists of the necessity of stronger organisation. Of these, Merrheim was the most articulate. He identified problems that made it necessary for workers to organise more strongly into unions, remain loyal and obey their leaders: the greater concentration of the employer class, growing international agreements between industrialists, and the development of trusts and cartels and their powerful influence over governments. In order to defeat its opponents, the syndicalist movement would have to match their organisational strength and structure. Siding with the reformists, he now encouraged congress to overturn its decentralist traditions. Although these reforms were partially introduced at Le Havre in 1912, there remained a fundamental tension between the attempts at integration by the confederal leadership and the strength of local autonomy.

Britain

The new model unionism of 1851 epitomises the evolution of British union organisation. It brought increased organisational strength, some degree of centralisation, but preserved the fundamental autonomy of local units. In this way, it superseded the local trade societies without fundamentally undermining the position of trade unionists in local life. Slow industrialisation and competition between employers allowed unions to operate on a largely local level. The characteristics of new model unions such as the Amalgamated Society of Engineers (ASE) and Amalgamated Society of Carpenters and Joiners (ASCJ) were portrayed as those of large efficient organisations concentrating power in the hands of a full-time head office, of economically liberal organisations with extensive friendly benefits and good relations with employers. The reality was that publicity, finance and the sanctioning of strikes were all the prerogative of the secretary, but wage demands, negotiation with employers, control of hours and apprentices and most aspects of workshop practice were in the hands of local officers. There was no effort to influence national variation in the 'standard rate' and, indeed, many 'new model unions' were disturbed by rank and file protest.[48] Much union activity was conducted in trade councils made up of small local unions. The new model unions may have represented a degree of centralisation but organisational autonomy with substantive issues decided at the local level remained the norm for most of the nineteenth century.

The legal recognition of unions during the 1870s consolidated these tendencies, but attempts at centralisation in less skilled sectors such as the Amalgamated Association of Miners tended to collapse during the economic slowdown post-1873. Those unions that survived were craft unions that combined central financial administration with decentralised trade policy. Systems of friendly benefits at a local level allowed craft unions to impose rules unilaterally where collective bargaining was not possible.[49] In the 1880s other patterns were to emerge in mining and cotton. Both were concerned with the negotiation of wages on a county-wide basis and national organisations were not so much federations as forums for discussion. Because of the geographical concentration of the workforce in local communities, strongly centralised organisations were created at a local or county level with full-time officers. Yet, in many respects, different county unions remained totally autonomous of a national authority. Clegg et al. are right to argue that the federal bodies of the cotton and mining unions were better informed and endowed with greater authority than the 'local' lay executives of the societies,[50] but it can be suggested that these organisations were merely the adaptation of the dynamic of autonomy to a less skilled and larger local labour market and community.

The 1890s saw the emergence of three related phenomena: new unionism, increased collective bargaining and stronger employer organisation. The heterogeneity of new unionism[51] makes it hard to draw any firm conclusions about its impact on the union movement apart from the clear failure of socialists and more militant unionists to impose a more integrated model on the union movement. In newly founded general unions of semi- and unskilled workers, a greater degree of centralisation was necessary, and socialists clearly played a role in mobilising and organising strikes. But the downturn of the 1890s tended to favour those new unions who could depend on homogeneous occupational communities and footholds in certain industries and large works. In other cases the remnants of new unions would provide the basis for subsequent centralised expansion in a later period. The impact of new unionism on existing unions was perhaps greater, leading to restructuring in coal, railways and cotton and a reform of the administrative apparatus of many of the craft unions. However, this restructuring and centralisation was linked more to increased collective bargaining and stronger employer organisation than the influence of socialists.

Technical change made craft controls increasingly unacceptable to employers who sought to improve their organisation. This resulted in the emergence of formal industry-wide collective bargaining 'at times the result of union pursuit of uniformity of conditions, more often the achievement of new and combative employers' associations seeking to contain grassroots challenges to union control'.[52] This was not entirely unwelcome since it strengthened national leadership against the branch level and weakened local autonomy. However, such attempts at integration were not entirely successful as they often created internal tensions at the shopfloor level and the eventual emergence of shop level representation.[53] Furthermore, the pattern of industrial relations incorporated a dimension of local autonomy in the dual system of collective bargaining in which substantive issues were dealt with at a local level, while procedural issues were dealt with at a national level. In addition, craft controls continued to exist alongside collective bargaining agreements.[54] The system of collective bargaining simultaneously left bargaining over conditions of employment at a local level, but created tensions between leaders and members through national negotiation of procedure, since employers saw national procedure agreements as devices for establishing their right to introduce new machinery and methods of working.[55]

These attempts at integration and greater interest by union leaders in industrial action (partly as craft controls became less effective and partly as the composition of the unions became less skilled) made little impact on the TUC which had been under challenge from the start and had based its activity around the organisation of deputations and lobbying. Its attempts at organising the union movement into a closely knit confederation had always failed when union autonomy had to be sacrificed.[56] Unlike the French and German confederations the centre had been unable to play any role in shaping the union movement. Even where the TUC had a constitutionally defined role such as in promoting union amalgamations it played no role in the significant groupings of the pre-war years in the NUR, the Transport Workers' Federation or the Triple Alliance. The tradition of voluntarism as opposed to statutory regulation tended to favour those unions that were already well-established in the workplace and ensured that the primary dialogue of industrial relations remained independent of the state and that the incentive to create a strong confederal presence did not exist.

The member unions themselves were facing their own problems with internal discipline in the period leading up to the First World War. Hyman identifies three elements of pre-war unrest: first, unorganised workers in weakly unionised industries; second, non-craft workers in strongly organised industries reacting against the constraints and discipline of collective bargaining; and finally, highly-skilled workers accustomed to considerable unilateral control over the labour process reacting against attempts by employers and union leaderships to impose new forms of discipline.[57] It was in the more skilled occupations that the shop steward movement established the structures of shopfloor autonomy that would continue to shape the organisation of the labour movement in face of the growing centralisation of strike funds of the 1920s.

III

In all three countries there was both diversity and competition between different organisational tendencies. The evolution of organisation within the three labour movements depended on the balance between groups in favour of open or closed unionism and local autonomy or national integration. It is this balance that we have sought to compare.

The conditions that favoured an industrial type of open unionism tended to be presence of radicalised skilled workers whose craft associations did not appear capable of protecting their skills, work conditions and wages against the influx of semi-skilled labour (or apprentices) and who were forced to turn towards interoccupational attempts at organising within the labour market based on periodic mobilisation rather than control of access. Yet it proved very hard for skilled workers to form interoccupational groups. Where open forms of unionism were successful it was because craft groupings were able to evolve in an interoccupational framework that gained its legitimacy outside the workplace as part of a wider political, economic or social project.

Where craft workers (or semi-skilled miners and textile workers) were able to establish effective organisations in local labour markets building on the resources in the local community, decentralised unions embodied the principle of autonomy. The capacity of these unions to resist the organisational demands of the less skilled and the corresponding pull towards integration from their leadership depended on the ability of these decentralised unions to shape the environment to their own organisational ends. In Britain craft unions were able to mobilise effective resistance at plant level to increase integration and, by doing so, forced many other integrated unions to adopt the shop steward system. In both France and Britain the strength of local communities and the weakly structured nature of interest group politics did not favour the concentration of power in a central confederation and hence this latter could never become an effective actor in the concentration process. The reverse was true in Germany: craft workers were unable to establish effective organisations in local labour markets, since rapid industrialisation and the hierarchical nature of German society did not favour community solidarities as a base for union mobilisation. The push towards integration was encouraged by the structure of interest group politics (in a regime where parliamentary politics was of particularly little relevance), by the early relevance of the national market to the understanding of the employer–union conflict and by the ideological commitment of socialist elites who had come to dominate the union movement under the *Sozialistengesetz*. The influx of less skilled workers reinforced this tendency.

In Britain a type of spontaneous collectivism was the dominant force in the development of the union movement, in which union organisation was able to reflect an occupational and employment-oriented logic. This fostered closed strategies of membership and the autonomy of local groups. The opposite was true in Germany where the weakness of spontaneous collectivism created a need for external mobilisation that often reflected the social, political and ideological projects of the organisers. This top-down approach, based on political, rather than labour market, needs favoured open strategies of recruitment and a push towards integrated organisations. At the same time it created political cleavages in the labour movement. The balance of forces was more equal in France producing a mixed model. Perhaps the most significant factor in explaining this is the legacy of trade socialism in the French labour movement and the role of the state in the politicisation of the organisation of the working class. This turned the search for autonomy within the workplace into a political project to be played out at the level of the state.

Notes

1. G. Sorel, *Pages Libres*, 21 March 1903, pp. 241–57.
2. P. Stearns, *Lives of Labour*, London, 1975; G. Marks, *Unions in Politics*, Princeton, 1989.
3. See H. A. Turner, *Trade Union Growth, Structure and Policy*, London, 1962. R. Hyman in *Industrial Relations*, London, 1975, p. 41 argues that 'two contradictory forces have operated: on the one hand towards breadth, unity and solidarity; on the other towards parochialism, sectionalism and exclusion'.
4. M. Pigenet, 'Le métier ou l'industrie? Les structures d'organisation et les enjeux au tournant du siècle', *Cahiers d'histoire de l'IRM*, 61, 1995.
5. B. Moss, *The Origins of the French Labour Movement*, Berkeley, 1976.
6. Ibid., p. 3.
7. *7ème Congrès de la CGT*, Montpellier, 1902, p. 144.
8. Ibid., p. 143.
9. Griffuelhes in *6ème Congrès de la CGT*, Paris, 1900, p. 149.
10. Péricat in *11ème Congrès de la CGT*, Toulouse, 1910, p. 143.

11. M. Leroy, *La coûtume ouvrière*, Paris, 1913, p. 184.
12. Ibid., p. 369.
13. The most significant opposition came from the mechanics and the printers. It is important to note that they opposed the principle of open unionism and not industrial unionism as such.
14. V. Lorwin, *The French Labour Movement*, Cambridge, Mass., 1954, p. 151.
15. K. Tenfelde, 'Germany', in M. Van der Linden, *The Formation of Labour Movements 1870–1914*, 1990, p. 253.
16. J. Kocka, 'Problems of Working Class Formation in Germany', in I. Katznelson and A. Zolberg, *Working Class Formation*, Princeton, 1986, p. 343.
17. G. Beier, *Geschichte und Gewerkschaft*, Köln, 1981, p. 252.
18. *Protokoll der Verhandlungen des Ersten Kongresses der Gewerkschaften Deutschlands*, 1892, pp. 31–5.
19. Ibid.
20. K. Schönhoven, *Expansion und Konzentration*, Stuttgart, 1980, p. 280.
21. Ibid., p. 281.
22. *Protokoll der dritten ordentlichen Generalversammlung des deutschen Metallarbeiter-Verbandes*, Stuttgart, 1897.
23. Schönhoven, *Expansion und Konzentration*, p. 280.
24. S. Pollard, 'New Unionism in Britain', in W. J. Mommsen and H-G. Husung, *The Development of Trade Unionism in Great Britain and Germany*, London, 1985, p. 49.
25. E. Hobsbawm, *Labouring Men*, London, 1964, p. 182.
26. H. A. Clegg, *The System of Industrial Relations in Britain*, Oxford, 1972, p. 52.
27. J. Julliard, *Autonomie ouvrière*, Paris, 1988.
28. See the series of articles by Hillmann in *Der Volksstaat* starting on 17 May 1873.
29. A. Förster, *Die Gewerkschaftpolitik der deutschen Sozialdemokratie während des Sozialistengesetzes*, Berlin, 1971, pp. 14–33.
30. M. Nolan, 'Economic crisis, state policy and working class formation in Germany, 1870–1900', in I. Katznelson and A. Zolberg, *Working Class Formation*, p. 384.
31. Beier, *Geschichte und Gewerkschaft*, p. 252.
32. Schönhoven, *Expansion und Konzentration*, p. 270.
33. D. Müller, 'Syndicalism and Localism in the German Trade Union Movement', in W. J. Mommsen and H-G. Husung, *The Development of Trade Unionism*, p. 240.
34. *Correspondenzblatt*, 23 May 1891.
35. G. Ritter and K. Tenfelde, 'Der Durchbruch der Freien Gewerkschaften Deutschlands', in *Vom Sozialistengesetz bis Mitbestimmung*, Köln, 1975, p. 88.
36. Schönhoven, *Expansion und Konzentration*.
37. M. Perrot, 'On the formation of the French Working Class', in I. Katznelson and A. Zolberg, *Working Class Formation*, p. 95.
38. Moss, *The Origins of the French Labour Movement*, p. 57.
39. P. Schöttler, *La naissance des bourses du travail*, Paris, 1985, p. 21.
40. It was only in 1910 that the CGT would comprise 51.4 per cent of unions and 56.6 per cent of unionists.

41. Leroy, *La coûtume ouvrière*, p. 137.
42. Ibid., p. 148.
43. Ibid., p. 158.
44. C. Rist, 'Les finances des syndicats ouvriers français', *Révue économique internationale*, 15 January 1911; M. Pigenet, 'Les finances, une approche des problèmes de structure et d'orientation de la CGT', *Mouvement social*, 1995.
45. Vezole in 1896 quoted in Leroy, *La coûtume ouvrièr*, p. 213.
46. Ibid., p. 157.
47. Ibid., p. 63.
48. E. H. Hunt, *British Labour History 1815–1914*, London, 1981, pp. 262–3.
49. H. Clegg, A. Fox and A. Thompson, *A History of British Trade Unionism since 1889*, 1964, p. 38.
50. Ibid., p. 39.
51. R. Hyman, 'Mass Organisation and Militancy in Britain', in W. J. Mommsen and H-G. Husung, *The Development of Trade Unionism*, p. 251.
52. Hyman, 'Mass Organisation and Militancy', p. 257.
53. Clegg et al., *A History of British Trade Unionism*, pp. 169, 471; Hyman, 'Mass Organisation and Militancy', p. 257.
54. Clegg et al., *A History of British Trade Unionism*, p. 155.
55. J. Lovell, *British Trade Unions*, London, 1977, p. 42.
56. B. C. Roberts, *The Trades Union Congress*, London, 1958, p. 359.
57. Hyman, 'Mass Organisation and Militancy', p. 262.

Index

Abbe, E. 205
Alsatian workers xii, 60, 68
Amalgamated Association of Iron, Steel and Tin Workers of North America (AA) 18–21, 25–6
Amalgamated Malleable Iron Workers of Great Britain (AMIW) 15–7, 19
Anseele, E. 99, 114, 117
apprenticeships 13, 72, 102, 125
arbitration 16, 97, 192, 207
Asquith, H.H. 193
Augsburg 92
automobiles 101

Bank of Labour 94
Barthès, I. 61, 77, 80, 86
Bebel, A. 141, 218, 240
Belgische Wekliedenpartij (BWP) 95, 115
benefits, trade union 215–30, 245
Berlin 123, 126, 130, 241
bicycles 101
Bielefeld 92, 100–6, 112–6
Bismarck, Prince Otto von 185, 198, 206
Blackburn 54, 56, 57, 64, 72
blacklegs 44, 50, 76
blacklists 69, 209
blanquistes 128, 129, 134, 145
Blondeau, M. 157
boilermakers 62
Bolton 54, 57, 64, 65, 72
bourse du travail: *see* chambers of labour
Bosch, R. 205
Bradford 92
Bremen 54, 55, 57–60, 64, 65–6, 68, 69, 71, 73–5, 77, 78, 146, 151
Bresca 108
brewing 124
British Steel Smelters Association (BSSA) 26
Brookland Agreement, 1893 56

Brussels 143, 154
building workers 55, 93, 124, 129, 133, 148, 235, 238
Burnley 54, 57, 64, 65, 71

Campbell-Bannerman, Sir H. 189
Catholic Church xii, 109, 127, 147, 159
Catholic Centre Party (Germany) 5, 130
Catholic workers 5, 61, 108, 110, 111, 126, 129, 132
Chamberlain, J. 199, 202–3
chambers of labour 108, 109–11, 115–6, 127, 129–30, 133–4, 135, 145, 149, 162, 191, 194, 196–7, 229, 235, 242
chemicals 92, 124
Chicago martyrs 155, 156
children 76, 80, 87, 94, 100, 113, 146, 158, 195
Christian trade unions 105, 108, 110, 111–2, 114, 129, 130, 135, 209, 211
Churchill, W.S. 188, 193
Clegg, H. 239, 245
closed shop 44, 61, 69, 84
coalminers 5, 25, 91, 147, 148, 152, 192, 198, 199, 207, 208, 233, 234, 236, 245, 247
Commune, The 156, 160 242
Confédération Générale du Travail (CGT) 38, 39, 61, 62, 77, 82, 134, 143, 155, 180, 191, 194, 200, 212, 235–6, 243
Confederazione del Lavoro (General Confederation of Labour) 110
cooperatives 94–5, 103–4, 135, 153, 222
Crane, W. 160

Darme, V. 136
Deutscher Metallarbeiter-Verband (DMV) 25, 103, 104, 105

Deutscher Textilarbeiterverband (DTAV) 57–9, 79, 84, 85
Disraeli, B. 188
dockers xi, 33–51, 125, 127–8, 131, 148, 238
Dormoy, J. 141
Douai 25
Düsseldorf 25

Elbeuf xii, 54, 55, 62–4, 67–8, 70, 71, 75, 77, 78, 81, 82–3, 85–6
employers 15–26, 40, 42, 46, 67, 70–2, 128, 135–6, 188–9, 204–13, 245
engineering 8, 65, 123, 125, 131, 194, 233, 244

female emancipation 79, 121, 131
female trade unionists 56, 58, 74, 78–81, 102–3, 131
Fourmies 155, 156, 157

garment industry 100–1, 102, 116
general strike, revolutionary 4, 153, 154, 162
Genoa 107
George, H. 127
Ghent 92, 93–9, 112–6, 143, 144, 147, 152, 154
Giolitti, G. 110
Gladstone, W.E. 187
glass 91, 124, 129, 133, 148, 149
Goodman, J. 128
guesdistes 128, 129, 130, 133, 134, 136, 143, 145, 148, 151, 154, 169, 182, 190, 242, 243
guilds 3, 4, 145–6
Gur, J. 149

Hamburg 43–6, 47–51, 123, 151
hatters 106, 107, 109, 110, 111
Henderson, A. 192
Hobsbawm, E.J. 156–7, 239
Hospital, People's 95
Housewives Crusade, 1911 39
housing 70, 94, 98, 123–4, 132
Hyndman, H.M. 144

immigrants xii, 60, 66, 68, 69, 73, 82, 100, 123, 159

Independent Labour Party (ILP) 79, 144
Irish workers 37, 82, 123, 125, 127, 132
iron and steel xi, 3–28, 91, 238
Iron and Steel Trade Confederation (ISTC) 26

joint committees 16, 97, 115, 192, 206, 213

Knights of Labour 127, 136
Krefeld 91

'labour aristocracy' 94
labour exchanges 109, 196
Labour Party 81, 85, 131–2, 153, 189, 192, 195, 210
Labour Representation Committee (LRC) xiii, 57, 188, 189
Lancashire 55–7, 64–5, 68, 70–1, 72–3, 77, 79–80
Lasalle, F. 218
Lavigne, R. 141
Layton, R.T. 9
law 184–200
leather 129, 133, 236
Leeds 92
Legien, K. 111, 237, 241
Le Havre 37–40, 47–51, 244
Lehmann, H.B.A. 131
libraries 103, 196
Liebknecht, K. 141
Liège 146, 147
Lille 92, 149
Liverpool 121–37
Lloyd George, D. 193, 199
London 34–7, 47–51, 143–4, 147, 150
Louis, P. 215
Lyon xii, 121–37

machine building 91–4, 100, 106, 112, 207
Mann, T. 192, 239
Martin, E. 63, 83, 86
Marx, E. 144, 147, 153
masons 62, 129, 178
May Days xi, 39, 126, 128, 129, 132, 133, 141–63, 170, 171

Mazamet 54, 55, 60–2, 68, 70, 76, 77, 78, 80, 82–3, 85–6
metalworkers 93, 96, 101, 111, 124, 125, 129, 133, 235, 236, 237, 243
Milan 107, 108, 109
Millerand, A. 194, 196, 212
Mole, J. 128
Mönchengladbach 92
Monza 92, 106–16
Montgomery, D. 8, 11, 13, 43
Morris, W. 160
Mundella, A.J. 192–3
Munich xii, 121–37
music clubs 68, 103
mutual aid societies 68, 70, 95, 107, 216–8

National Union of Railwaymen (NUR) 246

Oldham 54, 57, 64, 65, 71, 81
Osborne, W. 189
Ostend 94

Pankhurst, E. C. and S. 79
Paris xii, 126, 148, 162, 191
Parti Ouvrier Belge (POB) 143, 148, 152, 153
Partito Operaio Italiano (Italian workers' Party) 107
paternalism 70–1, 81
Pavia 108
Penrhyn, Lord 193
Perrot, M. 242
police, use of 39, 76
Prato 91
printing 96, 124, 131, 233, 236, 237
Protestantism 43, 68, 127, 132, 157

railway workers 125, 130, 131, 135, 189, 194, 199, 234, 238, 243, 246
Reina, E. 110, 111, 114, 119
religion xii, 5, 43, 61, 68, 82, 101, 105, 108, 109, 114, 115, 147, 159, 160, 201
revolutionary syndicalists 6, 62, 129, 132, 133, 134, 195, 211, 244

Ritchie, C.T. 193
Riva, G. 111
Rosebery, Lord 192
Rotterdam 40–3, 47–51
Roubair 67, 228
Ruhr xii, 7, 23, 25, 42, 208

St Etienne 92
St Petersburg xii
Salisbury, Lord 193
seamen 39
service sector 91–2, 121, 124
Severing, C. 103, 114
Sexton, J. 131
Shipbuilding 5, 65, 125
silk 100, 104, 105, 116, 124, 129
sliding scale agreements 16
Social Democratic Federation (SDF) 128, 144, 150
Socialist League 144
Sorel, G. 233
soup kitchens 76, 87
SPD (German Social Democratic Party) 5, 60, 81, 85, 95, 103–4, 105, 115, 118, 126, 130–1, 143, 144, 150–1, 153, 168, 210, 240–1
sport 68
steel xi, 3–28, 147, 148
Stradella 108

Taff Vale Judgement, 1901 xiii, 57, 189, 194
Taggart, J.G. 127
tariffs 199
textiles xi, 54–87, 91, 93–9, 100, 107, 109, 111, 129, 148, 208, 234, 237, 247
theatre 103
Thomas, A. 141
tobacco 65, 125, 133, 217, 236
Touraine, A. 168
trades councils 103, 105, 108, 127, 131, 144
Trades Disputes Act, 1906 xiii
Trades Union Congress (TUC) xiii, 177, 187, 188, 198, 219, 246
tramway workers 135–7
troops, use of 39, 109, 154, 155
Turner, B. 192
Turner, H.A. xiii, 234

unemployment insurance 115, 198, 199, 228
universal suffrage 95, 99, 152, 161
USA 3–32

Valenciennes 25
Verviers 91
Vlaamsche Socialistiche Arbeiderspartij (VSAP) 95, 96
Viani, O.G. 107–8

Vooruit 94–5

Webb, B. and S. 85, 239
white-collar workers 121–2, 124, 126, 129, 134
women 56, 58, 60, 73, 74, 78–81, 92, 93–4, 100, 102–3, 109, 112–3, 116, 123, 125–6, 128, 133, 146, 158, 160, 195, 208
Wuppertal 92

For Product Safety Concerns and Information please contact our EU
representative GPSR@taylorandfrancis.com
Taylor & Francis Verlag GmbH, Kaufingerstraße 24, 80331 München, Germany

www.ingramcontent.com/pod-product-compliance
Lightning Source LLC
Chambersburg PA
CBHW060623250426

43670CB00056B/1878